# IRELAND'S TERRORIST TRAUMA

**Interdisciplinary Perspectives**

# IRELAND'S TERRORIST TRAUMA

**Interdisciplinary Perspectives**

**Edited by**

## Yonah Alexander
*State University of New York and The George Washington University*

## Alan O'Day
*Polytechnic of North London*

St. Martin's Press
New York

First published in the United States of America in 1989

Printed in Great Britain

ISBN 0-312-02508-4

**Library of Congress Cataloging-in-Publication Data**

Ireland's terrorist trauma : interdisciplinary perspectives / edited
  by Yonah Alexander, Alan O'Day.
      p.  cm.
    Includes index.
    ISBN 0-312-02508-4
    1. Terrorism—Northern Ireland.  2. Northern Ireland—Politics
and government—1969–  I. Alexander, Yonah.  II. O'Day, Alan.
HV6433.G7175 1989
303.6'25'09416—dc 19                                          89-31390
                                                                   CIP

# CONTENTS

CONTENTS

6. The Ambiguous Dynamics of the Anglo-Irish
   Agreement                                              149
   *Paul Bew*

7. Northern Ireland: Corrupt Ideologies and the
   Failure of Government Cagebuilding                      159
   *Jerry DeGregory* and *John F. Galliher*

8. Northern Ireland: Internal-Conflict Analyses           166
   *John Darby*

9. Terrorised into Terrorist: 'Pete the Para' Strikes Again  178
   *Rona Fields*

10. War of Words: The *Belfast Telegraph* and Loyalist
    Populism                                               213
    *Michael Bromley*

11. Catholic Women and the Northern Irish Troubles         234
    *Catherine Shannon*

    Glossary and who's who                                 249

    Index                                                  254

# CONTRIBUTORS

Yonah Alexander (co-editor) is Professor of International Studies and Director of the Institute for Studies in International Terrorism at the State University of New York and the Elliott School of International Affairs, The George Washington University. He is author and editor of more than thirty books and editor of *Terrorism: An International Journal, Terrorism: An International Resource File,* and *The 1987 Annual on Terrorism.*

Paul Bew is Reader in Political Science at The Queen's University of Belfast. He has authored or co-authored more than half a dozen books the most recent being, *Conflict and Conciliation in Irish Nationalism* (1987) and published numerous articles. He was a contributor to *Terrorism in Ireland* (1984) (eds. Alexander and O'Day).

Michael Bromley was until 1987 a London leader writer for the *Belfast Telegraph.* He is now studying at Yale University on a Fulbright Postgraduate Award.

Steve Bruce is Reader in Sociology at The Queen's University of Belfast. He is the author of four books on the role of religion and politics, including *God Save Ulster! The Religion and Politics of Paisleyism* (1986).

John Darby is Professor and Director of the Centre for the Study of Conflict, University of Ulster. He has written or edited six books and many articles on the Irish conflict, the most recent of which is *Intimidation and the Control of Conflict in Northern Ireland* (1986). He is a member of the Standing Advisory Commission on Human Rights.

Richard Davis is Reader in History and Head of the Department of History, University of Tasmania. He has published three books, including *The Young Ireland Movement* (1987), and numerous articles. His work on Northern Ireland was undertaken at the Institute for Irish Studies, The Queen's University of Belfast.

Jerry DeGregory is Assistant Professor in Sociology, University of North Alabama-Florence, Alabama. He is co-author of *Violence in Northern Ireland* (1985).

Rona Fields has been Associate Professor of Psychology at Clark University and is a psychological consultant, Washington, D.C. She has published three books on Northern Ireland, including *Society Under Siege* (1977) and numerous articles.

Mark Finnane is Lecturer in History and Australian Studies, Griffith University, Queensland. His publications include *Insanity and the Insane in Post-Famine Ireland* (1981) and several articles. He has recently edited a volume on policing in Australia.

John F. Galliher is Professor of Sociology, University of Missouri-Columbia, Missouri. He has co-authored *Violence in Northern Ireland* (1985) and authored *Criminology and Human Rights* (1988).

Rosemary Harris is Reader in Anthropology, University College, University of London. Her numerous publications include *Prejudice and Tolerance in Ulster: Neighbours and 'Strangers' in a Border Community* (1972).

Alan O'Day (co-editor) is Senior Lecturer in History, The Polytechnic of North London. He has authored and edited ten volumes, including *Parnell and the First Home Rule Episode* (1986) and a substantial number of articles.

Catherine Shannon is Professor in History, Westfield State College, Massachusetts. Her publications include *Arthur James Balfour and Ireland* (1988).

Jim Smyth is Lecturer in Sociology at The Queen's University of Belfast. He has published several articles previously.

# INTRODUCTION – THE PERSISTENCE OF IRISH TERRORISM

For the past twenty years Northern Ireland has been a perennial trouble spot – one of the world's most important areas of politically inspired terrorism. Ulster has had its share of international attention, particularly from the media. The origins of the violence are not a mystery, but are rooted in the fact that the Roman Catholics of Northern Ireland have rejected the present political arrangements. If terrorists form only a tiny segment of the population of Ulster, there can be little doubt that Richard Rose's verdict – 'governing without consensus' – has been the hallmark and plague of Northern Ireland's regime.[1] Resort to terrorism has come from two directions. Extremists in the Republican – virtually wholly Catholic sector – see its use as historically justified and the only means of uniting Ireland in view of their own minority position in Ulster. Quite understandably they cannot see how the democratic process can bring about a united Ireland. At the other end of the spectrum, the Unionist, that is, Protestant, extremists have responded to terrorism against their community with periodic attacks on the supposed enemy. Successive Labour and Conservative governments in Britain have failed to resolve the impasse, although much time, money and rhetoric have been expended on this age-old problem.

Political terrorism has been a fast-developing field of academic inquiry – and rightly so. It deserves systematic investigation, and terrorism, with its effects in Northern Ireland, remains a key, but unresolved, difficulty in contemporary British political life. The terrorist threat stemming from Northern Ireland cannot, in terms of duration and scale, be compared with any era of Anglo-Irish conflict in the last 300 years or in twentieth-century Europe.

The terrorist threat, the trauma it has aroused and the impact of violence on society and the state are matters of fundamental importance, demanding the energies of investigators drawn from a number of disciplines, each having its own distinct perspective. This volume, which explores some of the crucial aspects of terrorism and its context in Northern Ireland, is the third volume on Irish terrorism from the joint-editors but the first to confine the discussion to the source of the violence, Northern Ireland.[2] Examination of Northern Ireland is especially timely for two reasons. First of all, after twenty years of disturbance, with no end in sight, this is a suitable moment to take account of the impact of Irish terrorism. And, second, the volume gives us an opportunity to assess the state of the academic discussion on Irish terrorism.

Paul Wilkinson, one of the most influential academic authorities on terrorism in the British Isles, has recently presented a weighty analysis of the contemporary situation.[3] He claims there is clear evidence that the strategy of policing and of judicial control 'is slowly but surely winning the battle against terrorism . . .' Its success, he believes, results from 'a well-defined and consistent approach [which] has been adopted by successive governments since the mid-1970s'. Its principles are:

1. A firm political will to uphold the rule of law and democratic government and to defeat terrorism.
2. Absolute refusal to surrender to terrorist extortion and demands.
3. Determination to act in accord with domestic and international law.
4. Treatment of convicted terrorists as common criminals with no special privileges, pardons, or amnesty.
5. The promotion of national and international measures to combat terrorists by minimising their rewards and maximising their costs and losses.

He points out that the means of making policy effective is twofold. On the one hand, policing and the judiciary have been strengthened; on the other, the British authorities 'have realised the importance of addressing the deeply felt and legitimate grievances of whole ethnic groups or communities'. Wilkinson then cites the Anglo-Irish Agreement (November 1985) as such an 'exercise in bridge-building, a framework for potential power-sharing co-operation [between the Catholic and Protestant communities] . . .' Although there have been lapses and shortcomings in implementation of policy, he concludes that 'the British approach is widely respected and has been highly effective and consistent'. Overall, he contends, 'the British government's record in combating terrorism is impressive. Indeed, it is one of the best in the democratic world.' Wilkinson makes two further points relevant to the discussion in this volume. First, he insists, 'in spite of the cries of doom by Ulster politicians, the long-term prospects for greater stability in Northern Ireland are better than they have ever been throughout the past seventeen years of conflict'. Second, he comments on the apparent futility of terrorism:

> The Northern Ireland conflict has also shown very clearly the severe limitations of terrorism as a weapon. Terrorist atrocities have secured plenty of publicity for the terrorists and their various threats and demands, but these propaganda 'victories' should not delude anyone into thinking that terrorists of either extreme have 'won' their wars. On the contrary, terrorism has only tended to stiffen the determination and intransigence of the adversary community. Violence and sectarian attacks by one set of extremists inevitably provoke counter-terror and defensive paramilitarism from the other.

So clear an exposition from an eminent authority deserves careful attention. How far does his decisive and optimistic account, published only in 1988, fit current realities? Taken as a group, the contributors to this book all address the same general questions, but, as readers of the present volume will find, they reach a rather more pessimistic conclusion than Wilkinson's.

Is, as Wilkinson suggests, terrorism a diminishing feature of the Ulster landscape? He produces impressive statistics that demonstrate a decline in fatalities, particularly for civilians, since the high point of the early to mid-1970s. But, he acknowledges blips in the pattern, notably for the years 1979 and 1981, the latter being a consequence of the hunger-strikers' deaths. Might it, then, not be more appropriate to treat the period 1972–6 as unusual and the years since as the norm – steady but less regular or massive tallies of deaths through terrorism? Also, fatalities are only a part of a mosaic which includes psychological and physical injury, intimidation and breakdowns of social order. At no moment can we claim that terrorism in Ulster after 1976 has been defeated. At best it has been contained. Several years ago David Carlton projected the emergent pattern of confinement of terrorist incidents to an 'acceptable' level as the prime aim of British policy.[4] Control of the level rather than abolition, then, was the objective. Events have conformed to the Carlton hypothesis. When the number of incidents has risen dramatically, further resources have been pumped into Northern Ireland. Additional concentration on security has led to a reduction in terrorism, but when the number falls to the 'acceptable' point, the security effort ceases to be increased. Little wonder that the loyalists have been disconcerted by successive governments' attention to security; indeed they remain highly suspicious of British commitment to the province.

Moreover, the pattern of ebb and flow in terrorism seems confirmed by the greater IRA activity that has occurred since the Anglo-Irish Agreement. The past years have seen an upsurge in the number of terrorist incidents. This development was vividly illustrated on Remembrance Sunday 1987, when in the worst bombing since 1982, the number of civilians killed reached double figures and the total of dead and injured exceeded seventy. Enniskillen's tragedy briefly seized the attention of the western world but, in reality, it was only the daily agony of Northern Ireland writ large. Had it not been for the failure of a second bomb, planted along the parade route of another town and timed to go off simultaneously with the Enniskillen device, the Remembrance Day casualties would have been even greater. Enniskillen's suffering proved to be a propaganda setback for the IRA. Its impact on public feeling paralleled the indignation aroused by the bombings in Birmingham in 1974, Regent's Park in 1982, and outside Harrods just before Christmas in 1983. After the Enniskillen tragedy there was general condemnation of terrorism. The Catholic hierarchy, as Richard Davis points out, often suspected by loyalists of equivocation on IRA terrorism, denounced resorting to violence in terms that no one could misunderstand. It was the strongest statement on terrorism ever to come from that body. However, as Davis observes, the relationship between clerical authority and republican terrorists is not, contrary to unionist demonology, one of servile obedience to the Roman Catholic church. Unshaken by these condemnations and by the propaganda disaster of the Enniskillen massacre, the IRA soon resumed its attacks and assassinations. A month after the Enniskillen bombing, Sir John Hermon, chief constable of the Royal Ulster Constabulary, warned that 1988 would see a rise in IRA terrorism.[5] His prediction has been fulfilled.

As has happened in the past after increases in violence, the British government responded by raising the security profile and allotted additional resources for the fight against the IRA.[6] If the pattern of the past is repeated, we can expect terrorism to diminish to 'acceptable' levels, after which security considerations will again be shifted into lower gear. In his article, Jim Smyth explains how the IRA was able to recover so rapidly after the error of judgement at Enniskillen. He also suggests that the tendency of British politicians to concentrate almost entirely on suppressing the IRA and Sinn Fein avoids the necessity of dealing with the heart of the longer-term problem.

One outcome of recent loyalist disenchantment with British policy has been the significant increase in the number of loyalist arms caches. Rather than getting bridges built, the Anglo-Irish Agreement, succinctly considered by Paul Bew, has complicated the maintenance of security. For some months in 1986, people in the Protestant community ceased aiding the police. Their action may have assisted the IRA – it certainly increased the difficulties of the civil authority in Northern Ireland. Probably the main outcome to date of the Agreement has been to enlarge the ever-present unionist mistrust of British politicians. Loyalists as a consequence, despite reservations about violence – neatly described by Steve Bruce in his article – have shown a greater disposition towards direct action. During 1988 there was mounting evidence that the loyalist paramilitaries had made impressive strides in catching up with the IRA in the arms race. Rocket launchers, armour-piercing grenades and large quantities of other weapons have been discovered. However, few observers doubt that these groups have ample reserves of arms in hand and, with well-developed supply routes, find it easy to get replacements. Because rival terrorist groups – real or potential – have such a huge military capacity, there is real danger of general civil war breaking out in Northern Ireland. We can certainly be sure that the violence will continue.

Though the outlook for eradicating terrorism in the next few years is unpromising, Paul Wilkinson is right to draw attention to the decline in numbers and severity of violent incidents since the mid-1970s. It remains unlikely that the IRA can bomb or assassinate the British out of Ulster, and it is doubtful if republicans have ever believed such a result were possible. As for the IRA, its objectives in using terror have been somewhat mixed. But it has certainly striven to weaken British commitment to Northern Ireland, to attract publicity for itself, to gain credibility and support within the Catholic community, and possibly to provoke a loyalist backlash that would make the current political boundaries impossible. In addition, IRA terrorism contains a primeval revenge element and is now difficult to halt, because a generation of youths cultured in traditions of violence know no other way to express dissent. Rona Fields's psychological study of Peter McMullen ('Pete the Para') shows the powerful impetus to terrorism that exists within certain people. What the British government can hope to achieve, as it has in the recent past, is a reduction of terrorism to 'acceptable' levels, and it is likely politicians will continue to pursue policies to that end. In Wilkinson's estimation the decline in terrorism has been the outcome of improved security techniques and firm, consistent policies. No doubt he is correct to place emphasis on the efficiency of the security forces. Without their vigilance, republican violence would flourish. But there is an alternative explanation for the restraint of wholesale terrorism in Northern Ireland. As we have noted, the IRA has been prepared to limit its own actions. It has done so for reasons of strategy in which considerations of government policy and security figure as two but not the sum of the explanations.

Steve Bruce, Richard Davis and Rosemary Harris, academics from three different disciplines, consider the in-built resistance to terrorist tactics in both religious communities in Ulster. Many people have been prepared to turn a blind eye to violence emanating from their own people or over ready to believe that such actions were, in fact, precipitated by the other side; but, as Steve Bruce observes, 'most people on both sides of the conflict in Northern Ireland are unhappy about murder and intimidation'. He points out, 'both sides have a problem in justifying terrorism to themselves and to their respective audiences, but unionists have considerably more trouble in this respect than do nationalists'. Richard Davis expands on this theme, showing the extent to which terrorism has generated internal conflicts within the Catholic community, especially between the clerical hierarchy and proponents of violence. His comments prove exceptionally timely in the light of the Enniskillen bombing and the attempts of the hierarchy to throw its weight behind peaceful and legal action rather than to condone or support terrorism by Catholics. Writing in a similar vein, but employing an anthropological impress, Rosemary Harris examines the limited sanction for violence within the cultures of Ulster. She observes, for instance, that permissible conduct does not support the slaughter of women and children of the opposite faith simply because of their religion. Tribal violence in Northern Ireland is internally accountable: it is more restricted by cultural constraints than similar conflicts in other parts of the globe. Commentators frequently note that the troubles in Ulster originated in the seventeenth century; but they are less quick to point out that the present-day version has not led to a wars-of-religion-style attempt to exterminate the enemy. In fact, republicans and unionists both predicate a future regime where none would dominate but the other continue to live. That goal necessarily supposes limits on violence against the opposition and longer-term co-operation. Whereas Wilkinson appears to emphasise the function of the British state in restraining violence in Ulster, essays in the present volume stress certain internally dynamic features of the various cultures in the province as factors that help to limit terrorism. The evidence suggests that Wilkinson's view is rather over mechanistic, attributing too much credit to government policy, though no one would wish to deny that state security has had a prominent part to play in curtailing terrorism.

Wilkinson's analysis, however, is at its most contentious when he credits control of terrorism to the 'well-defined and consistent approach' adopted by 'successive governments'. His outline of the principles of that approach is provided above and would command only modest assent within this volume or from a host of earlier commentators. His list of principles is no more than a re-statement of what the present home secretary, Douglas Hurd, has enunciated them to be. Moreover, it requires real sleight of hand to present policy as either consistent in itself or always adhering to the principles outlined by the home secretary. Successive governments in the Republic of Ireland have complained about aspects and applications of British policy in Ulster. Recently, the alleged

shoot-to-kill tactics of the Royal Ulster Constabulary, the conse-
quential murder of innocent youths that has resulted, the curious
affair of John Stalker's inquiry, and the decision not to prosecute
anyone involved in the police, led to consternation in Dublin and
considerable disbelief in Britain. Several of our contributors,
notably Paul Bew, Mark Finnane, and Jerry DeGregory and John
F. Galliher, examine government policies and their contradictions.
Also, John Darby's essay treats the topic in part. From the
evidence amassed by them and others, it would be overly kind to
credit British politicians with pursuing well-defined, consistent
policies. Bew, for example, even suggests that British policies have
contributed to an escalation of violence.

Rona Fields's exploration of how republican prisoners have
been tortured, with resultant long-term physical and psychological
repercussions, does not merit Wilkinson's appraisal of British
'determination to act in accord with domestic and international
law' any more than does a shoot-to-kill policy. For its treatment of
prisoners, Britain was indeed taken before the European Court by
the Irish Republic and its procedures were found unlawful. There
is scant scope for doubt that on occasion at least government
actions have been neither consistent nor lawful in the sense
declared by the home secretary. But, overall, the theme that
emerges from several essays is not so much routinised malevolence
on the part of successive British governments as muddle. British
policy has not been clearly aimed at suppression of terrorism,
resolution of grievances, conciliation of the Irish Republic, relief
of loyalist anxieties or development of governing instruments
commanding consensus support, though all of these requirements
have received attention at various moments. John Darby comments on the tendency of policy-makers to focus on so-called
political solutions when less earth-shattering but effective concrete
improvements in life might prove more enduring and build more
bridges.

Two contributions, those of Michael Bromley and Catherine
Shannon, give particular emphasis to the impact of the troubles on
the community. Bromley's study of a prominent, moderate
unionist newspaper, the *Belfast Telegraph,* reveals the pressures
towards polarisation in Northern Ireland. Ultimately the commercial survival of the newspaper hinged on attenuating its reformist
position. In many respects, as Bromley demonstrates, Ulster is

more pluralist and segregated in 1988 than it was in 1968.[7] That separation is both mental and physical, for recent population trends show that residential, indeed, inter-regional, segregation has been growing in all parts of the province. Catherine Shannon examines another crucial area – the way violence has impinged on the community, especially on women and their outlook. Her study assesses both the strains and resilience of a society under almost continuous stress.

Terrorism seems likely to remain a major theme in Ulster life. The present volume offers some insight into the workings of the community. It has no unified message, though individual authors offer a variety of perspectives. The future is not universally optimistic or pessimistic but the road ahead must surely be a long one. This volume seeks to contribute to, and act as a critical ingredient in, the academic and popular discussion of terrorism.

## NOTES

1. Rose, R., *Governing Without Consensus* (London: Macmillan, 1971).
2. See Alexander, Y. and A. O'Day (eds), *Terrorism in Ireland* (London: Croom Helm, 1984); *Ireland's Terrorist Dilemma* (Dordrecht, The Netherlands: Martinus Nijhoff, 1986).
3. Wilkinson, P., 'British Policy on Terrorism: An Assessment', Lodge, J. (ed.), *The Threat of Terrorism* (Hemel Hempstead: Harvester Wheatsheaf, 1988).
4. Carlton, D., 'The Future of Political Substate Violence', in Alexander, Y., D. Carlton, and P. Wilkinson (eds.), *Terrorism: Theory and Practice* (Boulder, Colorado: Westview Press, 1979); reprinted in Carlton, D. and C. Schaerf (eds.), *Contemporary Terror* (London: Macmillan, 1981).
5. *The Times*, 6 Feb. 1988.
6. Ibid., 22 Jan. 1988.
7. See Kennedy, L., *Two Ulsters: A Case for Repartition* (Belfast: Institute for Irish Studies, 1986).

# PART I

# THE DYNAMICS AND LIMITS OF TERRORISM

# 1 · PROTESTANTISM AND TERRORISM IN NORTHERN IRELAND

The purpose of this chapter is to explore some Ulster Protestant attitudes to political violence.[1] The first section examines Protestant involvement in political violence, the second discusses Protestant theories of force, and the third looks at the various Protestant reactions to the tension between the reality and the theory. It should be noted at the start that considerable simplification is involved in talking about the beliefs and attitudes of a population of a million people, divided by class, regional, and denominational loyalties, and having quite varied experiences of the Troubles.

## PROTESTANT VIOLENCE

Although it is useful to divide the past into discrete periods, the common-sense notion of the Troubles should not lead us mistakenly to assume that Northern Ireland was peaceful from shortly after partition (1922) until the violent response to the civil rights marches in 1969.[2] There were riots in the 1930s. In November and December 1956, the IRA launched a series of attacks on police stations and other government buildings. By the end of 1957 there had been a total of 366 incidents, and three RUC men and seven republicans had died.[3] By then the IRA had been beaten, but it continued its campaign at a low level until February 1962. In total, eleven republicans and six RUC men had been killed. Damage estimated at a million pounds had been caused, and spending on security in the North had been increased by some ten million pounds. The absence of civilian Protestant reaction during the campaign suggests that it was not seen as a serious threat to the stability of the state (largely because it attracted little or no support from the wider Catholic community), but it did enough to remind Protestants of the precariousness of their position and to provide the more militant with the rationale for their later judgement of the civil rights campaign as merely being the old nationalist and republican wolf in sheep's clothing.

The first acts of violence in the modern Troubles were committed by Protestants. In May 1966, the petrol bombing of a Catholic bar caused the death of an elderly (ironically) Protestant woman. Three weeks later a group of loyalists set out to murder a local IRA activist. They could not find him and instead shot John Scullion, a drunk who was wandering home singing republican songs. Then, on 26th June, the same gang murdered a young Catholic barman in Malvern St, Belfast. Gusty Spence and other Shankill Road loyalists calling themselves the Ulster Volunteer Force (UVF) were convicted of the crime.

In March and April 1969 there were explosions at an electricity sub-station just outside Belfast and at the Silent Valley reservoir in the Mournes. Ian Paisley's *Protestant Telegraph* was quick to blame them on first the IRA and then the Irish government and presented them as the expected fruits of the reformist unionism policy put forward by Terence O'Neill, then prime minister of Northern Ireland. In fact, it is almost certain that they were caused by members of Paisley's Ulster Protestant Volunteers (UPV), a 'mass movement' created to demonstrate against O'Neillism, some of whose members had links with Spence's UVF.[4] Thomas McDowell, a member of the Kilkeel Free Presbyterian Church and the South Down UPV blew himself up while setting a similar charge at an electricity sub-station across the border in Donegal. Although there is some confusion about exactly who played what part in those explosions, there is no doubt that they were set by militant Protestants to dramatise the claim that Terence O'Neill's reforms (or, as they saw it, appeasement) would simply encourage the IRA to take up the campaign that it had stood down four years earlier.

Between December 1970 and December 1971, leaving aside members of the security forces, six men had been assassinated, all by the IRA. Five were Protestants, one was a Catholic. Large numbers of people in Belfast unlucky enough to live in the 'wrong' area or on a street that formed a border between Catholic and Protestant areas were intimidated into leaving their homes.[5] The year closed with the first mass killing – the bombing of McGurk's – a Catholic bar in Belfast, in which fifteen people died. Although this was initially described as an IRA accident or 'own goal', a loyalist was convicted in 1978 of the murders.

On 24th March 1972, the Stormont parliament was closed and direct rule from London was imposed. In the twelve months that followed something like 200 civilians were killed. After an exhaustive examination of the circumstances of what were often described as 'motiveless killings', Dillon and Lehane concluded: 'that the bulk of the assassinations were carried out by Protestant groups, and that these started as an organised and concerted campaign of sectarian killings'.[6]

An overall impression of the nature of fatal violence can be gained from Table 1.1, which shows the figures for murders between 1969 and 1986.

Despite the shift in the IRA campaign from large bombings to more selective attacks on the security forces, the majority of deaths have been of civilians. As the religion category shows, most of these have been Catholics. Not all the Catholic deaths have been caused by Protestant paramilitaries; many were caused by the security forces and a number were caused by nationalist paramilitaries, either in the random violence of large bombs or in assassination of informers in their own ranks. Similarly, a number of the deaths caused by loyalist paramilitaries, especially between 1973 and 1975, were other loyalist paramilitaries. But even with these sorts of qualifications, there is no doubting the basic point I want to make; loyalists have been responsible for a lot of the fatal violence in Northern Ireland.


## THE THEORY OF LEGITIMATE VIOLENCE

Ulster Protestants are not pacifists. The particular strains of their situation might have made them a little more militant than other Christians, but Ulster Protestants are firmly in the mainstream of Christian thought in believing that there are many occasions on which it is perfectly justifiable to use violence. If one wishes to find intellectual sources, one can go to Luther and Calvin. Luther

**Table 1.1** Murders in Northern Ireland, 1969–87

| | | |
|---|---:|---|
| (1) Victims | | |
| Civilians | 1,418 | (56%) |
| Security Forces | 785 | (31%) |
| Paramilitaries (Nat) | 202 | (8%) |
| (Loy) | 50 | (3%) |
| (2) Religion of victims (excluding army) | | |
| Catholic | | 54% |
| Protestant | | 45% |
| (3) Agents of civilian deaths | | |
| Loyalist Paras | 587 | (41%) |
| Nationalist Paras | 523 | (37%) |
| Security Forces | 167 | (12%) |
| Unclassified | 141 | (10%) |

*Source:* Irish Information Partnership[7]

endorsed the German princes crushing the Anabaptists. Calvin was not only not a pacifist; he also believed in the morality of rebellion. The citizen had certain obligations to the state – Calvin's 'civil magistrate' – but such obligations were conditional on the civil magistrate acting in a godly manner. The English puritan leader Thomas Cartwright (1535–1603) thought the death penalty suitable for the obdurately irreligious. Although most strands of Protestant thought abandoned the idea of enforced religious orthodoxy around the early eighteenth century, few thought that the use of force was entirely wrong.[8]

In their thinking about violence Ulster Protestants are almost entirely conventional. They believe that force and violence are 'bad things'. They share the modern democratic view that the state should have a monopoly of legitimate violence. Even Ian Paisley, regarded by many of his critics as an important cause of the de-stabilisation of Northern Ireland, is a constitutionalist. This should not necessarily be read as a great virtue. It is easy to be a constitutional supporter of law and order when one's beliefs and values are enshrined in the constitution and when one's own people are in power.[9] Nevertheless, Paisley has usually been unequivocal in his condemnation of private initiatives. For example, he was quick to respond to the 1966 Malvern Street murder:

> Like everyone else, I deplore and condemn this killing, as all right-thinking people must. Incitement, direct or indirect, must be treated with the full rigour of the law. Under the Special Powers Act the

government has the full authority to act and has failed to do so. If it continues to abdicate its responsibilities then the British government must act immediately in its place.[10]

Although he could not resist inserting an attack on O'Neill's government, his constitutionalism is quite clear here. It is the responsibility of the state to maintain the rule of law and to justify its monopoly of legitimate violence by protecting its citizens.

The third element of Protestant thinking about force is also clear from Paisley's own actions. Calvin was quite clear (although at times he tried to disguise the revolutionary implications of this conclusion) that the individual's duty to obey the civil magistrate was part of a matching pair with the magistrate's duty to obey God. The legitimacy of the state and its monopoly of violence are *conditional* because the duty to obey the civil power is less pressing than the duty to obey the word of God. If the state fails to act righteously (and the protection of its citizens is righteous), then private citizens have the right to undertake their own defence. In the thinking of most Ulster Protestants, their call to arms is purely defensive, a 'last measure'. Paisley has always been clear that his various paramilitary ventures, most recently in his Third Force, are intended to be preparatory. Although the Third Force undertook one or two publicity exercises involving stopping cars and asking drivers for proof of identity, the aim (never achieved) was to create a framework and a degree of readiness so that, come the civil war, Protestants would be ready.

The other circumstance in which the use of force is legitimate is related. If the British army withdrew because the government was intent on forcing Ulster into a united Ireland, then the government would have forfeited its right to a monopoly of force. Many Protestants reason this way on purely democratic grounds. Most people in Northern Ireland do not want a united Ireland. The creation of such a state would be such an infringement of their democratic rights that they would be justified in resisting what would amount to tyranny. Thus Paisley could say in 1972 'if the British government attempted collusion with the Irish government to put us into a unified Ireland, every Protestant would fight'. Asked if he would back them in that fight, Paisley added 'I would lead them.'[11]

More theologically conservative Protestants would also add that the subordination of 'Protestant' Ulster to 'Catholic' Ireland would be unbiblical and unChristian and hence should be resisted.

## PROTESTANT REACTIONS TO PROTESTANT VIOLENCE

The conflict between the reality outlined in the first section and the theory described in the second raises the general problem of how Protestants maintain their self-image of being law-abiding, decent, and loyal citizens in the face of the knowledge that some of them, in the name of Protestantism and unionism, have undertaken private acts of murder, many of them grotesque in their cruelty. Clearly the nature and extent of the problem of 'accounting' for such actions varies with involvement in, as well as attitude towards, them. The problem can be clarified by dividing Protestants into four groups:

1. Those who commit terrorist acts.
2. Those who unreservedly support such acts.
3. The larger group which feel ambivalent but who may sometimes tacitly support the political use of violence.
4. Those who denounce loyalist terrorist acts.

This paper is hardly concerned with the first or second groups. There are undoubtedly Ulster Protestants who have no moral problem justifying violence because they like it and think it appropriate. In so far as such people are considered in what follows, it is because they may still have the problem of accounting for their actions to others who are appalled by their callousness.

People in the fourth group, like those in the first, are not central to my concerns. They consistently denounce all forms of violence, security force, nationalist and loyalist. Such consistency is generally to be found only among liberal Protestant churchmen and those mainly middle-class Protestants for whom they speak.[12]

The third group – the bystanders – share with the first and second the problems of formulating some sort of coherent account of acts that their self-image should lead them to condemn, even though it is not their own but someone else's behaviour that needs recasting and neutralising. Sociologists of deviance have long been interested in the ways in which people who are labelled as 'deviant' and dishonourable attempt to deny their deviance, reduce the negative connotations of the label, or justify their actions. Although the majority of Protestants – the third group – are not themselves involved in such deviance disavowal, the fact that they share a common religion, ethnic identity, and (largely) political agenda with those who actually commit terrorist acts suggests that the ideas developed initially in considering how deviants neutralise their own deviant labels are also appropriate, not only for the active supporters and condoners of terrorism, but also for those who either feel or have imputed to them common identity with terrorists.

To put it simply, many Protestants who are not active in paramilitary actions are under some pressure to reconcile the Protestant stereotype of law-abiding citizenship with those actions, and the categories developed in the study of deviance disavowal seem to offer a fruitful approach to the study of the accounting work which forms the basis for such a reconciliation.

Although it may appear to confuse the issue, it is worth saying that some of my observations below are not so much about the responses to loyalist terrorism of four different groups as they are about changes in location within the four groups. As will become clear below, the major issue of reaction – to justify or denounce – is settled by the same people in different ways on different occasions. However, I will suggest that such shifts were not entirely random or idiosyncratic but followed discernible patterns.

The various ways in which Protestants respond to the reality of Protestant terrorism will now be described under a series of headings drawn from the sociology of deviance; but first I will describe responses to one event that include many of the features I will later highlight.[13]

## A CASE STUDY: McGURK'S BAR

On 14th December 1971, a bomb wrecked McGurk's Bar in North Queen St, Belfast, killing fifteen people, all of them Catholics. Three were women; two were children.

Despite the claims of a boy selling papers outside the pub that he saw a car stop and a man get out and plant the bomb, and an anonymous phone call claiming that the 'Empire Loyalists' were responsible, the army and police decided that the IRA had scored an own goal. *The Times* ran the official version:

> Police and Army intelligence officers believe that Ulster's worst outrage, the killing of 15 people, including two children and three

women, in an explosion in Belfast bar last night was caused by an IRA plan that went wrong . . .

The Army's theory is that the bomb in McGurk's Bar was 'in transit', that it had been left there, probably without the knowledge of any of the people who were killed or injured, by a 'carrier' for another person to pick up, and that the second person was unable to keep his rendezvous because of the security operation.[14]

Not surprisingly, given its source and its confirmation of their stereotypes of the IRA, most Protestants believed this version of events. John McKeague, a leading activist in the loyalist paramilitary groups of west Belfast, repeated it in his *Loyalist News:*

Now to the truth about McGurk's pub. What terms can we use . . . poetic justice? Yes . . . a bomb in transit, meant for another building, and we believe it was for the Co-op in York street. Over the past weeks we have had the sneers and gibs from Republican elements, in reference to the fact that business will be brought to a stand still before Christmas, and when it happens to themselves they don't like their own medicine . . . the blast at McGurk's need not have happened, if the 'slugs' responsible for the bomb, had not called for a wee something to boast their moral.
IRA CAUGHT IN THEIR OWN TRAP.[15]

The important point to note in this account is the elision of Catholics and IRA men. Republican elements who threatened a bombing campaign do not like a touch of their own medicine. With no discussion of, or justification for, it (in fact in the whole article those who died are never referred to as Catholics but just as 'people'), the victims are assumed to be identical to Republicans and the 'slugs' responsible for planting the bomb.

Another loyalist publication with ties to the paramilitaries, the *Dundonald District UDA News,* also took the own-goal line. It followed its report that Gerry Fitt, then SDLP MP for West Belfast, was condemning the bomb as the work of Protestants by saying:

We are awaiting the day when you (so concerned for your people) will come out and condemn the thugs and animals who have brought about destruction and death on a scale not seen since the Belfast Blitz, this is one that backfired and without a doubt, this one was meant for the Protestant People. What bar would it have been, we wonder, Yea, this one backfired.[16]

The report in the *Woodvale Defence Association News* was significantly different:

> Many lies, and much IRA propoganda, have been circulated since the explosion at McGurk's bar, where fifteen people, some of whom were innocent, and probably had no connection with the IRA died. But, what many people outside Belfast, and all outside the province, do not know, this bar, on numerous occasions, was a meeting place for terrorists. It was also situated in the centre, and surrounded by an IRA fortress, particularly Artillery Flats, where IRA Snipers and machine gunners have reigned terror on Army patrols . . .[17]

It continues to give reasons why it was hardly likely to be a Protestant bomb and it repeats the army and police theory. It then goes on:

> We would wish it to be known, while sympathy is extended to the families of those killed, it should be noted that these people have never once condemned the IRA. In fact, they claim the IRA would have given a warning. Let us remind those people the IRA gave no warning at the Springfield Road Police Station, where a 30lb bomb was placed just one foot from children standing in the hallway . . . Is it possible that the Roman Catholics believe that the IRA only give warnings when they, the Roman Catholics, are in danger? This is possible, for the hatred they possess for the Protestant Community leaves them blind to anything else, and they will at all times support any organization or army whose sole purpose is to destroy anything or anyone who is Protestant.[18]

The Woodvale version is more explicit in its view that at least some of those who died deserved it. Only some are 'completely innocent'. It is also more specific in linking the clientele of McGurk's with the IRA and thus justifying the death of at least some of those who died. But, then it offers another principle which almost undermines the distinction between deserved and undeserved dead. All Catholics hate Protestants.

These themes will be discussed in a typological examination of the ways in which Protestants tried to reconcile their claims to be law-abiding with the reality of loyalist violence.

## DENIAL OF THE OFFENCE

The most common first reaction of Protestants confronted with evidence of Protestant violence is to deny that it occurred. When members of the Free Presbyterian Church were being tried in 1969 and 1970 for explosives offences connected with the 1969 bombings, most Free Presbyterians simply refused to believe that there was any substance to the charges. The fact that Thomas McDowell killed himself with one of his own bombs was not enough to shake many of them from the notion that the criminal charges were part of a plot, instigated by O'Neill, to discredit Ian Paisley. Time and again, they either completely dismissed reports of Protestant paramilitary activity as 'lies and IRA propaganda' or insisted that minor incidents had been 'exaggerated'. That a number of Catholic deaths were IRA killings of informers and others who defied the organisation gave warrant for seeing many of the killings that the police described as 'motiveless' as the work of the IRA, even when all the circumstances made such an explanation unlikely.

The denial of the offence was an extremely common reaction to the intimidation that produced forced population movements. Thus *Loyalist News* asserted that Catholics had themselves set fire to Bombay Street and burned themselves out of homes.[19] As we have seen loyalists rejected Fitt's claim that the McGurk's Bar bomb was planted by loyalists as 'lies' and 'IRA propaganda'.

Only in late 1973 when the Ulster Volunteer Force (UVF) and Ulster Freedom Fighters (UFF) began to claim responsibilities for murders did many Protestants accept that their people also did that sort of thing.

## DENIAL OF THE VICTIM

When an offence is not denied, its significance can be altered, it can be 'neutralised', by challenging the character of the victim. The challenge here is not to the *corpus delicti* of the offence but to its moral quality. By re-defining the victim, one also re-defines the seriousness of the event. It is easy to suppose that the victims of violence deserved what they got. Thus in the *Woodvale Defence Association News* version of the McGurk's Bar bombing the claim is made that IRA terrorists used the bar. Sarah Nelson in her analysis of interviews with working-class loyalists points to the often made claim that those who acted violently did so selectively; the victims were deserving. As an example, she offers the young man who followed his rather candid admission that: 'Everyone knew the police and the B Specials were for us. You know, the Protestants, against the Catholics; we were on the same side . . .'[20] with the claim that the security forces could distinguish between 'good' and 'bad' Catholics. They did not harass Catholics indiscriminately but rather kept an eye on known troublemakers. 'The B Specials discipline was renowned. Going on the rampage was against their whole tradition. It was the IRA they were against, not the ordinary decent Catholic.'[21] It follows that the Catholics they did harass must have deserved it.

The unionist assumption that the IRA had only temporarily ceased military action in 1962 was the foundation for the 1969 belief that the civil rights marchers were really just the IRA in a new disguise. For all that they usually portrayed the Protestant people as victims of aggression, many of the roneoed publications of the period were considerably more candid than the responses presented to the mass media. Many display a crude triumphalism, nowhere more so than in the song lyrics they frequently published. A song called the Battle or Burntollett, commemorating a brutal attack on a civil rights march by a large number of men (many of them off duty B Specials) armed with clubs and sticks, glories in the way a small 'fearless crowd of men and Loyal to the Crown' broke up the march:

> The true blues they attacked them, it was a glorious sight
> To see the hoards of rebels, being put to flight
> They ran and jumped the hedges, pursued by Bunting's men
> Down fields and cross a river, into woods and glen
> They cried have mercy on us, The Lord protect us too
> And we'll never come again to loyal Killaloo
>
> When the fight was over the victorious Bunting's men
> Assembled at Burntollett and not a man was slain
> The Major thanked them one and all and said 'Long Life to you
> God Bless you loyal Ulstermen who live round Killaloo'
>
> Now our task is over, you're finished for today
> You've shown to all the world at large, this is the IRA.[22]

The reality of the matter is inadvertently given away by the composer of the doggerel. An earlier verse describes the students gathering:

With arms joined together and their girl friends hanging on
A most pathetic sight indeed to see them march along.

Leaving aside what this sub-Kipling sort of song, with its 'Horatius on the Bridge' tone, tells us about loyalist views of themselves, the justification for the attack on unarmed students, many of them female, is clear. It wasn't an attack on unarmed students, many of them female. It was an attack on the IRA, even though, as the lyrics admit, the IRA wasn't actually there. It was an attack on the IRA because the Civil Rights Association was really the IRA. While in public many unionists denied the seriousness of the attack, in private many loyalists glorified it while justifying it by insisting that the Catholics attacked were really IRA supporters and as such had forfeited their right to be treated as ordinary decent people. It was not a deviant act or a dishonourable attack because the victims did not possess the appropriate moral character to be victims.

Precisely the same denial of the victim is made in considering more recent paramilitary activity, the random killing of the Shankill butchers notwithstanding. The claim to know a great deal about the IRA and to have good intelligence is part of the image of military competence that the Protestant paramilitaries wish to project, and many Protestants seem to be willing to accept such claims. In a speech made shortly before the worst period of loyalist murders, right-wing unionist politician William Craig said:

> We will be launching a fighting fund setting up an organisation that could intensify a trade war with the Irish Republic and identify the real enemies within Ulster. And we will establish a more sophisticated intelligence service than is available at the moment . . . If the politicians fail it will be our job to liquidate the enemy.[23]

Those Protestants who wanted to endorse the killings when they came could reason backwards that, if the UDA or the UVF attacked a Catholic, then they must have had good reason for so doing. Thus the victim must have deserved it.

An idea of where the line lies for many Protestants was given by Paisley when asked about UDA claims to have bombed in the Republic. He said that 'the vast loyalist majority were behind the UDA going in – not to destroy life – but to destroy the places where bombs were made'.[24] Clean surgical pre-emptive strikes, preferably not involving killing people (although he later said that it was necessary to kill the killers before they killed) were fine. Random killings were not. This is certainly the majority view. The problem is that the notion of a surgical strike is almost always utopian and, with most attacks by the UDA and UVF, ludicrous. None the less, the belief persisted and could be sustained by assuming, at least in the case of individual assassinations, that the paramilitaries knew what they were doing.

And even apparently random murders of Catholics could be partly justified in this way. Protestants widely believed that the residents of the Catholic ghettoes in which the IRA was strong actively supported the IRA. If they didn't, why didn't they eject it and drive out the gunmen? This is the final theme in the response to the bombing of McGurk's Bar. For those most sympathetic to loyalist violence – generally other members of the working-class ghettoes in which the paramilitaries were strongest – the 'good' and 'bad' Catholic distinction is maintained in one compartment while, in another, the failure of the Catholics to denounce the IRA is used to define all Catholics as bad Catholics who deserve all they get.

An element of the ethnic stereotyping found in the more candid columns of loyalist publications is the de-humanising of their opponents. This often begins with the IRA but then casually slides till it refers to all Catholics. Quite tasteless asides are common. In describing a funeral of a Catholic victim of the troubles, McKeague's *Loyalist News* said:

> Wednesday of last week saw another animal on his way to Milltown [a cemetery] . . . What the Protestants want to know is . . . what do they really do with the ones we never see in boxes? Rumour has it that the IRA are exporting them as animal flesh to the continent via Dublin![25]

Most Protestants outside the working-class ghettos of Belfast (and many of the more 'respectable' loyalists, such as those who began their political involvement in local defence associations before joining Ian Paisley's Democratic Unionist Party, the DUP) rejected the Protestant paramilitaries once enough had become known about their campaign for the romantic myths to have been discredited. Interestingly, it was the feuding within the paramilitaries, which could not be neutralised by denying the offences (which were sometimes openly admitted), or by denying the victims (who were Protestant), which changed a lot of people's perceptions. In the autumn of 1974 a number of loyalist politicians in west and north Belfast spoke out against paramilitary feuding and racketeering. For their pains, two were attacked by loyalist gunmen. In March 1975, Paisley delivered a long statement condemning the paramilitaries:

> Mr Paisley, in his call for the Protestant community to withdraw all support from Loyalist paramilitary groups, said that all right-thinking Protestants should repudiate and condemn groups which had openly claimed, or had been proved to be murderers. He said that what really stunned the decent Ulster Protestant was that a section of his own community would engage in crimes 'just as heinous and hellish as those of the IRA' under the guise of Protestantism and loyalty . . . 'No group of people has the right to force their view on any other section of the community by the gun or the bomb, and what is more, the Protestant community will not bow to intimidation, either from the IRA or any so-called Protestant paramilitary group'.[26]

## CLAIMS TO A HIGHER MORALITY

A third strategy for deviance disavowal is to admit that one did the deed in question, that one deserves the deviant label, but that some higher morality justified the action in these circumstances. The private use of violence can be justified as the only way to avoid some worse outcome; violent attacks on one's own people, for example. Here Ulster Protestants are divided, not on the theory of justified violence, but on the question of whether the situation yet calls for it.

Most middle-class unionists do not see the present situation as justifying private initiatives. Hardly surprisingly, the closer people are to actual violence, the more they see violent reaction and even pre-emptive strikes as necessary. This can be illustrated with the expulsion of George Seawright from the DUP. Officially, Seawright was expelled from the party for refusing to retract an outburst about buying incinerators to burn Catholics and their priests. In its formal statement, the DUP said:

> [The DUP] maintains that Protestantism in religion stands for liberty and in the civil and political sphere maintains as a spin-off from

religious liberty the complementary civil liberty. It holds that no man should be persecuted because of his religion. What Protestantism has won for itself by the blood and burnings of its forefathers it freely gives to all men.[27]

As far as Seawright was concerned, it was not his outburst which was at issue. He quite happily told reporters that:

I neither said, thought nor believe that Roman Catholics should be incinerated. My wrath was and is directed at the armed and murdering forces of republicanism which I believe should be eradicated.[28]

In his view the conflict between himself and the DUP leadership arose because he represented the working-class loyalists of West and North Belfast – the people who were being murdered or intimidated out of their homes:

We would like to be law-abiding but if you analyze it, there's a war going on. The Republican movement declared war on our people and everything we stand for and I stood in Stormont and openly supported the shooting of Gerry Adams. I was definitely doing what the rest of the DUP were saying privately. They saw publicly that they couldn't condone murder but that's not what they say privately.[29]

This last point – that he was only saying what others thought when he applauded the UVF for trying to assassinate the Sinn Fein president Adams – will be considered in a moment. Here I want to make the obvious point that the same principle – that reactive and defensive violence is justified – produces different assessments of actual actions because different elements within Protestantism have different evaluations of how threatening the situation is. It is not accidental that the Free Presbyterian minister most active in Paisley's Third Force was Ivan Foster, whose church is in a part of Fermanagh that has seen regular fatal attacks on Protestants. Loosely we might describe four positions on a continuum. At the end, supposing there exists an actual 'state of war' that justifies murdering Catholics, one finds many working-class loyalists. Around the middle one finds the Paisleyite position, which is very occasionally sympathetic to the first view but generally is not and confines itself to sabre-rattling. At the other end one has the position of those middle-class Protestants least involved with the troubles who, for the obvious reason that they have little day-to-day contact with violence and intimidation, have a much more sanguine view of the conflict and are thus easier able to be strict constitutionalists. But even here there are two identifiably different positions that can be illustrated from the views of Protestant clergy.

Many of the ministers of the mainstream churches played a noble role in the worst periods of communal violence, patrolling the streets, trying to diffuse rumours before they provoked violent reactions, persuading groups intent on marauding to go home, trying to maintain fraternal relations with Catholic clergy, and using their pulpits to calm fears and cool tempers.[30] Almost without exception the clergy consistently condemned vigilante and terrorist activity. But the debates within the Presbyterian Church about the wording of Presbytery and General Assembly motions show a clear political and theological division. Those ministers who were theologically and politically liberal (and thus supporters of ecumenism) talked about the need for 'peace'. Conservative ministers talked about the need for 'law and order'. While neither group supported loyalist violence, the second group was closer to doing so and was to be found offering more political support for acts of resistance such as the 1974 Ulster Workers' Council strike, which brought down the power-sharing executive. Although neither group saw the present circumstances as justifying the taking of matters into one's own hands, the 'law and order' group were clearly more sympathetic to the idea that a time might come when what is unacceptable would become necessary.

## OUR LADS

Even when no justification is offered for an act of violence, there may still be a response which is importantly different from total and outright condemnation. Although the act is not condoned and may even be condemned, there is a silence, a qualification, or an explicit statement of understanding which is absent from reactions to similar acts when committed by the other side. Here we have the simple facts of common aims and ethnic solidarity. Although there was initial disbelief and then horror that 'our lads' could act like the IRA, many of those who condemned the use of violence none the less found it possible to 'understand' such acts. In this they were only practising the common human failing of explanatory 'dualism'. We often divide the world of things needing explanations into those we like and those we dislike. Acts in the former class may be 'unreasonable' but we still find them 'reasoned'. Acts in the second class are not treated with such explanatory generosity; they are unreasoned, irrational, barbaric, the products of mindless psychopaths, and so on. What I have in mind here is the 'but' which tends to follow the condemnation of an act of terrorism by one's own side, as in 'but if the British government insists on ignoring the democratically expressed wishes of the people of Ulster, we will see more and more of these acts . . .'.

This partiality may not be as conscious as Seawright suggests when he says that, when he congratulated those who had tried to murder Gerry Adams, he was speaking what other Protestants were thinking. None the less, it is a fact of political life that people rarely reject prizes because they abhor the tactics that won them. For all its condemnation of IRA and INLA terrorism, the SDLP is happy to accept the political gains which have resulted from that activity. Similarly, even Protestants who regard themselves as opponents of loyalist terrorism have at times candidly admitted some pleasure at the results of such activity.

## AN ASIDE ON MOTIVES AND JUSTIFICATIONS

A common problem in sociological explanation is to establish the links between motives, actions and justifications. Against the more common idea that one explains behaviour by seeking from actors an account of the motives which led them to act as they did, some sociologists have followed C. Wright Mills's observations about 'vocabularies of motives' to argue that such accounts may owe more to a desire to justify their actions after the act than to explain their initial motives. Some have gone so far as to insist that we cannot know the motives which informed any act, because all actors' accounts are contaminated by a desire to present their acts as reasonable. This view, advanced by ethnomethodologists and conversation analysts, accidentally matches the view of people who are critical of any particular action. It would be easy to see the above strategies as being only or primarily devices used, after an act has been committed for some less honourable reason (such as a hatred for Catholics), to present the act in the best possible light. There is no doubt an element of that in such strategies. However, I would want to challenge the idea that motive, act and justification should be radically separated. One of the key assumptions of symbolic interactionism is that humans are capable of formulating their intentions in a process of interaction with themselves. An element in our decision to act in a particular way is the result of the debate we have with ourselves about how our act might look to others. The ability to draw on some publicly acceptable rhetoric to define and defend our planned action is itself part of the motive to act in that way rather than in some other.

There may be occasions on which people act for one reason and then defend their action on quite other grounds. For the obvious reason of a lack of evidence as to 'real' motive in such cases, our suspicion that the person is guilty of disguising their real grounds for action remains just that and we have to record a verdict of not proven. But usually, there is considerable continuity between motive and justification because our ability to justify an act is one of the factors which allows us to commit it.

## CONCLUSION

Many nationalists are critical of the actions of the IRA and INLA. However, there is far less ambivalence on the nationalist side. Sinn Fein, for example, consistently refuses to condemn IRA action and IRA acts themselves have a logic and a consistency which seem to be missing from the more sporadic and less well-directed terrorism of working-class Protestants. The reason for the lack of symmetry is obvious. The actions of the IRA are congruent with republican analyses of the history of British imperialist rule in Ireland and will be retrospectively validated by a future all-Ireland Republic just as the Easter Rising was validated by the government of the Free State. The problem for Protestants is that their cause is the preservation of the union with Great Britain. Their self-image is one of contrast between their law-abidingness and loyalty and the rebelliousness of nationalists. So long as the security forces continue to operate, they provide something for law-abiding Protestants to support and hence erode potential support for vigilante activity on the Protestant side. Although the statistical data required to test the notion is not yet available, it seems there is an inverse relationship between the perceived strength and determination of the security forces and both incidence of, and support for, Protestant paramilitary activity.[31]

Although some Protestants can offer various justifications or explanations for vigilante action in terms of being loyal to the Protestant monarchy rather than to this particular British government, they are extremely short of public support for this analysis. For all that recent Irish Republic governments have condemned and outlawed the IRA, its supporters can point to acts of armed rebellion as recent as sixty years ago which are now endorsed by the Republic. The present Prime Minister, Charles Haughey is widely believed to have been involved in plans to supply guns to nationalists in the north less than twenty years ago. Loyalists have to search considerably further back in their traditions to find anything comparable. There is little or nothing in recent British attitudes towards Ulster which can provide a justification for private acts of violence. If one considers the question of what future state of affairs might provide retrospective validation of the actions of the UDA and UVF, the only possibility is an independent Ulster: the antithesis of unionism.

Most people on both sides of the conflict in Northern Ireland are unhappy about murder and intimidation. Probably few of even those actively involved in such acts enjoy them. Both sides have a problem in justifying terrorism to themselves and to their respective audiences, but unionists have considerably more trouble in this respect than do nationalists. The nationalist past and hoped-for future both give considerable scope for the justification of present violence. In so far as force has a place in the unionist past, it is 'state' and quasi-state force which is lauded in unionist hagiography. In so far as any imaginable future is likely to provide retrospective justification for what is presently defined as 'terrorism', that future is not the one desired by most unionists. In a position of such ideological dissonance, not only those Protestants who engage in terrorism, but also those who are forced to respond to it, are faced with considerable problems of 'accounting' for their own people doing the sorts of things their stereotypes of republicans have always regarded as characterising the other side.

It is the accounting problems which explain the need for the various rhetorical devices described in this paper.

## NOTES

1. This paper has benefited considerably from the comments of John Brewer and Dr Steven Yearley of the Queen's University of Belfast; William McCurrie; the editors; and Dr Seamus Thompson of Columbia University, New York.
2. Lippmann, M., 'The abrogation of domestic human rights: Northern Ireland and the rule of British law', Alexander, Y. and K. A. Myers, *Terrorism in Europe* (London: Croom Helm, 1982), p. 183, for example, says that 'in the early sixties, violence in Northern Ireland was limited to sporadic vandalism'. The shooting of a policeman is hardly sporadic vandalism.
3. Farrell, M., *Northern Ireland: the Orange State* (London: Pluto, 1980), p. 217.
4. This does not mean, as many of his critics claim, that Paisley was in any way involved in acts of terrorism. The only claim that Paisley knew of the links and of the supply of weapons came in the evidence of an informer whose word on related matters was twice rejected by juries. For details of the incidents and the claims made about them, see Boulton, D., *The UVF: 1966–73* (Dublin: Torc Books, 1973).
5. Darby, J., *Intimidation and the Control of Conflict in Northern Ireland* (Dublin: Gill and Macmillan; Syracuse, New York: Syracuse University Press, 1986).
6. Dillon, M. and D. Lehane, *Political Murder in Northern Ireland* (Harmondsworth: Penguin, 1973), p. 10.
7. *Fortnight* (19 Feb. 1987), p. 15. Obviously there is an element of uncertainty in the classifications of both victims and agents but there seems no reason to suppose any consistent direction in the errors.
8. For detailed discussions of reformed thinking on force and rebellion, see Little, D., *Religion, Order and Law* (Oxford: Basil Blackwell, 1970) and Walzer, M., *The Revolution of the Saints: A Study in the Origins of Radical Politics* (Cambridge, Mass.: Harvard University Press, 1965).
9. As this essay deals with attitudes towards vigilante violence, it is not the place to discuss the complex question of the links between Protestant attitudes towards the security forces and towards the paramilitaries. A broader discussion might usefully explore the similarities and differences in Protestant attitudes to the security forces and in Catholic attitudes towards the IRA.
10. Bruce, S., *God Save Ulster! The Religion and Politics of Paisleyism* (Oxford: Clarendon Press, 1986), p. 79.
11. *Irish Times,* 23 Oct. 1972.

12. The failure of the Peace People to have any significant impact on the troubles, although it had its own idiosyncratic causes, shows how little support there is among working-class people for a position of non-violence.

13. For very obvious reasons there are no good survey data on attitudes towards paramilitary activity in general or towards particular acts of criminal violence. The 'data' which inform this discussion are the impressions derived from a decade of research interviews, informal discussions, and simply from living and working in Northern Ireland.

14. *The Times*, 6 Dec. 1971.

15. *Loyalist News*, 11 Dec. 1971, p. 1. The many loyalist publications of this period were 'rough and ready' and the standard of writing, typing and proof-reading was generally very low. In quoting from them, I have corrected a few typographical errors that would have been grossly misleading but have otherwise been faithful to the originals. To avoid giving the impression of making fun of the authors, I have omitted the usual *sic* after mistakes.

16. *Dundonald District UDA News*, 11 Dec. 1971, p. 8.

17. *Woodvale Defence Association News*, 20 Dec. 1971, p. 5.

18. Ibid.

19. *Loyalist News*, 16 Oct. 1971, p. 7.

20. Nelson, S., *Ulster's Uncertain Defenders* (Belfast: Blackstaff Press, 1984), p. 89.

21. Ibid.

22. *Loyalist News*, 8 Jan. 1972, pp. 4–5.

23. Dillon and Lehane, op. cit., p. 62.

24. *Irish Times*, 23 Oct. 1972. This was before the 17 May 1974 car bombs in Dublin and Monaghan Town, which killed thirty-one people.

25. *Loyalist News*, 30 Oct. 1971, p. 1.

26. *Irish Times*, 20 Mar. 1973.

27. *Belfast Telegraph*, 29 Dec. 1984.

28. Ibid.

29. Private interview, Mar. 1985.

30. Gallagher, E. and S. Worrall, *Christians in Ulster 1968–1980* (Oxford: Oxford University Press, 1982), p. 50.

31. Dr Seamus Thompson of Columbia University has constructed a machine-readable data base comprising basic details of 'political' murders in Northern Ireland and plans to publish material that will allow us to consider such relationships.

# 2 · IRISH REPUBLICANISM v. ROMAN CATHOLICISM: THE PERENNIAL DEBATE IN THE ULSTER TROUBLES

## REPUBLICANISM: PUPPET OR ADVERSARY OF ROME?

Behind the spectacular violence of the current Ulster Troubles a bitter ideological dispute has persisted between the IRA and the Catholic hierarchy. This dispute has been confused by the traditional loyalist insistence that Irish republicanism is masterminded by the Roman Catholic church. As the chief loyalist argument against a united Ireland, belief in Romanist aggression is essential to this philosophy. Republicans, on the other hand, assert their immunity from clerical pressure, while appealing to Catholic opinion by declaring their actions compatible with true religion. Loyalist paramilitaries have similar problems with Protestant churches. Many of the debate's arguments are mirror images of those on the other side. Extreme loyalists and republicans agreed that the Catholic hierarchy was not even-handed: loyalists deploring a blatant bias to the IRA, republicans denouncing a craven subservience to Britain. Such patterned opposition requires analysis. In examining the church v. paramilitary contests of the 1970s and 1980s this chapter discovers in the classic issues ostensibly dividing Catholic and Protestant – confession, excommunication, last rites, church reform, revolutionary clergy – some surprising convergence.

Both republicans and loyalists began the 1970s with prepared scripts. Republicans cited a history of resistance to clerical condemnation dating back to the twelfth century. The loyalist counter-script also traced Roman aggression to twelfth-century Ireland. By World War I and the first Irish revolution anti-Catholic writers such as M. J. F. McCarthy and J. A. Kensit lumped all current evils – Prussianism, Bolshevism, Sinn Feinism – into one colossal Vatican conspiracy, 'the Celibate internationale', against the British Empire.[1] In applying their scripts to the Northern Irish events of the 1970s, there was mirrored agreement between republicans and loyalists. The former listed honourable exceptions to traditional Catholic hierarchical opposition to Irish nationalism; the loyalists cited the same names, but insisted that they represented the true policy of the church. When republicans produced catalogues of unpatriotic clergy, loyalists complained that these men rejected republican methods, not ideals. In the 1970s, republicans denounced clerics who condemned their activities as exceeding their spiritual powers, while loyalists complained that Catholic churchmen refused to apply their legitimate religious sanctions.

## THE ANTI-NATIONAL TRADITION OF IRISH BISHOPS

In early 1971, less than a year after the Provisionals had established their press, the tradition of republican resistance to clerical denunciation was invoked, and the list of exceptions sketched.[2] During the next decade numerous articles delineated a detailed picture. Irish bishops, declared the republicans, gravitated naturally towards British interests. The English Pope Adrian IV's dubious Bull *Laudabiliter* (1155), granting Ireland to Henry II,[3] demonstrated an early liaison between the English monarchy and the Holy See. On the other side, however, the Orange Order Grand Master, Martyn Smyth, like Paisley, used *Laudabiliter* to typify Rome's initial interference in Irish affairs.[4] Opponents were at cross purposes. Republicans, moreover, insisted that Rome altered its policy to suit circumstances. In 1600, for example, when England had rejected Catholicism and made it illegal, Pope Clement VIII granted a plenary indulgence to the liberators of Ireland.[5] Republicans endorsed the embattled bishops of the eighteenth-century penal era, but portrayed the British government's establishment[6] of the Maynooth seminary in 1795 as a blatant liaison between church and occupying power. The Official Sinn Fein journal, the *United Irishman,* which usually ignored the Catholic church except on education, pointed out that bishops had condemned both the 1798 rebellion and that of Robert Emmet in 1803.[7] Fr. John Murphy, one of the leaders of the Wexford rebellion of 1798, was a good priest according to the Provisionals,[8] but a typical political cleric to loyalists.

In the nineteenth century clear polarisation between nationalism and the official Catholic hierarchy seemed evident. The Young Irelanders were stigmatised as 'infidels' by numerous clerics and the church condemned their 1848 rebellion. The rise of Fenianism in the 1860s posed particular problems for the Catholic church, apparently experiencing a 'devotional revolution' and 'Romanisation' under the determined Cardinal Paul Cullen. The Provisionals have followed a well-worn nationalist tradition in condemning Cullen as being 'largely to blame for the peculiar type of snobbery and intolerance of priests which, unfortunately has survived to our own day'.[9] Cullen's alleged protégé, Bishop David Moriarty, was duly remembered for his famous statement that 'Hell was not hot enough nor eternity long enough' to punish the Fenians.

## CULLEN v. THE FENIANS

Though the debate of the 1970s and 1980s cited the struggle between Cullen and the Fenians as a typical phase in a long tradition of hostility, it became an important precedent. The short-lived Fenian journal, the *Irish People,* operated in 1865–7 under the shadow of Dublin Castle, much as the Provisionals' *Republican News* and *An Phoblacht* later functioned under the aegis of British army patrols and helicopters. The *Irish People,* moreover, conducted a debate with Cardinal Cullen analogous to that between the Provisionals and the Northern Irish bishops in the 1970s and 1980s.[10] The Fenians delegated their defence to Charles J. Kickham, a devout Catholic, who sought to demonstrate that Catholic clergy were exceeding their functions in condemning a movement, compelled by repression to act secretly, but seeking the God-given right of Ireland to self-government. Cullen was not impressed. He tried to implement a long-ignored

papal rescript of 1844 by ordering his priests to abstain from
politics and instructing confessors to refuse absolution to penitents
who had taken the Fenian oath. In 1870 Cullen secured a papal
rescript condemning the Fenians by name. The movement,
however, continued, even after the dismal failure of the 1867
Rising. Not all Catholic clergy obeyed Cullen in questioning
penitents on the Fenian oath: there were religious orders and
bishops outside his control. The precedent of finding patriotic
confessors to absolve republicans was thus established at a time
when the physical force preached was in many cases theoretical.
Cullen was nevertheless condemned and disparaged by his
opponents. They accused him of being an agent of Britain and
enriching his family in Carlow.[11] The propaganda was true in the
sense that Cullen, who had no love of the British, certainly
demanded government action against Fenianism. Cullen, however, considered himself a prince of the universal church rather
than an Irish patriot.[12] Republicans have never appreciated this
distinction. To them churchmen must be either advocates of an
independent Ireland or traitors bought by the British. As
Professor Donal McCartney, in an article published shortly before
the beginning of the current Ulster Troubles, argued of the
Fenians, Cullen merely employed 'the sort of clever but distorted
argument against them which they had used against him'.[13] Such
misunderstanding occurred frequently in the 1970s.

McCartney's article, 'The Church and the Fenians', amplified in
1979 by R. V. Comerford's, *Charles J. Kickham,* places the church
and Provisionals in perspective. They show, first, that Kickham in
his polemic used strong language but avoided theological questions, insisting on the separation of religion and politics, a
proposition condemned by Pius IX's *Syllabus of Errors* in 1864.
Kickham, however, argued that by the 1860s the Irish had shed the
old dependence on the clergy necessitated by 'fiendish' British
tyranny. Better-educated Irish could judge for themselves 'in all
worldly concerns'. This was not far from the Protestant principle
of 'private judgement', which can only with difficulty be abstracted
from the realities of the Reformation period. Second, the *Irish
People*'s comment, shortly before its suppression in 1865, that 'the
people are now so used to denunciation there is no room to fear
they will be frightened of it when time has come for the final
struggle', is relevant.[14] The *Irish People* was only partly correct.

Bishops were slower to condemn thereafter, but they eventually came out against Parnell. Only seven denounced the 1916 Rising, while twenty-two remained silent. A third precedent was the Fenian insistence that Vatican condemnation was based on errors fostered by British diplomacy; it proved of value when the pope came in person to Ireland in 1979. Finally, the Fenians played an essential part in insisting that the onus was on the church, not the individual penitent, to prove that patriotic activities were immoral. Comerford may not have overstated the case when he awarded Kickham's defence 'a permanent place in Irish republican tradition and in Irish historiography'. Even more significantly, the president of Maynooth, also writing of the church and the Fenians, concluded that clerics, even after the nominative condemnation of Fenianism by the Vatican in 1870, remained much divided on the issue. As Cardinal Tomas O'Fiaich, this ecclesiastical historian was to play a leading role in a similar contest in Northern Ireland.[15]

## NATIONAL AND ANTI-NATIONAL CLERGY AFTER 1916

Not all the arguments of republicans in the 1970s were based on a clear understanding of the Fenian debate as summarised above, but much of its spirit filtered down through other insurgents. Cullen's great enemy in the Irish hierarchy, Archbishop John MacHale of Tuam, was excepted from this tradition of anti-national prelates. So too was Archbishop Croke of Cashel, though originally recommended for the episcopate by Cullen and, despite much ambiguity, in agreement with the latter of the need to defeat Fenianism at the polls. Dr O'Fiaich cited these clerics in his argument. In the aftermath of the Easter Week Rising Bishop Thomas O'Dwyer of Limerick and Archbishop Daniel Mannix of Melbourne were the obvious heroes. Of lesser status, Fr. Michael O'Flanagan, briefly president of Sinn Fein and disciplined by his superiors, was a model cleric to the Provisionals.[16] During the Irish revolution Bishop Michael Fogarty of Killaloe had associated himself with Sinn Fein, in its non-violent form. After partition Cardinal Joseph McRory, denounced by loyalists for denying true Christianity to Protestants and asserting that no Protestants would survive fifty years of a united Ireland,[17] was regarded as basically patriotic in his sympathies. A somewhat surprising inclusion in the canon of good clerics was the Englishman, Cardinal Henry Manning, whose letter to Gladstone (24 February 1865) was quoted: 'I am convinced that we hold Ireland by force, not only against the will of the majority, but in defiance of all rights, natural and supernatural'.[18]

Opposed to these were many prelates accused of following the pro-British tradition. Bishop Daniel Cohalan of Cork was singled out as the one authority in the first Irish revolution who had excommunicated IRA men in his diocese.[19] When the Irish civil war began, many republicans opposed to the new Free State government were excommunicated. This was a double-edged precedent. According to James Connolly's earlier prediction, whatever the hierarchy's actions during a revolutionary struggle, it would very soon rally behind the ultimate victor. On the other hand it appeared a particularly vicious instance of perennial anti-republicanism. A final example of the anti-national tradition before the Ulster Troubles was revealed in 1982 when the newly released cabinet papers of 1951 showed that Archbishop John Charles McQuaid of Dublin had asked the British ambassador to prevent the release of IRA men gaoled in England.[20] Though not realised by republicans, this was analogous to Cullen's letter to Gladstone asking for the suppression of the Fenian *Irish People.*

Irish republicans could thus make out a fairly effective historical case against the Irish bishops. This case was partly for home consumption, to enable young Catholics to join the IRA without jeopardising their immortal souls. But there was another side. Republicans needed to refute the Rome Rule argument so dear to loyalists. During the Irish revolution the *Irish Bulletin,* directed at foreign opinion, laid great stress on the unpatriotic character of the Irish hierarchy; it portrayed traditional Irish nationalist non-sectarianism as inevitably condemned by bishops.[21] Similar arguments in the Provisional press of the 1970s and 1980s were extensively disseminated in the USA and other countries. Profes-sor McCartney claimed, ironically, that the outspoken Fenian dialogue with the Catholic bishops rendered sectarianism 'largely irrelevant'. It was not quite eradicated in 1865, 1921, or 1989. Opponents ridiculed the notion of non-sectarian republicanism;

even less prejudiced outsiders were sceptical of distinctions between religion and politics. Sometimes the Provisionals, moreover, appeared to protest too much. If really free from clerical influence why reject it so vehemently? The tradition of counteracting clerical denunciation seemed to require refurbishing in every generation.

## CATHOLIC BISHOPS AND ULSTER TROUBLES: POLITICS AND PERSONALITIES

The Catholic bishops themselves had no easy task. In the initial stages of the Ulster Troubles, the *Protestant Telegraph* gloated that republicans rejected the clergy in political celebrations such as the fiftieth anniversary of Easter Week in 1966 and the Connolly commemoration of 1968. Paisley's paper attributed this to the advance of socialism in the ecumenical age; no longer could the Roman Catholic church claim to be a bulwark against communism.[22]

In Northern Ireland, though six dioceses touched on the area, only two sees were restricted entirely to the Six Counties. Three bishops had the main responsibility for the embattled nationalist population: the primate, the bishop of Derry and the bishop of Down and Connor. In 1968 the cardinal archbishop of Armagh and primate of All Ireland was William Conway (born in Belfast), a prelate of the old school, appointed in 1963 after the normal career of pastoral and academic life. Conway was born in 1913 in Belfast, in a street between the Protestant Shankill and the Catholic Falls. He had played no notable part in the Second Vatican Council and might have found adjustment to the new reforms sufficiently difficult without any political disturbances. His cautious ecumenical advances, however, appealed to Protestant ecumenists.[23] But in the 'cruel see' of Down and Connor was a very much more controversial figure. William Philbin was born in 1907 in Mayo, educated at Maynooth, where he eventually became a professor of theology before appointment as bishop of Clonfert and Galway in 1953. There he demanded a reduction in the political influence of the five per cent Protestant minority and insisted that the republic was a Catholic state. He was translated to

Down in 1962. A theological conservative, he protested at Vatican II against a more liberal interpretation of revelation. Working closely with Monsignor Patrick Mullally and Canon Padraig Murphy (according to Labour prime minister James Callaghan 'a wonderful leader of his flock, who constantly strove for peace'), Dr Philbin built schools and reorganised church property. He was accused of encouraging the building of the notorious Divis Flats to populate the parish from which he derived most of his revenue. Republicans complained that Philbin worked closely with the unionists, especially when Terence O'Neill was prime minister. In 1970 he and Conway appointed a Catholic chaplain to Stormont. To some an ecumenical gesture of reconciliation, to republicans it was a blatant sellout of nationalist principles. Inevitably, Paisley's *Protestant Telegraph* was equally irate: 'a Priest of Baal cannot be at the same time a Minister of God'. It demanded protest from all Protestants and subsequently denounced Dr Philbin for part-authorship of a draft on ecumenism.[24] Thus a diametrically opposed, though mirrored, interpretation reflects from opposing extremists. To Philbin republicans attributed offences similar to those of Cullen: personal or family enrichment, association with the British government – especially dinner with the queen and attendance at a royal garden party – and valuing stained-glass windows above Catholic lives.[25]

Two other prominent bishops were men of different styles. Bishop Cahal Daly was born in 1917 and served a long apprenticeship as professor of scholastic philosophy, not in a Catholic seminary, but at the non-denominational Queen's University of Belfast. Before succeeding Philbin in Down in 1982 he was appointed bishop of Ardagh and Clonmacnois, a diocese outside the Six Counties. Daly's background soon established him as a spokesman on Northern Ireland. In 1973 he published *Violence in Ireland and the Christian Conscience*.[26] The bishop denied the Provisionals legitimacy as successors of the IRA of the first Irish revolution, arguing that the latter were supported by the Sinn Fein victory at the 1918 general election. His acceptance of the 1916 Rising, however, was controversial. In 1974, Dr Cahal Daly was joined in the northern episcopate by a namesake, Dr Edward Daly. The latter's background was less academic but he had considerable media experience. Daly was appointed in the wake of Derry's 'Bloody Sunday', where he gained TV publicity and later gave evidence to the Widgery Commission on the nightmare shooting of thirteen people in ten minutes. Edward Daly, born in Fermanagh in 1933, the son of a grocer and undertaker, was educated at the Irish College in Rome. He felt 'shattered' when appointed, as a mere curate, bishop of Derry. His Bloody Sunday experience 'highlighted the obscenity of killing' and made him abhor all violence. His outspoken condemnations of violence enraged Provisionals; he figured almost as prominently in loyalist demonology. However, after Dr Cahal Daly's appointment to Down in 1982, he drew most Provisional fire. According to *An Phoblacht*, the new bishop was 'more intellectually sophisticated but every bit as reactionary' as Philbin. His father, it was claimed, had supported the Black and Tans.[27]

Arriving later in the Northern Irish hierarchy was Cardinal Tomas O'Fiaich, who was born in the strongly republican town of Crossmaglen on the south Armagh border in 1923. He succeeded Cardinal Conway in Armagh on the latter's death in 1977. The appointment gave rise to the Ian Paisley gibe that you can take a man out of Crossmaglen, but you can't take Crossmaglen out of a man. Many loyalists were apprehensive of a new primate originating from what they regarded as Provisional-dominated 'bandit country'. Did he not sign his name in Irish and please republicans by his views on language?[28] Even ecumenists lamented the loss of the less doctrinaire Conway. In fact, soon Cardinal O'Fiaich incurred the wrath of republicans, who discovered that the prelate had been a ruthless disciplinarian as president of Maynooth. Meanwhile Dr O'Fiaich's tentative offer to engage in dialogue with Dr Paisley evoked a ferocious sermon at the Martyrs' Memorial, which asserted the Free Presbyterian moderator's readiness for public debate, but no dialogue, with Antichrist's representative.[29]

The bishops of Clogher, Dromore and Kilmore, whose dioceses contained part of the Six Counties, were less frequently drawn into the revolutionary debate. Occasionally other southern bishops who, like Dr Cahal Daly, had initially no direct responsibility for the northeast, participated. Generally, the primate, the bishop of Derry, and the bishop of Down and Connor, plus their personal clerical lieutenants, were the embattled prelates. Drs Eric Gallagher and Stanley Worrall, eminent Methodist ecumenists, epitomised the hierarchy's problem when describing the republican view that Cardinal Conway was a government agent as a 'mirror image' of the loyalist belief that he was a crypto-Provisional.[30]

# THE EARLY TROUBLES:
# THE PEACEMAKERS' DILEMMA

In the early years of the Troubles, before the republican propaganda war gained momentum, Cardinal Conway tried to moderate passions. When Paisleyites and Civil Righters clashed at Armagh in November 1968, Conway and the Church of Ireland primate issued an unprecedented joint appeal for restraint. Nevertheless, at the Methodist conference in June 1969 the cardinal was rebuked for his silence. When he did speak out on the conditions in Derry, which led to the explosion in August 1969, Conway received a characteristic blast from the *Protestant Telegraph:* 'instead of making an appeal for peace, (he) is actually revealing the plan of campaign . . . He cants with the hypocrisy dripping from his polluted lips about the manifest injustices of 40 years . . . his corpulent belly, his extravagant (albeit effeminate) dress and luxurious surroundings, give the lie to this indictment of the Protestants of Ulster.' Bishop Philbin, later criticised by republicans for persuading Catholics to remove their barricades in Belfast, was denounced, before the emergence of the Provisionals, by Paisley's journal for whitewashing Roman Catholic murders: 'Well may the Pope be indicted as a man of blood and the Papacy as a system of murder'.[31]

Roman Catholic bishops were in a quandary in the Northern Ireland of the 1970s and 1980s. If their duty lay in neither uncritically defending the union nor devoting all energies to a united Ireland, what could they do? They had, first, as the Provisionals recognised in their fairer moments, to condemn outrages on both sides. Second, they had to maintain communications with both the British government and the nationalist community. Conway was pressured by unionists to accept *de jure* the northern regime by publicly attending government functions. But this would have neutralised his influence in Catholic areas and he had to act very cautiously, talking quietly to the authorities when necessary. Cardinal Cullen had faced a similar dilemma.

From another perspective, the issue was a new opportunity for the Roman Catholic church to demonstrate its superiority over the rival force of secular nationalism. Neither side, however, wanted to provoke mutually destructive confrontation.

Ecumenism was a new element in the history of Irish nationalist activity. At the very beginning of the Troubles the precedent had been set for joint church appeals for peace. With Conway's support, such declarations and services of intercession continued. The churches involved were generally the Roman Catholic, the Church of Ireland, the Presbyterian, and the Methodist, or at least some members of them. A number of clergy in the latter three churches took the Free Presbyterian position. These conservatives belaboured many joint initiatives as a sellout to Rome. As late as 1985 the theologically conservative Presbyterian minister of Limavady, David Armstrong, was hounded, at Paisleyite instigation, from his parish. He had invited the local Catholic priest to say 'Happy Christmas' to his congregation. When ecumenism did occur it was often directed, in joint church statements, against the Provisionals. The latter, opposed to the 'Two Nation' theory, bracketed Cardinal Conway with the Church of Ireland Archbishop Simms in their counter-denunciations,[32] and were prepared to negotiate through ecumenical Protestants, as at Feakle in late 1974. There was no simple Catholic versus Protestant dichotomy, but a more fluid division, cutting across individual churches, between Roman Catholics (radical and conservative), Protestant ecumenists ('Prot-ecums'), and Protestant statists ('Prot-stats').

In 1968–70, therefore, Cardinal Conway and the other Roman Catholic bishops endeavoured to steer cautiously between outright support for the government and encouraging revolt by the Catholic community. Conway insisted[33] on the need for reforms to be implemented, but was prepared to attend meetings at Stormont. He also distanced himself from Fr. Denis Faul's demand for English and Scottish judges to replace biased Northern Irish counterparts.[34] In April 1970 the cardinal appealed to his community for 'dignified silence' in the face of provocation.[35] The policies of Bishop Philbin and Bishop Farren of Derry were similar. Certainly, such admonitions were unlikely to promote the revolution; Conway was later accused, like his predecessor Cullen, of assisting Stormont in return for total control of Catholic education. On the other hand, when Conway praised the people of Bogside in 1969, a *Protestant Telegraph* correspondent in Australia accused the cardinal of ignoring the 'diabolical petrol bomb throwing'.[36] Even Conway's dissociation from Faul did not appease the Paisley paper, which complained that Conway had asserted that the remarks on the judiciary were 'unauthorised and unfortunate' but not a lie.[37] Not surprisingly the *Protestant Telegraph*, reporting that 'Mr Philbin' had been booed off the Falls Road,[38] failed to draw the conclusion that, as the Catholic authorities could no longer count on the uncritical support of their flocks, fears of Rome rule were obsolete.

## PROVISIONALS CHALLENGE THE HIERARCHY

By 1971 the emergence of the Provisionals as an urban guerrilla army inaugurated insurgency proper. Meanwhile, Conway, who claimed on UTV to have already condemned violence twenty-three times,[39] broke a fifty-year precedent by conducting, at his own request, private discussions with the Northern Ireland prime minister. He also met the British home secretary, James Callaghan, when the latter visited Northern Ireland later in the year. Such interviews could not stop the escalation of violence, which led to internment on 9th August. This turning-point embarrassed the cardinal and his bishops, who had virtually acknowledged the existing regime as all Prot-stats and many Prot-ecums wished. When internment was mooted earlier in the year, the *Republican News* complained that only Bishop Philbin had refused to protest. Cardinal Conway appeared to condemn internment on 14th August and criticised the brutal treatment of innocent people by the security forces. Though a radical priest later complained that the protest was not against internment as such, Prot-stats were furious.[40]

But the Provisionals were even more irate about what followed. On 12th September, the cardinal and six bishops issued a statement condemning the IRA for disgracing noble causes. It contained the famous rhetorical question, how could a million Protestants be bombed into a united Ireland? The Provisionals' IRPB (Irish Republican Press Bureau) issued an immediate retort, accusing the bishops of double standards. There had been no condemnation, it claimed, when 500,000 Catholics were forced to live under a regime condemned by 80 per cent of the country's population. The American, Fr. Sean McManus, recently fined for disorderly conduct at Enniskillen, was quoted on the illegal and violent origin of the Six County regime. Moreover, the Provisionals insisted that they were not forcing Protestants but fighting the British army. Somewhat inconsistently, the Provisionals invited the bishops to provide defence against 'marauding British troops, partisan police forces and extreme Unionist mobs'.[41] The 'bombing of a million Protestants' was long remembered; as late as 1976 the *Republican News*[42] attributed to Conway 'one of the most unfortunate phrases' by a recent political figure. It claimed that the 1971 census, which showed 625,000 Catholics to 865,000 Protestants, demonstrated the phrase's inaccuracy.

The bishops' statement of September 1971 was even-handed. It criticised the brutality of internment and asked Protestants to heed the very strong adverse reaction in the Catholic community. Moreover, it anticipated the power-sharing experiment by suggesting a reform of parliament to allow something other than the strictest majoritarian democracy. Interrogation in depth by torture was condemned as un-British by Conway and other bishops in October and November. Even the Provisionals were constrained to admit that their bête noire, Bishop Philbin, had spoken out against the British army's interference with the funeral of an IRA lieutenant, Terence MacDermott, and had demanded the investigation of CS gas in the precincts of St Agnes Hall.[43] Earlier in the year, the bishop had refused to open his suitcase when challenged by the army.[44]

Hopes of rapprochement were dashed in late October by another condemnation of the Provisionals, this time by the whole Irish episcopal conference of 30th September.[45] It aroused the fury of the *Republican News,* which used language that would have horrified the more circumspect C. J. Kickham in 1865. The 'episcopal vipers' were told that their previous efforts had been sufficiently bad but 'the back-stabbing edict issued this week by the Irish hierarchy's commissars must rank as the greatest act of premeditated treachery against an innocent people since Judas betrayed his Saviour with a kiss. That so-called men of God should issue such a damnable lie, on the very day that two young innocent

women were being buried, defies understanding.'[46] Invective
could scarcely be stronger. Once again, the conference statement
had been balanced in the sense of attributing much of the current
violence to internment. Revolutionaries, however, have no use for
'balance', but require total endorsement: 'Bas go Bua' (Death or
Victory).

## THE CHURCH CONFRONTS INTERNMENT
## AND BLOODY SUNDAY

In the wake of internment some of the Catholic clergy seemed
prepared to endorse PIRA. 'Each week', rejoiced the *Republican
News,* 'gives new evidence of more clergy throwing their full
weight behind us'.[47] Though the hierarchy 'was as reactionary as
ever', it was 'clearly becoming more and more isolated as every
day brings news of the ordinary clergy rejecting the false doctrines
of their superiors and rallying to the support of their people'.[48] It
quoted Fr. Murray of St Paul's, Falls Road, who could not
distinguish between a murderer and a patriot, and Fr. C.
O'Donnell, former rector of the Holy Cross community, Ardoyne,
who believed the people considered the IRA their only
protectors.[49] Eight priests on 24th November identified with
internees by refusing to pay fines for boycotting the census.
Earlier, on 25th October, sixty Armagh diocesan priests signed a
protest against brutality at the Holywood Barracks. Fr. Faul was
as usual particularly active in campaigning against torture; with Fr.
Brian Brady of St Joseph's Training College and Fr. McEvoy of
the New University of Ulster. Faul was congratulated by the
*Republican News* for his work on behalf of the internees and their
families.[50] Sympathy from Catholic educationalists like Fr. Brady
may have defused ominous talk in Provisional ranks of abandoning
segregated schools and enforcing strict separation of church and
state in a united Ireland.

Conway's even-handed policy was ultimately wrecked by
internment. On 10th May, Fr. Padraig Murphy had claimed 50,000
signatures for peace. But after internment the nationalist community became so aroused that even the loyalty of priests to their
ecclesiastical superiors was put at risk. Though the British and
Stormont governments hoped that the Roman Catholic church

would be a moderating factor in the nationalist ghettoes, the authorities themselves had revived the traditional rejection of clerical leadership in times of great patriotic excitement. The republican rhetorical excesses against any church criticism were based on a deep understanding of this tradition. Republicans, unlike the two governments, read the relevant history. Stormont and Westminster contrived to fall simultaneously into the loyalist trap by making Catholic clergy behave as the rebels the Prot-stats traditionally asserted them to be. Some years later, in changed circumstances, several of the militant priests were to reverse their direction. As Oliver MacDonagh has shown, Irish churchmen shared the dilemmas and evasions of their congregations.[51]

Ironically, the Catholic hierarchy was saved from further exploitation of its difficulties by another outrage, Bloody Sunday, 30th January 1972. As Cardinal Conway led the obsequies of the thirteen dead on the Catholic side, there could be no breach in the unanimity of the community's abhorrence for an act regarded as wilful slaughter. Even unionists, according to Gallagher and Worrall, with the usual exception of Dr Paisley, were sufficiently shocked to await an enquiry at the beginning of this cruel and brutal year.[52] The Catholic consensus soon disintegrated. Conway duly condemned the Official IRA's retaliatory bombing at Aldershot in February 1972; the logic of the action was accepted by the Provisionals. The cardinal described the men of violence in his community as but a microscopic minority. Accordingly, in an RTE interview on 2nd April, after the fall of Stormont, he insisted that most northern Catholics were opposed to the IRA and demanded a ceasefire. Two days later about a hundred Andersonstown women met to support Conway, but, on 16th April, 800 people, mainly men, also gathered in Andersonstown to support continuance of the Provisional campaign. The *Republican News* recited the traditional list of unpatriotic prelates. Its columnist, Seamus O'Kelly, warned the primate that 'no churchman, be he bishop, cardinal, or even the pope himself, has a right to deny our claim to nationhood'. Conway was to be respected as a cardinal, but not as an advocate of 'Imperialism or British Dominionism'. Fr. Sean McManus insisted that 'to be against the Provisionals is to be against Ireland'.[53] Conway, however, persisted in his assertion that only one per cent of the Northern Irish population supported violence.[54] In August 1972 the cardinal was appalled by the

Bloody Friday bombings. The Provisionals, insisting that adequate warnings had been given, maintained that Conway's silence on the twenty deliberate killings of innocent Catholics by the UDA was evidence of double standards.[55]

## CATHOLIC BISHOPS v. LOYALIST PARAMILITARIES

Such criticism was hardly justified. On 18th August Conway and other heads of leading churches condemned the 'appalling assassinations', the vocabulary of disapproval beginning to run down. In November the cardinal was more explicit, complaining of a second campaign of extermination directed against the Catholic population, sixty of whom had now been shot, while hundreds were forced out of their homes.[56] Even the *Republican News* admitted that Conway had at last spoken out against violence to the Catholic community. Nevertheless both primate and Catholic bishops had been 'strangely silent on the whole question of the sufferings of the nationalist people'.[57] This was very far from the truth. Indeed the difference between the cardinal and Fr. Faul, author of numerous protests and pamphlets on the harassment of Catholics, was less than appeared at first sight. Conway certainly continued his denunciations of increasing loyalist killings into the following year. On 9th November 1973 he used the very argument that the Provisionals had used against him by accusing the authorities of a 'muted' response to the problem.

Loyalists needed to divert accusations from themselves. The Rev. Roy Magee, a Prot-stat Presbyterian minister and president of the UDA auxiliary, the Loyalist Association of Workers, agreed with the Provisionals that the Roman Catholic church was ambivalent on violence, but detected bias towards the IRA, not the loyalists. He denied that the Catholic church, was a true New Testament church.[58] This mirrors Cardinal MacRory's rejection of Protestantism. The *UDA News* claimed that Conway had said that it was no murder to kill a British soldier; in a war situation the intention of the act was the vital factor.[59] It also emphasised the use of the confessional[60] to absolve murderers from dastardly crimes. Paisley's paper named an Australian, Fr. W. Creede of Clonard Monastery, willing to give absolution to Provisionals.[61]

Paisley himself, despite an attack in parliament on sixty-five priests who had claimed that army undercover men shot innocent Catholics to provoke IRA exposure, admitted loyalist assassinations. When stigmatising, in late 1972, the Roman church as 'drunk with martyrs' blood', he warned Protestants not to copy the enemy. Perhaps the most useful diversion at this time was the visit of the archbishop of Dublin, Dr Dermot Ryan, and his predecessor, Dr McQuaid, to the Provisional chief of staff, Sean MacStiofain, then on hunger strike in a southern gaol. This was long remembered as proof that the Roman Catholic church connived at terrorism, though, at the time, the *Protestant Telegraph* also condemned an ecumenical Church of Ireland cleric, the Rev. Joseph Parker, who tried to secure MacStiofain's release.[62]

In 1973 Cardinal Conway himself emphasised the Protestant assassination campaign in his most publicised public utterances and enthusiastically supported the government's plans for power-sharing, partly anticipated by the Catholic bishops in 1971. Everyone who believed in democracy, said the Catholic primate in December 1973, should back the Sunningdale agreement.[63] Power-sharing was the logical outcome of the cardinal's work for inter-church co-operation after Vatican II. His stand meant effective support for the constitutionalist Social Democratic and Labour Party (SDLP), the eternal rivals of the Provisionals in Catholic areas. Provisional propaganda was now geared to demonstrating that the Catholic hierarchy and SDLP were working together in collaboration with the British. As for the more immediate struggle between republicans and clerics, a front-line priest was Fr. Aquinas, CP, of Holy Cross Church, Ardoyne.

## THE CONTRASTING TRIBULATIONS OF FATHERS AQUINAS AND WILSON

Fr. Aquinas, in August 1972, argued in his parish magazine that eighty-five per cent of his congregation opposed violence. This conceded a higher percentage of supporters for physical force than that suggested by his primate. In March 1973 Aquinas extended his attack on the Provisionals.[64] In an open letter he claimed to speak for the majority of his people, who wanted protection by troops but were afraid to speak out in the face of Provisional intimidation. This struck at the roots of Provisional propaganda; Aquinas was answered by Provisional leaders such as Billy McKee and Martin Meehan, who insisted that violence was used mainly in defence against Orange mobs burning Catholic homes.[65] Aquinas was also attacked by republican prisoners.[66] In May Aquinas was removed from his position as editor of the parish journal; the *Protestant Telegraph* complained that this was for opposing the Provisionals.[67] Three years later Paisley's paper noted that Aquinas had been sent to Dublin for his own protection: 'I have got on a confidential telephone, I have informed the authorities that such and such a person had done such and such a deed.' Even this was not enough for the Free Presbyterian newspaper, which accused Aquinas of failing, with 'Jesuitical dexterity', to offer full co-operation to the security forces or to condemn the ideals of the Provisionals. It also rejected an alleged admission that he had used material obtained from the confessional.

Without accepting the full *Protestant Telegraph* rumour, Fr. Aquinas's apparent support for established authority prejudiced him in the eyes of his congregation. Provisionals insisted that his use of the confidential telephone had sent Catholics to RUC torture compounds. But Aquinas, who had worked with Protestants in England, Scotland and Australia, had previously spoken out against the Stormont regime, internment and torture. Like Bishop Cahal Daly, he distinguished between the Easter Week insurgents and the modern IRA. Aquinas cannot therefore be dismissed as a unionist sympathiser. His case has been used by Frank Burton to illustrate the tension in the Ardoyne between the Provisionals and the Catholic church. Burton maintains that about one-third of the Catholic community, frequently the nominally religious, consistently supported the Provisionals, while the rest had a 'see-saw relationship' with them. The IRA and the church were 'persistently at variance'.[68]

The year 1973 also saw a countervailing internal Catholic division on the left. The priest involved was Fr. Desmond Wilson of Ballymurphy, 'the worst housing estate in the British Isles'.[69] Fr. Wilson, an ecumenist before Vatican II, identified completely with the extreme poverty of many of his congregation. Wilson came to the conclusion, like many Latin American Catholic priests, that the official church was doing little or nothing to relieve the real needs of its people. In January 1972, a few days before Bloody Sunday, Wilson created a furore by stating, contrary to the efforts of Cardinal Conway and other bishops, that no one had the right to denounce violence unless they could offer something in its place.[70] He had also organised the sixty-five priests attacked by Paisley for condemning British army under-cover operations against Catholics. In August 1973 Fr. Wilson was involved in a public dispute with Fr. Mullally, representing Bishop Philbin, over the issue which, in a different context, led to Fr. Aquinas's precipitate departure for Dublin. Wilson accused certain Catholic army chaplains of abusing their position by giving information to the authorities. Mullally did not justify such activities but claimed that Wilson should not have made public criticism without proof.

In 1975, after criticising British influence on the Vatican, another perennial republican complaint, traceable to the 1860s, Fr. Wilson resigned his ministry and continued in Ballymurphy as a social worker. He was supported by a public meeting of 1,500 people and a petition signed by 2,000. The affair provoked widespread controversy. The former priest, Fr. Terry O'Keefe, defending Wilson, claimed that the Down and Connor diocesan establishment 'exactly mirrors the pre-1968 State in Northern Ireland'. Wilson similarly compared Belfast church procedures with those of the Unionist party before the current Troubles. He complained that in 1971 Edward Heath as prime minister had secured, via Philbin and London, a new Irish channel of communication with the Vatican, bypassing the traditional link between Conway and the Irish nuncio. These were weighty criticisms indeed. Nevertheless, in 1982 Bishop Cahal Daly, as Philbin's successor, lost no time in restoring Wilson's clerical faculties. Rehabilitation failed to diminish the vigour of Wilson's denunciation of British militarism and his insistence on episcopal condemnation of institutional violence, ideas expanded in his *An End to Silence* of 1985. Bishop Cahal Daly subsequently suspended another radical, Fr. Pat Buckley, equally willing to confront publicly loyalists, republicans, and his own bishop. The *Orange Standard* compared Buckley with the sixteenth-century Reformers.[71]

On the loyalist side, the *Protestant Telegraph* compared Wilson with the 1916 leader James Connolly and contrasted the priest's adherence to socialism with Conway's repudiation of it. The *Orange Standard* noted the great support accorded to Wilson by his community.[72] Again it failed to draw the conclusion that the Catholic church had thus demonstrated it was not the monolith claimed in loyalist propaganda. However, John McKeague's bitterly anti-Catholic *Loyalist News* saw this initial revolt against the hierarchy as a good omen. McKeague, ironically a personal friend of Wilson, was posthumously praised in the latter's 1982 novel, *The Demonstration*, as a unifying force. Fr. Wilson, as the Provisionals admitted, did not endorse their physical-force campaign; he appears, nevertheless, a genuine exponent of liberation theology.[73]

## POWER-SHARING AND HUNGER STRIKES: TWO BISHOPS DALY EMBATTLED

The church-nationalist dispute grew vituperative in 1974, when the power-sharing executive, upon which so many hopes were set, collapsed under the Ulster Workers' strike. Conway did what he could in January to aid the executive by denouncing, as a mortal sin, the taking of life without the sanction of elected representatives. In this, said the *Republican News,* he surpassed himself. The Provisional reply rehearsed the familiar story of church opposition to Irish nationalism, attacked the bishops for their apathy under the Stormont regime, and warned that there existed patriotic priests willing to provide spiritual consolation.[74] Nevertheless, the Provisionals had to endure what was virtually an episcopal 'spring offensive' led by the primate. From St Mel's Cathedral in Longford across the border came the admonitory voice of Bishop Cahal Daly comparing contemporary Northern Ireland with Al Capone's Chicago, suggesting that republicans were irreligious, and offering to talk to the Provisionals at the risk of his own life.[75] This 'immoderate sophistry', said a *Republican News* columnist, was 'nothing more than a sycophantic sop to the forces of British Imperialist oppression with which the Irish church has invariably sided against its own people'.[76]

The Provisionals could expect no better from Bishop Philbin, who in January 1974 asked Irish Americans not to contribute to funds that brought increasing misery rather than protection to the

Catholic minority in the Six Counties. Surely the new bishop of Derry, Edward Daly, who had experienced British imperialism at first hand on Bloody Sunday, would have something better to offer? On 19th April Dr Daly, less than a month after his consecration, did indeed produce a peace plan of three points, applicable in the first instance to Derry: a Provisional ceasefire, release of internees, and British army withdrawal to barracks. There was no political honeymoon for the new prelate. The bishop, declared the *Republican News,* had entered the political arena on the side of the English. The trade-off suggested was a 'despicable attempt to help the English divide and conquer the Irish people'. It agreed only with the third point.[77] The *Protestant Telegraph* also ridiculed the peace plan, which it wrongly believed 'will give the guerrillas a chuckle of delight' as the security forces would stop raiding and arresting while the internees were released. Thus it disagreed with the third point. Moreover, Dr Daly appeared in bad company as Dr Michael Ramsey, the former archbishop of Canterbury, whose service in Belfast was disrupted by Free Presbyterians, supported his plan.[78] The bishop of Derry found the onslaughts from both sides in his first weeks a recurrent challenge.

The Provisionals met their episcopal critics not only with abuse but also with rival authorities such as Bishop Thomas Drury of Corpus Christi, Texas, who, like Archbishop Mannix of Melbourne, in the first Irish revolution, endorsed from a distance. Drury was 'heart-sick to know that some of our Irish bishops have become so calloused not even to ask for prayer for our prisoners'.[79] The republicans had an excellent issue at this time to counter the attraction of the power-sharing executive, with Catholics (the tokenistic Dr G. B. Newe, who was appointed during Stormont's last months, excepted) for the first time in the state's history in ministerial positions. They emphasised the hunger strikes of the Price sisters, Marion and Dolours, and Michael Gaughan, all seeking repatriation to Ireland from their prisons in England.

The Catholic church was again in a difficult position. Cardinal Conway made private representations on behalf of the Price sisters, and Dr Edward Daly asked for their repatriation, pointing out that the British were not without guilt in their relations with Ireland. Both bishops publicly stated their hope that the women, serving life sentences for bombing in England, would not be allowed to die. Dr Cahal Daly also believed that repatriation would be yielding to humanity rather than violence, though, to the Provisionals' annoyance, he added that the hunger strikers were 'misguided' and 'culpable'.[80] The Price fast did not end in tragedy because the sisters ceased their strike in June and were sent to Northern Ireland in spring 1975. Even the Red Hand Commandos had supported repatriation. Both women were eventually released on grounds of ill-health. 'A public disgrace beyond all description', roared Paisley's paper.[81]

Not so lucky was Michael Gaughan, who died in 1974 after a sixty-five-day hunger strike. His funeral divided the Roman Catholic church. The priest who held a requiem Mass for him in London, Fr. Michael Connolly, was subsequently suspended for anti-British remarks by his superior, Archbishop Dwyer of Birmingham. In November the same prelate refused to allow the body of James McDade, killed by the bomb he was planting in Coventry, to lie in his cathedral on the way back to Belfast for burial. The *Republican News* denounced this 'despicable' contradiction of all Catholic teachings. Catholic prelates in England and Ireland faced different pressures. The *Protestant Telegraph*, unwilling to give any credit, maintained that in the end Archbishop Dwyer did say Mass for McDade.[82] Fr. Connolly joined its catalogue of priests proving the interchangeability of Romanism and revolution. Regardless of all condemnation, loyalists continued to insist that the Catholic church always gave last rites and failed ultimately to excommunicate the IRA. When, however, Catholic churches refused tricolour-draped IRA coffins, the Provisionals were outraged; when union jacks were banned from Catholic RUC coffins the *Protestant Telegraph* attacked Bishop Philbin.[83]

The fall of the power-sharing executive to the loyalist workers in May 1974 did not end the antagonism between the Provisionals and the Catholic hierarchy. The *Republican News* in July claimed that the bishops were 'in full swing behind the British'.[84] It accused Philbin of following the Ulster Workers' Council's demand for a condemnation of the IRA by a statement of 'utter fanaticism' in declaring the violence satanic and perpetrated by 'devil people' 'in full revolt against God'. Edward Daly, who denounced the purposeless violence that destroyed Strabane, was stigmatised as neutral only in name: he failed to take account of institutional violence by governments.[85] These ecclesiastics, in Provisional eyes, were on a par with the Church of Ireland bishop of Down and Dromore, Dr George Quin, who described the IRA as 'scum-like fiends'.[86] Many important politico-theological issues were vehemently debated at this time. The difference between the two Dr Dalys on the 1916 Rising – Edward against, Cahal for[87] – was openly ventilated. Much was also made of the Catholic church's desire to control its schools.

The relations between republicanism and the Catholic church were now deadlocked. In 1977 the Provisionals contrasted prelates like Cardinal Conway, Edward Daly, Philbin, and Casey of Galway with Des Wilson, Fr. Sean McManus, Fr. J. McDyer (known for the Glen Columkille co-operative which provided local employment), Faul, Camilo Torres, and Dr J. Newman of Limerick, the only bishop to demand straight British withdrawal. Dr Newman, an outspoken opponent of state secularism, believed the 1916 Rising had regenerated Ireland religiously as well as politically. Cardinal Conway, who had fought bravely for a politically untenable *via media* in one of the most troubled primacies Ireland had ever experienced, died in April 1977. His condemnation of the assassination of the British ambassador to the Irish Republic, Christopher Ewart-Biggs, in 1976 received the usual cries of partiality from republican sources. Why had he not protested when the SAS murdered Peter Cleary?[88] The debate was nothing if not repetitive.

New issues in the second half of the 1970s were the emergence of the Peace People and the prison protest against criminalisation. The Peace People raised the same question that had already been canvassed in so many forms, co-operation with and reform of the establishment or a 'zero-sum' insistence on full revolutionary objectives. Fr. Des Wilson empathised with the Provisionals when he declared himself 'blazingly angry' at the Peace People's desire for a settlement that would leave society as it had always been.[89] Cardinal Conway, however, participated in peace marches, and Wilson himself later apologised for the severity of his words. The prison protest was longer-lived and led to the hunger strikes of 1981. Here again the bishops' effort to steer a middle road proved extremely difficult. When Dr Edward Daly visited the H-Block at the Maze prison in 1978, describing it as a health hazard, but arguing that the miseries were self-inflicted, he was accused by the Provisionals of enemy propaganda at its most blatant.[90] When Cardinal O'Fiaich was shocked by the H-Block several months later, the *Protestant Telegraph* used the self-inflicted argument on him. Edward Daly became a front-runner for the northern Catholic bishops, with Conway dead and Bishop Philbin facing more opposition from his flock. The latter was picketed after Mass at Twinbrook in November 1977 by demonstrators demanding his condemnation of the H-Block.[91]

Dr Edward Daly, with a less conservative image than Philbin, was also heavily involved in the hunger-strike debate of 1981. More than Cardinal O'Fiaich, he incurred the violent opposition of the Provisionals. Though Daly in 1980 supported political prisoners demanding their own clothes, in March 1981 he bluntly declared the hunger strikes morally unjustified.[92] He was subsequently accused by *An Phoblacht* of 'vicious attacks on the dying hunger-strikers at critical periods',[93] and of 'hysterical euphoria' when the mother of a striker set the precedent by having her son treated.[94] In 1982 the battle continued, with Bishop Daly calling on Catholics to give information to the security forces. The issue had been anticipated in 1865 by Charles Kickham in the *Irish People*.[95] The Provisionals challenged the bishop to give evidence himself. Daly promised to supply information received as a private citizen to the authorities.[96] Thus from his initial attempt to maintain a balance between the nationalism of the Catholic community and the requirements of order, Bishop Daly seemed closer to the latter. However, later in 1982 the cycle continued when his attack on plastic bullets incurred the wrath of unionists like the rising lawyer Robert McCartney. The problem was exacerbated by the fact that in 1974 Catholic power-sharing ministers were potentially involved in the maintenance of order, while in the early 1980s the possibility of this soon recurring seemed remote.

## PIRA REPUDIATES FR. FAUL

The association of Fr. Faul with Bishop Daly as an enemy of the hunger strike is particularly significant. Though Faul never endorsed Provisional violence, his criticism of the security forces was always comprehensive; witness his twenty reasons why Catholics should not support the RUC, originally published in the *Irish News*.[97] Yet Faul found that Christ's injunction, 'those who are not with us are against us', especially applicable in a revolutionary situation, and agreed with Bishop Daly that evidence be given to the authorities to avoid both violence and arrests.[98] The priest who had published so much on the brutalities suffered by prisoners and internees over the decade discovered that none of this was remembered by Provisionals, who placed him with Dr Daly and Cardinal O'Fiaich in the 'treacherous trio', and by some irate 'blanket' men, who rejected him as 'a conniving, treacherous man, not in the least shy about twisting the truth to achieve his own ends'.[99] The *Protestant Telegraph* would have been delighted at this confirmation of its assertion that Faul's complaints were worthless and that there could be no neutrals.[100] Ironically, the Irish secularist *Church and State* accused Faul and Murray of encouraging the hunger strikes. Ultimately, however, Faul's opposition to the Provisional pressure on the relatives of dying hunger-strikers helped to end the protest.

Faul was not the only supporter of republicanism to become disillusioned. Such cases had apparently occurred even in the first Irish revolution, Bishop Fogarty being an example. Fr. Sean McManus, a comfort to the Provisionals in their early days, eventually condemned them.[101] Few Catholic clergy, despite the lists regularly drawn up in the *Protestant Telegraph,* could be wholehearted revolutionaries, and at the same time true to their calling. Even the radical Fr. Wilson was unable to reconcile his vocation with membership of a political party.[102] Camilo Torres, quoted by both republicans and loyalists for opposite reasons, may have died as a guerrilla in Colombia, but he renounced his clerical office first. However, as *An Phoblacht* correctly pointed out, he did so to be more truly a priest.[103] The hunger strikes are a classic example of the divergence of religion from social revolution. To a social revolutionary many people must accept death and bereavement, willing or unwilling, for the ultimate secular welfare; to the religious the nurture and the passage of the individual soul is the highest good. Hence the continued insistence of Conway and the other bishops on the sacredness of life, which, the Provisionals correctly asserted, they linked with anti-abortion. In 1979 the bishops had powerful confirmation of their position when Pope John Paul II, clearly acting on their advice, denounced violence on Irish soil.

## THE POPE ON THE SPOT

Though John Paul did not, like his predecessor Pius IX, repudiate the Irish revolutionary organisation by name, he made his position reasonably clear. 'I proclaim . . . that violence is evil, that violence is unacceptable as a solution to problems, that violence is unworthy of man. Violence is a lie, for it goes against the truth of our faith, the truth of humanity.' This was merely to repeat what the bishops had been saying for many years, in both Irish revolutions and earlier. It certainly conflicted with the romantic view of violence expressed by 1916 insurgent leader Patrick Pearse's rhapsody on 'the red wine of the battlefield'.

The pope's next sentence, 'Violence destroys what it claims to defend: the dignity, the life, the freedom of human beings', was also rooted in Irish history. This was the objection of some churchmen during the Irish revolution to the early IRA: the latter's hit-and-run tactics left the civilian population exposed to reprisals. The same point had been made in the Ulster Troubles. Canon Padraig Murphy, for example, in a Sunday plea for peace on 20th May 1972, argued that violence was not only against God's law but encouraged revenge against innocent people.[104] There was the related problem of bystanders killed in cross-fire or bombs exploding at the wrong time. The Provisionals had anticipated such criticism in the first issues of *Republican News,* when they quoted a famous passage from Sean O'Casey's *Drums Under the Windows,* describing the 1916 Rising: the dying young man clutched at a lamp-post, 'a young lassie' lying prone with 'a purple patch of death' on the back of her white blouse, an old woman's blood seeping through the floor of her tenement: 'all the goodly company of the dead who died for Ireland. Jesu, have pity! You didn't want to die. I know, I know. You signed no proclamation; you invaded no building; you pulled no trigger; I know, I know. But Ireland needed you all the same. Many will die like that before Ireland can go free. They must put up with it.'[105]

'Jesu, have pity' and 'they must put up with it' encapsulate the essential difference between Catholic theology and secular revolution which John Paul II, albeit indirectly, appears to have distinguished at Drogheda. In 1922, the future Catholic primate, Bishop O'Donnell, stated clearly the objection of many churchmen to guerrilla warfare as killing of the soul as well as the body by leaving those in mortal sin no opportunity for repentance.[106] The 'young lassie' surprised when returning from her holiday would indeed be dependent on the pity of Jesus. The secular revolutionary, on the other hand can call, without compunction, for the innocent to deliver up their lives for the great society to come.

The pope at Drogheda, when appealing on his knees to the men and women of violence, raised another relevant issue: 'You may claim to seek justice. I, too, believe in justice and seek justice. But violence only delays the days of justice. Violence destroys the work of justice.' This seems a direct reference to the slogan, 'Peace with Justice' that the Provisionals had used against the Peace People, accused simply of working for the status quo. It also recalls Bishop Edward Daly's contemplation of the ruins of Strabane, which he attributed to terrorism. In his short address the pope could only call generally for a 'return to Christ'.

The Drogheda address appealed, moreover, for people to leave organisations caught up with violence and ignore leaders preaching 'hatred, revenge, retaliation'. This again evoked traditional episcopal hostility to secret organisations whose demands were often incompatible with Catholic moral teaching and church authority. Leaving aside innocent victims – the 'murdering of defenceless people' according to the pope – no violent revolutionary organisation, despite all disclaimers, can operate without 'retaliation' against informers or dangerous opponents. Similarly, power of 'revenge' is vital in ensuring the safety of supporters, while the fostering of 'hatred' is an essential part of a political propaganda campaign. The Provisionals made no secret of these activities, however strongly they denied intentional injury to civilians. The pope, however, both at Drogheda, where he denied that the state could set aside the moral law, and at a Dublin ecumenical meeting, moved some distance towards answering the traditional republican complaint that Catholic authorities were one-sided in their condemnations of force. It was not difficult to read into these remarks a criticism of interrogatory torture, loyalist assassinations, and SAS stakeouts (ambushes prepared for IRA suspects), plus an endorsement of the untiring investigations of Frs. Faul and Murray. Indeed Paisley attacked the pope for these remarks.[107]

A pope had at last spoken on Irish soil. No student of republican propaganda, however, expected Provisional submission to arguments already rejected from Irish prelates who had obviously briefed the pontiff. As early as 1972 the *Republican News* had declared that not even the pope himself had the right to deny 'our claims to nationhood'.[108] Secret contacts with Provisionals were apparently made before the address, but after Drogheda, *An Phoblacht* proudly asserted that 'no apology was due'.

'P. O'Neill', speaking officially for PIRA, insisted on force as the only means for removing the British presence. Church leaders, politicians and the establishment had patently failed to resolve the massive social and economic problems created by the British. Moreover, other colonial countries – Zimbabwe was approaching its crisis – had demonstrated the high chances of success based on popular support. Finally, 'we know also that upon victory the church would have no difficulty in recognising us'. The maverick cleric, Fr. Des Wilson, agreed with the latter point in a *Hibernia* article. Danny Morrison, editor of *An Phoblacht,* took up the defence in person. Despite Paisley's complaints, Morrison was not satisfied that the pope had shown balance by condemning the institutionalised violence of the British. He also questioned the media emphasis on the pope's condemnation of violence rather than his reassertion of Catholic moral standards. Were the 400,000 Irish women, estimated to be on the pill, about to give it up?[109]

The papal visit to Ireland therefore settled nothing. Carefully analysed, John Paul's remarks helped to re-establish the basic issues, so often overshadowed by smokescreens of rationalisation. Perhaps, as two Catholic bishops argued, some young men were dissuaded from joining PIRA.[110] Inside clerical ranks the pope's visit probably made it more difficult for priests to take a republican line. In early 1980 Fr. Edmund Hogan of Cork complained that a number of Catholic priests were supporting the Provisionals, contrary to the church's stand on violence, and also lamented the Provisionals' response to Pope John Paul. Fr. Hogan was challenged in *Furrow* by Fr. Des Wilson.[111] The *Protestant Telegraph*[112] was glad to note an apparent confirmation that its links between popery and revolution were valid. Similarly, the UDA *Ulster* quoted Bishop Cahal Daly's complaint that four priests from America were in the IRA. The secularist *Church and State* saw a developing rapprochement between clericalism and Provisionalism.[113]

## RELIGIOUS AUTHORITY v. REVOLUTIONARY MANDATE

How was all this possible? For Prot-stats, who considered the Roman Catholic church an authority structure, based on total submission to the pope, the pontiff's appearance in Ireland should have been decisive. The only loophole was ambiguity of utterance. Yet the Provisionals and those clergy who continued to support them seemed to be deliberately rejecting ambiguity as a defence. It has been argued above that there was a clear line between revolutionary and Catholic doctrine. Why then the continued confusion? In fact the Roman Catholic church exhibited a far more uncertain authority than appears on the surface. This may be demonstrated in another look at the issues of the revolutionary mandate, the cluster of problems associated with confession, excommunication and last rites, and the principle of hunger-striking.

'By what authority?' The question has frequently been posed by Bishop Edward Daly and others in the condemnation of a particular IRA action. The answer inevitably comes pat: the same authority as Pearse and Connolly in 1916. Republican journals have repeatedly demonstrated that the insurgents of Easter Week were attacked by the clergy of that period for lacking a mandate for insurrection. This, as has already been mentioned, was a clever argument. The Irish Republic bases its authority on the Easter Week Rising, and those who rejected the rebellion as unjustified, be they cleric or lay, could not but appear unpatriotic Irishmen or even unionist fellow-travellers. By the 1970s, however, the revisionist history, already mentioned, was eroding the use of Pearse and Connolly as incantations to prove nationalist ortho-doxy. In 1971 Fr. Frank Shaw made 'Pearse a skittle'.[114] Others like John Hume of the SDLP and the writers, Ruth Dudley Edwards and Conor Cruise O'Brien, were accused of disparaging

1916.[115] Republicans had therefore to explain themselves more fully. What exactly was Pearse's mandate?

Clearly Pearse was not an elected representative, the Irish parliamentary party still possessing the field. Fr. Art O'Neill denied that any theologian required a revolutionary to be a legislator in the regime he endeavoured to supersede. To Fr. O'Neill, Pearse's mandate was found in the 1916 proclamation. This evidently meant a 'mandate of history'[116] to which the Provisionals and supporters like Fr. Sean McManus sometimes appealed. So vague a concept meant endorsement by the risings of the past, showing that British rule had never gained legitimacy, plus the support of a future popular consensus. Alternatively, the mandate might be justice, fidelity and nationality, another vague formula amounting to much the same thing. Loosely attached to the mandate of history was the ballot box. Regardless of clerical or contemporary opinion on the legitimacy of 1916, surely the seventy-three Sinn Fein representatives elected in the December 1918 election provided sufficient retrospective validation? Though accepted by churchmen like Bishop Cahal Daly, this is a double-edged weapon that could destroy the moral effect of the present-day church. Many loyalists have the same problem. As the republican Frank Gallagher complained in 1922, the bishops in 1918 campaigned strongly against Sinn Fein and even when that party had won the election still refused to accept the 'mandate' of the people implicit in Dail Eireann's declaration of war.[117] As the astute Fr. Des Wilson shows, contemporary republicans can appeal from Bishop Cahal Daly's current denunciation to the endorsement of churchmen in the future, assuming that ultimate victory is achieved. Hence the Provisional retort to the pope was based on historical realism. The fact that black terrorists in Rhodesia were metamorphosing into responsible Zimbabwe statesmen reinforced the argument.[118] However, another difficulty, affecting both churchmen of the Cahal Daly school and republicans, was that historians endorsed Arthur Griffiths's insistence in 1922 that the Irish people had not voted in 1918 for maintaining the republic of Easter Week.[119]

Provisionals also claim the mandate of the Irish revolutionaries of 1918–21. Bishop Cahal Daly and some old IRA men declared that there was no connection. Similarly, *Visor,* the British army magazine in Northern Ireland, claimed that there was no resemblance between the original UVF and the thugs of the new UVF. Yet this was not easy to prove on either side. Were the guerrillas of the first Irish revolution less ruthless? The Provisionals published a pamphlet, *The Good Old IRA,* to prove they were not. Circumstances simply required new methods. The flying columns of 1920–1 were replaced by the tactics of the modern guerrilla. They argued that, according to Catholic theology, the new war was even more justified than the 1916 Rising. Then the country was prosperous, Home Rule was imminent and there was no prospect of insurrectionary success. By the 1970s, however, the Provisional war, after 50 years' deprivation of rights, was obviously just, had a good chance of success, and was based on the support of the people. According to Fr. Wilson, in 1975 some Catholic clergy had accepted this argument. The primate, Cardinal O'Fiaich, created a diversion in 1984 by asserting that it was not morally wrong to join Sinn Fein, because of its work on housing and community projects.[120] Shortly afterwards Cahal Daly denied that the votes obtained by Sinn Fein when it contested elections after 1981 proved support for the IRA's fight. In reply, *An Phoblacht* quoted Gerry Adams, then Provisional Sinn Fein president and abstentionist MP for West Belfast: 'I don't think the IRA need a vote to continue their campaign' as the British presence in the country was a sufficient mandate.[121] Bishops and Provisionals tacitly converged in their distinction between the Armalite rifle and the ballot box.

In such quasi-theological arguments the Provisionals held their own. They claimed that only total pacifism, condemning alike state and revolutionary violence, was a valid argument against them. As Desmond Fennell argued against Dr Enda McDonagh of Maynooth, non-violence was feasible only under a leader like Gandhi, striving for positive change. The Catholic bishops, he asserted, had plainly failed to give any such direction in the early days of attacks on Catholic homes. Hence they were in no position to denounce the Provisionals who provided that defence.[122] As the loyalists were never tired of pointing out, sometimes citing controversial articles from the Irish revolutionary period, Catholic theology did make provision for violence. Provisionals would have said amen to the *Protestant Telegraph*'s evocation of Suarez (the sixteenth-century Spanish Jesuit theologian): 'When an oppressed people are left with no alternative but to resort to the use of force

in pursuance of legitimate basic human rights, then they are
entitled to do so.'[123]

## PROT-STAT AMBIGUITIES ON VIOLENCE

Paisley could not consistently exploit Catholic disagreement as he
faced the same difficulties with Protestant paramilitaries. He too
condemned sectarian murders very forcefully on occasion, but
found the UDA and UVF extremely unresponsive and, like the
republicans, apt to talk back to the clergy. On the other hand, if,
as some believe, Paisley was once very close to the UVF, he
emerges as a Prot-stat Camilo Torres. While Catholic bishops
were accused of not defending their communities, Paisley and his
colleagues were accused of talk and inaction. The UDA from the
start repudiated clerical advisers, associating them with the feeble
'fur coat' affluent unionist politicians, as the Provisionals identified their clerics with the collaborationist SDLP. Paisley
frequently accused the Catholic bishops of hypocritically denouncing violence; the same accusation was made against him. Again,
the giving of the last rites to IRA terrorists was a constant
complaint of Prot-stats against the Roman Catholic church, yet
Paisley officiated at the funerals of UDA leaders like Tommy
Heron.[124] The pope condemned retaliation; so too did the UVF
*Combat*, which distinguished it from legitimate resistance.[125] The
UVF journal agreed entirely with the Provisional insistence on
avoiding civilian casualties. It asserted that the Protestant tradition
required the 'greatest charity and compassion to non-combatants'.
This tradition was the loyalist 'mandate of history', but not
accepted by those Prot-stats who claimed that there were no
non-combatants.

## SACRAMENTS: CATHOLIC
## AND PROTESTANT

If there was such convergence in confusion over violence between
loyalist, republican and clergy, why were the related issues so
divisive? Confession, excommunication and the last rites of the
Catholic church seemed to Prot-stats positive proof that clerical

condemnations of violence were insincere. Here were powers, which the bishops possessed, to snuff out revolution like a candle flame if they so desired. The issue was a Morton's fork or Catch 22. If the church did snuff out the IRA by its authority, Prot-stats would fight its total control of the priest-ridden papists and resist a united Ireland to the death; if on the other hand the IRA persisted it was proof that, as Paisley's sometime correspondent Avro Manhattan (a well-known critic of the Catholic church) pointed out in 1971, Paul VI's master plan for the domination of Ireland was on the move.[126]

The confession-excommunication problem was thus not quite what it appeared to Prot-stats. In the days of Cardinal Cullen and the Fenians, revolutionaries had usually found loopholes to evade excommunication. Very few became atheists like the Fenian 'Pagan' O'Leary, whose English warders, to Karl Marx's indignation, ultimately compelled him, by a diet of bread and water, to attend Mass.[127] A relevant example is that of Cardinal Cullen's interlocutor, Charles Kickham. On release from a long prison sentence Kickham returned to the movement and became president of the supreme council of the Irish Republican Brotherhood. Archbishop Croke of Cashel, however, insisted that he could have no absolution unless he renounced the IRB. Kickham refused. According to his colleague, John Devoy, Kickham declared that he would trust to God's mercy and die without confession. Though Croke then relented, according to the story, the significant fact is surely Kickham's apparently 'Protestant' reliance on direct intercession with the deity.[128] Other revolutionaries seem to have resolved this problem in the same way. As Eamon de Valera said of himself, he had such a strong belief in the justice of his cause that he refused to believe it was wrong.[129] A priest during the first Irish revolution accepted the assurance of a member of Collins's assassination squad that he sincerely believed he was doing right. Cardinal Conway was attacked by the *Ulster Militant* for upholding a similar position. In 1974, the Provisional sympathiser, Fr. Art O'Neill, explained the doctrine.[130] The British, he argued, had an interest in keeping Irish Catholics as confused as possible on church teachings relating to insurrection and contraception. Conscience, however, was supreme. In confessional, the priest must explain the teaching of the church but the penitent must decide on its application to his or her behaviour. Thus killing is permissible in self-defence, the execution of a criminal, or a just war. 'The church has always insisted that under no conditions whatever may a Catholic priest attempt to control events through the confessional.' Thus it might be considered improper to ask a penitent if he belonged to a proscribed body. In fact, the Provisionals argued that the Catholic clergy of the 1970s hesitated to excommunicate republicans as in the past, not only because the latter had the support of the community, but because such excommunication was impossible after Vatican II.[131] It was thus logical for Prot-stats, who rejected ecumenism, to demand Vatican I conduct from the Catholic church.

Much now falls into place. The sacraments or last rites of the church could hardly be denied when the intention, or private judgement of the individual, was ultimately a matter between himself and God. The same factors applied to hunger strikes. Loyalists could sneer at the argument that there might be no intention to commit suicide, but what became of private judgement? One more example of such convergence must be mentioned. The Provisionals in the midst of controversies with opponents like Paisley and the socialist Noel Browne remembered for once their ultimate model, Theobald Wolfe Tone. As an admirer of the French Revolution, Tone wanted to apply the ruthless civil constitution of the clergy, which reduced the priesthood to dependence on the state, in the independent Ireland of his dreams. Fr. Wilson and the UDA's *Ulster* emphasised this. Desmond Fennell, writing for *An Phoblacht,* considered Tone's project out of date. Instead he suggested a reorganisation of parish and diocesan boundaries and councils containing elected lay representatives. Clergy and bishops would be vetted by the representative body and political bishops disciplined.[132] While obviously tongue in cheek, this proposal for turning the Irish Catholic church into something like the Presbyterian Kirk or the Church of Ireland is yet another example of mirror vision.

# SUMMARY: CATHOLIC AND REPUBLICAN LOYALISTS DIVIDE

The Anglo-Irish Agreement of November 1985 created some new alignments. The Catholic bishops, including Cardinal O'Fiaich, were generally supportive of the Accord as raising nationalist morale. The radical Fr. Wilson, who believed the Agreement likely to lead to the demise of the Irish Catholic church, joined loyalists, lay and clerical, and Provisionals in total opposition. The Provisionals' support for divorce in the Irish referendum of June 1986, and their partial endorsement of abortion in 1985, did not prevent Paisley's paper, totally opposed to both divorce and abortion, from discovering papal approbation for the IRA in May 1986.[133]

In a debate apparently impervious to current realities, certain facts stand out. First, the controversy between the Provisionals and the official Catholic church was fundamental and contained relatively little shadow-boxing. In the end, there was a line beyond which a churchman could not go in support of revolution. On the other hand the Catholic bishops maintained a consistent, slightly right-of-centre position from the outbreak of the Troubles in 1968 till the 1980s. Cardinal O'Fiaich was minimally to the left of his colleagues.[134] The pope's visit in 1979 simply confirmed the stance maintained by the Irish bishops. The loyalist complaint that the Catholic church connived at PIRA's actions is unjustified on the evidence for the bishops but partly true of a handful of lower clergy. The PIRA counter-charge of collusion with the established authorities is true from the republican viewpoint. Second, a number of very important issues, nearly all based on past disputes between Irish revolutionaries and the Catholic church, re-emerged with a post-Vatican II twist. Compared with the debate between Charles Kickham and Cardinal Cullen, the dispute between *An Phoblacht/Republican News* and Cardinals Conway and O'Fiaich was more wide-ranging and bitter. Despite the ostensible secularity of the Provisional credo, republicans were intensely concerned with parrying episcopal barbs. An increasing strain was placed on the old, comfortable, but theologically unjustified, distinction between religion and politics. As always there was tacit inconsistency when urging this principle: churchmen were sternly admonished for unpatriotic politics, but welcomed heartily when their message was favourable. In the 1860s, as Comerford has shown, Kickham did not oppose priests in politics as such, but only when they criticised Fenianism.[135] This indicates that to ask whether nationalism or religion is the stronger force in the Irish context is unprofitable: both occupy their own areas of the mind and clash in a mental no-man's-land. As Oliver MacDonagh says, priests and people shared the same ambiguity. Usually, the Prot-stats, despite the capital they made out of divisions in the Roman Catholic community, found themselves involved in mirrored disputes with their own paramilitaries, and sometimes their bishops. Moreover, the very vigour of the intra-Catholic dispute undermined their basic argument against a united Ireland, namely domination by a Catholic monolith. Cardinal O'Fiaich's conclusion, that the church of the 1860s was divided on Fenianism, is equally applicable to the 1970s and 1980s.

## NOTES

### Newspaper Abbreviations

| | |
|---|---|
| AN | *Andersonstown News* (Republican/Prov.), 1972–6 |
| AP | *An Phoblacht* (Provisional) |
| C | *Combat* (UVF) |
| IN | *Irish News* (SDLP?) |
| IT | *Irish Times* |
| LAW | *LAW* (Loyalist Association of Workers) |
| LN | *Loyalist News* (UVF – Red Hand Commando), 1970–7 |
| OS | *Orange Standard* |
| OUDAN | *Official UDA News* |
| PBP | *Protestant Blu Print* (Paisley) 1985– |
| PP | *Peace by Peace* (Peace People), 1976–7 |
| PT | *Protestant Telegraph* (DUP) |
| RI | *Republic of Ireland* (Anti-Treaty, 1922) |
| RN | *Republican News* (Provisional) |
| SDLPN | *SDLP News* |
| U | *Ulster* (UDA) |
| UDAN | *UDA News* |
| UI | *United Irishman* (Official) |
| UL | *Ulster Loyalist* (UDA) |
| V | *Volunteer* (Provisional Andersonstown), 1971–6 |
| Vi | *Visor* (British army), 1974 |
| VU | *Voice of Ulster* (DUP), 1982–4 |

1. McCarthy, Michael J. F., *The British Monarchy and the See of Rome: The Tragedy of Ireland* (London: Protestant Truth Society, 1922?) and Kensit, J. A., *Rome behind Sinn Fein?*, (London: Protestant Truth Society, 1921). See also Davis, R., 'The Manufacture of Propagandist History by Northern Ireland Loyalists and Republicans', Alexander, Y. and A. O'Day (eds.), *Ireland's Terrorist Dilemma* (Dordrecht: Martinus Nijhoff, 1986), pp. 145–77.

2. RN 1–2.71.
3. AP, 9.5. and 18.7.75. As early as 1821 even ignorant Catholics knew that the pope had encouraged Henry II to invade Ireland. Garvin, Tom, *The Evolution of Irish Nationalist Politics* (Dublin: Gill and Macmillan, 1981), p. xiv. See also *The Nation* on *Laudabiliter*, 4.11.1843.
4. UI, 14.11.74.
5. RN, 1.2.75.
6. AP, 10.71; RN, 14.1.74.
7. UI, 1.74.
8. RN, 1–2.71. Fr. Murphy is also a popular subject for AOH (Ancient Order of Hibernians) banners.
9. AP, 6.8.74.
10. See McCartney, Donal, 'The Church and the Fenians', Harmon, M. (ed.), *Fenians and Fenianism* (Dublin: Scepter, 1968), pp. 11–23. AP, 25.11.82 (Kickham and clergy).
11. Davis, op cit., pp. 1–2.
12. I am indebted to Professor Desmond Bowen for this point.
13. McCartney, op. cit., p. 22.
14. 16.9.65.
15. Comerford, R. V., *Charles J. Kickham: A Study in Irish Nationalism and Literature* (Co. Dublin: Wolfhound, 1979), p. 65. O'Fiaich, Tomas, 'The Clergy and Fenianism', *Irish Ecclesiastical Record*, vol. cix, no. 2 (Feb. 1968), pp. 81–103.
16. RN 1–2.71, AP, 15.3.74. The Provisionals do not appear to have emphasised O'Flanagan's original desire to leave Ulster to the unionists.
17. PT, 1.5.71., 31.5.69. For Croke's ambiguities, see MacDonagh, O., *States of Mind: A Study of Anglo-Irish Conflict, 1780–1980* (London: Allen & Unwin, 1983), pp. 100–1.
18. RN, 28.4.74.
19. RN, 9.4.72.
20. AP, 7.1.82.
21. Davis, R., 'Ulster Protestants and the Sinn Fein Press, 1914–22', *Eire-Ireland* (Winter 1980), p. 47.
22. PT, 8.68.
23. Gallagher, E. and S. Worrall, *Christians in Ulster, 1968–1980* (Oxford: OUP, 1982), p. 117.
24. PT, 2.1.71. and 29.3.75. For Philbin and southern Protestants see White, Jack, *Minority Report: the Protestant Community in the Irish Republic* (Dublin: Gill and Macmillan, 1975), p. 112. According to Callaghan, James, *A House Divided: The Dilemma of Northern Ireland* (London: Collins, 1973), p. 72, he talked Conway into appointing the chaplain. For Fr. Murphy, see p. 103.
25. Belfast Workers Research Unit, *Belfast Bulletin No. 10: The Churches in Northern Ireland* (Spring 1980), pp. 27–8 for a very critical account. RN, 1.2.71 and 30.10.71, 11.5 and 6.7.74; PT, 29.31 and 11.5.75.

26. Daly, Cahal B., *Violence in Ireland and the Christian Conscience* (Dublin: Veritas, 1973), pp. 40–1, criticised in AP 31.5.74.
27. Interview with Alf McCreary, Radio Ulster, 21.2.82. Widgery Report (HL 101 and HC 220), p. 16. AP, 6.1.83 & 21.7.83 (against Cahal Daly).
28. RN, 1.2.75.
29. PT, 2.79.
30. Gallagher and Worrall, p. 118.
31. PT, 30.8.69.
32. AP, 6.6.72. Armstrong, David with Hilary Saunders, *A Road too Wide: The Price of Reconciliation in Northern Ireland* (Basingstoke: Marshalls, 1985).
33. 17.11.69. Deutsch, R. and V. Magowan, *Northern Ireland, 1968–74: A Chronology of Events,* 3 vols. (Belfast: Blackstaff, 1974 & 5).
34. Deutsch and Magowan, 17.1.69.
35. Deutsch and Magowan, 3.4.70.
36. PT, 25.10.69.
37. PT, 6.12.69.
38. PT, 27.9.69.
39. Gallagher and Worrall, p. 60.
40. RN, 3.71. According to Wilson, Fr. Des, *An End to Silence* (Cork: Mercier, 1985), p. 75, Conway protested against torture, but not internment as such.
41. AP, 10.71.
42. RN, 3.4.76.
43. RN, 9.10.71.
44. RN, 3.71.
45. Gallagher and Worrall, p. 63.
46. RN, 30.10.71.
47. RN, 5.12.71.
48. RN, 6.11.71.
49. RN, 5.12.71.
50. RN, 9.10.71, 25.9.71.
51. See MacDonagh, op cit., p. 101.
52. Gallagher and Worrall, p. 64.
53. RN, 9.4.72.
54. Deutsch and Magowan, 24.5.73. and 17.3.74.
55. RN, 8.74.
56. Deutsch and Magowan, 14.11.72.
57. RN, 1.12.72.
58. *LAW* (1, 28) 72. McRory's statement was quoted in IN, 18.12.31. See Arthur, Paul, *Government and Politics in Northern Ireland* (London: Longmans, 1980), p. 42.
59. UDAN (18) 72.
60. UDAN (13) 72.
61. PT, 7.10.72.
62. PT, 15.12.72. *LAW* (2, 40) 72.
63. Deutsch and Magowan, 10.12.73.

64. Deutsch and Magowan, 16.3.73.
65. AP, 6.4.73. For Aquinas's leaflet and reply, see Burton, Frank, *The Politics of Legitimacy: Struggles in a Belfast Community* (London: Routledge & Kegan Paul, 1978), pp. 94–5.
66. RN, 24.3.73.
67. PT, 26.5.73.
68. PT, 2.10.76. Burton, op cit., pp. 8, 93 and 103 for non-religious natures of Provisionals, p. 85 for 'see-saw relationship', and p. 94 for Aquinas on Connolly and Pearse. See also IN, 11.8.72 for Aquinas interview on opposition to Stormont. See V, vol. 2, no. 3, 1976, for republican opinion.
69. An academic quoted by The *Sunday Times* Insight Team Ulster (Harmondsworth: Penguin, 1972), p. 202.
70. Deutsch and Magowan, 4.1.72.
71. PT, 7.3.70. For details of the dispute between Wilson and Philbin see AN, 21 and 28.6.75. The article causing the trouble was published in AN, 19.4.75 and quoted from *Hibernia*. For Terry O'Keefe, AN, 5.7.75. A booklet, *Open the Window, Let in the Light,* was published by Wilson's followers.
72. OS, 8.75. See also Wilson, *An End to Silence,* p. 80. For Buckley, OS, 11.85.
73. AP, 9.5.75. According to Nicky Tamin of AN, 5.7.75, Provisionals thought Wilson an Official, while the latter were convinced that he supported the Provisionals, and the IRSP considered him a supple reactionary. For McKeague, LN, 1.7.75.
74. RN, 19.1.74.
75. Deutsch and Magowan, 18.3 and 20.3.74.
76. RN, 18.5.74.
77. RN, 4.5.74 and 11.5.74.
78. PT, 27.4.74.
79. RN, 29.5.74.
80. RN, 2.2.74.
81. LN, 22.6.74 and PT, 5.81.
82. PT, 30.11.74.
83. AP, 19.12.75 and PT, 29.3.75.
84. RN, 6.7.74.
85. For Philbin (25.6.74) and Daly (23.6.74), RN, 6.7.74 and Daly's failure on institutional violence RN, 24.8.74.
86. AP, 9.8.74.
87. AP, 21.3.75 and RN, 12.4.75.
88. RN, 3.4.76. Newman, J., *The State of Ireland* (Dublin: Four Courts Press, 1977, pp. 66–7 (British withdrawal), p. 123 (1916).
89. RN, 15.1.77. PP, 25.3.77 (Wilson) and 22.4.77.
90. AP, 6.5.78.
91. RN, 12.11.77.
92. AP, 7.3.81.
93. AP, 10.10.81.
94. AP, 22.8.81.

95. See Comerford, *Kickham*, p. 71. *Irish People*, 16.9.1865.
96. *Fortnight*, 187, Nos. 7–8, July–August 1982. In an interview 16.9.82 Daly said that he believed that large numbers used the confidential telephones.
97. IN, 18.11.75, quoted in PT, 11.3.78.
98. AP, 19.11.81.
99. AP, 10.10.81.
100. PT, 18.9.76.
101. AP, 11.8.79., 5.1.80. *Church and State: A Forum of Irish Secularist Opinion* (Cork, Autumn 1981), p. 4.
102. PT, 10.1.76. – Fr. Michael Connolly – PR's Holy War, 2.10.76. Fr. Burns Fell and McManus (sympathy too weak to express feeling for IRA), Fr. Connolly, Fr. McGriel (gun sacramental in Ireland), Fr. Kane, Fr. O'Duill (blessed IRA man), Archbishop Ryan (visited MacStiofain), Fr. Faul, Fr. Marcellus Gillespie, Fr. Burns (Glasgow arms case), Fr. Fell (imprisoned in Coventry). Wilson, *An End to Silence*, p. 48.
103. Provisionals emphasised Torres, 'the Catholic who is not revolutionary is living in mortal sin', but he did ask for lay status before joining the guerrillas. See Gerassi, J. (ed.), *Revolutionary Priest: the Complete Writings and Messages of Camilo Torres* (London: Jonathan Cape, 1971), pp. 28–9. For Torres, RN 31.1.76. and 6.3.76., 22.1.77. (radical interpretation of *Populorum Progressio*), 24.9.77.; AP, 5.7.74., 27.7.77. (took off cassock to be more truly a priest), 14.12.77., 29.4.78., 23.2.80., 30.5.81., PT, 7.3.70., 12.5.73.
104. Deutsch and Magowan, 20.5.72. For John Paul II at Drogheda, see *The Pope Teaches – including Speeches made in Ireland, September, 1979* (London: Catholic Truth Society, 1979, pp. 390–9, esp. p. 392.
105. O'Casey, Sean, *Drums under the Windows* (London: Pan, 1973), p. 283. RN, 3.71. and 23.8.75.
106. Davis, R., 'The Advocacy of Passive Resistance in Ireland, 1916–1922', *Anglo-Irish Studies*, III, Cambridge, 1977, pp. 48–9.
107. Gallagher and Worrall, p. 122. *The Pope Teaches, 27 September 1979*, 'Christian Unity', p. 402. He opposed 'all violence and assaults against the human person – from whatever quarter they come'.
108. RN, 9.4.72.
109. AP, 6.10.79.
110. Gallagher and Worrall, p. 123.
111. AP, 10.5.80.
112. PT, 5.80.
113. U, 2.80. *Church and State*, op. cit. (Autumn 1981), pp. 1–8, 'The Catholic Church in the H-Block Campaign'.
114. AP, 6.1.79.
115. RN, 7.5.77.
116. AP, 10.2.82. and RN, 9.4.72.
117. RI, Dublin: 27.4.22. Nelson, Sarah, *Ulster's Uncertain Defenders* (Belfast: Appletree, 1984), p. 90.
118. AP, 19.4.80. and 10.5.80. Wilson, *An End to Silence*, p. 56.

119. See, for example, Farrell, M., *The Founding of Dail Eireann: Parliament and Nation Building* (Dublin, 1971).
120. AP, 6.6.72. Wilson, *An End to Silence*, p. 57. O'Fiaich on RTE Radio, 15.1.84.
121. AP, 9.2.84.
122. AP, 6.72. 'Freeman' identified as Fennell.
123. PT, 12.5.73. and 15.2.75. They evoked the 'Killing No Murder' article of Charles Diamond in the *Catholic Herald* and the theology of Marianus de Luca, both mentioned by Kensit (pp. 22–3) in 1921.
124. UL, 29.9.73.
125. C (1,33) 74.
126. See Manhattan, Avro, *Religious Terror in Ireland* (London: Paravision, 1971), pp. 87–90. The book was 'a must' according to a writer in OUDAN (1,13) 72 but to AN, 30.8.75, it was 'a Goon Show script from beginning to end'.
127. Marx, K. and F. Engels, *Ireland and the Irish Question* (London: Lawrence & Wishart, 1978), p. 257.
128. Comerford, *Kickham*, pp. 158–60.
129. See speech at 1917 Sinn Fein Ard Fheis, *Gaelic American*, 17.11.17.
130. RN, 6.4.74. For Conway, *Ulster Militant*, first issue (1972).
131. RN, 30.10.71., AP, 16.8.74., UM, 1 (1972), LN's attempt (16.8.75) to distinguish between Protestant and Catholic conscience by assuming that the latter was 'the collective conscience of the Catholic clergy, which is dictated by the Pope', does not answer these arguments.
132. AP, 16.5.75. Wilson, *An End to Silence*, p. 35 (Tone and church), Ulster, 12.85/1.86 (Paul Loane).
133. Wilson and Accord, AN, 23.11.85. & AP, 20.11.86. Pro-divorce, AP, 19.6.86.; abortion, 7.11.85. PBP, vol. 1, no. 41, 2.5.86. (Paisley).
134. Wilson, *End to Silence*, pp. 36 & 75: Wilson considered O'Fiaich's demand for the removal of abuses and their cause an improvement on Conway. AP, 14.3 & 25.7.85, while admitting that O'Fiaich believed British withdrawal the answer to Ulster's problems, complained that he did not justify the Provisionals. Ironically, an apparently tactless O'Fiaich statement blaming Protestants for 90 per cent of Northern Ireland bigotry (IT, 20.7.85), was later echoed by a remarkable article in the UDA's *Ulster*, 6.86 (written under the pseudonym 'Connall').
135. Comerford, *Kickham*, p. 74.

# 3 · ANTHROPOLOGICAL VIEWS ON 'VIOLENCE' IN NORTHERN IRELAND

We breakfast with a peaty Irish voice
And think of those young men, scarce more than boys,
Imprisoned in the Maze for so-called crimes,
Severing so-called legs and so-called arms.
Out in the Punjab, turbanned freedom-fighters
Have commandeered a bus of wives and daughters,
Fathers and sons, old men and women, born
And unborn babies. All await their turn
As freedom-fighters separate them out,
The Hindus from the others who are not.
Then line the Hindus up and shoot the lot.
The Archbishop says that England's lost her soul.
A good day for religion on the whole.

John Whitworth[1]

Guided by the model of Jesus' patience, forbearance, and compassion, law is no longer confined to the reasonable expectations of human mutuality and reciprocity. It obligates the disciple to go to any length for the sake of a fellow human being: to love the enemy; to bless the persecutor; to forgive the one who has injured; to give freely, more than is required, to the one who makes oppressive demands. With stipulations such as these, law no longer functions simply to sustain community, to maintain the minimal requisites of social order; it functions to extend and enlarge community and to renew it when it breaks down. Its thrust is to turn enmity and hatred into mercy and mutual forbearance.[2]

In this article I shall explore one aspect of the problem of terrorist violence in Northern Ireland – its manifestation by men embedded within communities that emphatically claim to be Christian. Clearly such violence is antithetical to the Christian gospel: what are the implications of this violence for our understanding of the relation of religious belief to social organisation? Can we conceptually isolate the 'men of violence' from the religious communities and so exonerate these from responsibility? Should we rather conclude that religious ideals are without influence except on a few individuals and that in so far as others claim to be followers of the gospel they are simply hypocrites? The two quotations provide not merely ironic comment on each other but raise a central debate. On the one hand are those who say that religious beliefs and practices are significant for the kind of reasons the French sociologist Emile Durkheim suggested – they serve social purposes by making the group itself 'sacred', effectively transforming it by religious symbols so that it itself becomes the mystified object of worship, thus making group self-interest morally justified. On the other hand are those who credit religious ideals with an independent and at times transforming power. Christian theologians like Thomas Ogletree assert that Christian morality must not be limited by the boundary of any social group but must extend beyond it. David Martin, as a Christian sociologist, examines the tension between these ideals and 'Civic Religion', with its 'straightforward Durkheimian unity of cult and culture' where 'religion and culture are isomorphic' and '(t)he secular has sucked the divine into its maw'; he sees through the ages a dynamic dialectic between this religion and Christianity that repeatedly breaks up these 'homogeneities and intertias' and then succumbs to them, only to break them up again.[3] Other kinds of sociologists and anthropologists, simplistic Marxists or Durkheimians, denying any independence to religious concepts, see no problem in such situations as the Catholic/Protestant conflict in Ulster. For them, two groups with conflicting economic and social interests are simply expressing them in ideological terms that serve so to 'mystify' the real situation that very few of those involved perceive that reality. In opposition to this viewpoint I, like Martin, see a tension. But my particular anthropological interests lead me to focus both on the nature of the social relationships that keep so many as perplexed adherents of 'civic religion' and on the extent to which the assertion, even if only by a minority, of Christian ideals may nevertheless exert an effect on such people at the point of greatest tension, the issue of violence between 'neighbours'. I also want to explore the nature of the particular branch of 'civic religion' to which they are attached, for I would label it as a particular sub-species, 'ethnic religion'. To lay the foundations of my discussion I shall start, in characteristic anthropological fashion, by setting the whole issue in cross-cultural terms, beginning therefore with a very brief digression on the nature of religious belief and on practices in non-Christian contexts.

Undoubtedly those involved in savage ethnic disputes may define themselves in terms of their religious adherence: Sikh and Hindu in the Punjab; Moslem and Christian in the Lebanon; Hindu and Buddhist in Sri Lanka; Sunni and Shiah Moslem in the Persian Gulf; the issue this raises depends on whether we assume that all religions take, in principle a moral stand on such matters. The tenets of Buddhism require its followers to be peaceful; and Christian belief imposes two inextricable laws: the love of God and the love of the neighbour, archetypically the Samaritan, a member of the 'other' community. Therefore, where a Buddhist people is involved in violence, or where Christian communities are involved in mutual terrorism there we have a problem. I would argue, however, that religious belief is so central to the cultural identity of many groups that as a kind of shorthand they identify themselves in religious terms; but I would have to go on to say that as there is nothing particularly moral about 'religion' in general there is nothing very surprising that violence should be committed in the name of religion. Looked at in a broad cross-cultural perspective, it is in fact very difficult to define 'religion'.[4] But it is not so difficult to generalise about the 'functions' of religious beliefs; and a concern with what, in our culture, we regard as ultimate moral questions is by no means necessarily significant. Rather, religious beliefs explain the nature of the human condition and set out a programme that, in a particular context, tells adherents how to attain felicity. This necessarily implies that in the religious account of the world are embedded explanations of the evil in the world – but this 'evil' may be primarily misfortunes that seem to threaten people's very existence. Because these points are important to my later argument I illustrate them here by reference to the Mbembe of southeast Nigeria, whose beliefs I studied in the 1950s.[5] The Mbembe were monotheists in that they believed in Ibinokpabi as Creator and final cause; but Ibinokpabi interfered very seldom in human affairs and had delegated most influence for good to the Dead. Ancestors were unconcerned with the morality of the living; indeed I was thought to be very naive to ask if they were concerned with the rules of kin groups; I surely knew that people were selfish, so why should I think they would be different just because they were dead? The Dead could be cajoled by sacrifices into giving such things as good harvests, and would inflict misfortune on those who failed to perform the proper rites; they did not capriciously cause harm but they did not normally bother about the affairs of the living. The Dead, as a collectivity, were identified with the Earth in its ritual aspects, and there were joint rituals for Earth and Dead that symbolised the whole group; its priest's ultimate curse, which brought down punishment by the Dead, lay on those who shed blood within the group; his blessing had been at the service of those who went head-hunting into other groups. But, normally, intermediary spirits were needed to help the living motivate the Dead into taking an active role in human affairs. Each subordinate group acquired shrines of these inter-mediaries for its own purposes, and rites at these shrines in turn often symbolised the group concerned. 'Medicines' from these shrines might be used with social approval to punish those who committed certain offences; theft and adultery were not punished by irate spirits but by irate husbands and owners, who used these forces as mercenaries to protect their rights. However, most misfortune, serious illness and many forms of 'bad luck', were thought due to the malevolence of human beings who attacked others with supernatural violence. This violence came from two rather different kinds of person, the sorcerer and the witch, and the differences believed to exist between them are important for various arguments that I want to develop.

Ambitious men, who were ruthless but rational, were thought to acquire wealth by joining a sorcerer's society – recurrent fees being the souls of close kin, which each member gave as feasts for the group. The victims had to be kin because to kill an unrelated person would have incurred the vengeance of such a victim's sorcerer kin (at this fantasy level the Mbembe retained pre-colonial ideas of kin-group rights). People were wary of kinsmen they believed to be sorcerers, but as suspicion naturally fell on those who were most affluent and powerful, direct action was seldom taken against them, although if suspicions were very strong a kin group might go in a body to extract from the sorcerer a promise to desist from his attacks. Just because they were rational, sorcerers could be constrained by group opinion. Witches, male and female, were quite different. They were motivated by sheer malevolence that meant they derived pleasure from the sufferings of others; they were pathological killers indwelt by an ineradicable substance that might be inherited but was sometimes said to take root in people who were naturally malicious. Special envy might direct their attack to particular victims, but they were inherently irrational, for they neither derived any benefit from the harm they did nor could they restrain themselves in the face of public threats.

Witchcraft beliefs played a crucial role in Mbembe religious concepts, because witches were the main cause of undeserved misfortune that was the primary evil in the world. For this reason I classify beliefs in witchcraft as central to the religious beliefs of the Mbembe. Less threatening misfortunes, whether bad luck or sickness, were believed due to transgressions and could be coped with relatively simply by proper sacrifices that would, infallibly, result in cures. Persistent, life-threatening misfortunes were, normally, blamed on witchcraft. Thus within Mbembe religious belief the whole range of human ills was explained and beliefs in witches sustained faith in the essential beneficence of non-human forces. Where anything was so horrendous that it threatened the existence of the people with a kind of ultimate evil, there religion stepped in. Politically the ultimate threat was unrestrained warfare between villages that made up the group, and here the curse of the Priest of the Earth could kill offending villagers. In everyday life ritual 'medicines' had formerly provided the means for a poison ordeal that killed witches; and the most terrifying kind of epidemic – smallpox, was rationalised as the one occasion of God's intervention in human affairs, for it was believed that all who died of smallpox were witches. (Not surprisingly the great crime of the British was that they were the friends of witches, for had they not sought to eradicate smallpox, and made it an offence not to be a witch but to accuse someone of being a witch?)

I shall return at the end of this paper to the significance of religion in relation to evil that threatens the very identity of a people. For the moment I want simply to use the Mbembe notions of witches and sorcerers in relation to violence in Ulster. Sometimes at its worst it is called 'mindless'. If this were true then, however horrifying, there would be no problem, for we should be dealing with the irrational acts of psychopaths. The term is usually used when an observer concludes that violence stems from individual malice that the majority must condemn. That would be like Mbembe witchcraft; but it cannot be dismissed as being like that of the witch, the irrational indulgence of a malicious pleasure. Rather, at their worst, the violent are almost always to be placed in the category of the sorcerer, quite rational: their violence is meant to achieve something. Further they are not beyond the influence of people in their community. This is important for our argument: it implies that those who use violence will do so in ways calculated not to so alienate their own people that they will cease to tolerate such activities. It follows that acts of violence can be properly analysed only in the context of an analysis of what is regarded as acceptable or unacceptable behaviour within the group: hence the necessity for the careful, detailed, analysis of the place of the violent within their own groups and the implications of their apparently well-founded belief, that behaviour that seems 'mindlessly violent' to the outside world will be tolerated. We have to explore the parameters that set bounds to what the violent man may do without so alienating his own community that he is seen as horrifying and is, like the witch, rejected. This, in turn, necessitates a careful examination of the 'community' itself, for we need to know how strong the boundaries are that Christian benevolence is supposed to transcend.

The very nature of the violence is itself evidence that those who commit it believe in the strength of these boundaries. Acts, commonly called 'mindless' by outsiders because they seem irrational, can be, from the viewpoint of the activist who knows his people, not mindless but rather Machiavellian, because he calculates that it will produce a reaction he regards as desirable. Our interest lies in drawing out the assumptions in terms of which the action is rational. The type case, of course, is that of the action calculated to produce confrontation and a backlash. Frank Burton, the sociologist, whose detailed work on the IRA in Belfast in the early 1970s I shall look at in more detail,[6] concludes that the IRA have been too readily accused of such action. Certainly, however, such acts have taken place on occasions; and what is significant for us is the obvious fact that any such act is based on the belief in the potentiality of a group identity that can be strengthened and set in opposition to the authorities. A similar kind of rationality has motivated sectarian killings by Protestants. I am not here referring to killing of those believed to be in the IRA. Such beliefs may be mistaken but, since IRA members neither wear uniform nor are listed as such in DHSS files, mistakes are scarcely surprising, and from the viewpoint of those paramilitaries involved the logic of the act is obvious. Rather I am referring to those killings, not the result of mistaken identity, which have involved killing people because of their religion. To such murders only the adjective 'mindless' seems applicable. To the outside observer the seeming irrationality of the violence is so appalling that it looks as if the only explanation for events must be the existence of extraordinary bigots who can operate simply because public opinion is itself extraordinarily bigoted. It may be true that some of these murders have been carried out by psychopaths, for on occasions each side has attracted them to its paramilitary ranks. What is important, however, is that clearly many must have been killed by sane terrorists who, by definition, must operate with some regard to public opinion.

The implication of much of the worst violence is that 'the other side' is seen as such an undifferentiated group that an attack on any one of 'them' may seem justified by the hope of teaching 'them' a lesson and making 'them' control their violent men. As this is a factor in conflict ranging from that between tribes to that involving modern states and may, sometimes, serve to make groups desist from violence, it cannot always be considered irrational. In practice, of course, such violence may have precisely the opposite consequence to that intended, creating among 'them' that very solidarity 'we' fear so much. This is what outside observers in Ulster often think they see happening as the result of paramilitary activity. The people seem not only bigoted but incredibly blind not to realise that their acts of violence must be against their own interests. The initial task of the anthropologist is thus to show, not in historical terms but in the existential experience of people within local communities, how it is possible for those who are psychologically normal and may be well intentioned towards members of 'the other side' to excuse where they do not support, deplorable violence towards them. The task to be faced is to explain how it is that Catholics and Protestants in Ulster should perceive themselves to be so divided as to constitute two distinct communities between whom benevolence is not expected. In terms of the quotation from Ogletree we might think that the very existence of two distinct communities provided evidence for the lack of influence in the life of the people of the characteristics of the 'Christian community' that he sets out. Certainly the men of violence seem to operate with quite different ideas about the nature of their groups and of the people within them. We have to answer the question as to whether the fact that the people at times behaved as if 'the other' were totally hostile is in itself evidence for the non-significance of the Christian ideology of community. As a beginning I shall examine a peaceful community.

I had the good fortune to study Ballybeg[7] in a relatively peaceful period when, for an outsider, easy contacts with both Catholics and Protestants was possible. Because it was a rural area where the religious groups were intermixed, I had the opportunity, through close observation, to analyse relationships within and between them. Under these circumstances it was possible to recognise how much they shared common values, and how far they were separated by factors other than the hatred and enmity of bigotry. Although we must face the issues raised by violence within the urban areas it is important to set this in the context of a very different rural area.

In the Ballybeg district Protestants and Catholics had so much in common that it is virtually impossible to think of any cultural traits that unequivocally separated them. In the area there were two economic categories: relatively prosperous lowland farmers and poorer hill families. A majority of lowland farmers were Protestants and a majority of hill farmers were Catholics but, as this implies, some Catholics were lowlanders and more prosperous than some Protestants. In any case their common characteristics were striking. Despite the fact that the members of the two religious groups seldom intermarried they shared totally patterns of kinship that distinguished them from, say, rural England. For example, kinship ended with first cousins: 'Our fathers were cousins but we're not related' was a phrase I often heard. Both groups expressed their general egalitarianism in addressing almost everyone but married women by their christian names. All joined in condemning the irritating manners and bureaucratic attitudes of outside officials. Moreover I noted that Protestants shared certain aspects of the Catholics' hostility to the Unionist government; Catholics thought the local Protestants were favoured by officials, but the Protestants thought the government gave its favours on a territorial basis, helping areas close to Belfast and neglecting those, like Ballybeg, more distant.

Few of the factors commonly thought to be the cause of strain between the religious groups had any real significance in this area. The farmers were not competing for land: land was seldom sold between Protestants and Catholics but it might be leased between them – and as farming was not very profitable few wanted to buy more acres. Neither were jobs a local source of contention since men who did not acquire land expected to have to go away to work, mostly to unskilled jobs in England. Economic competition occurred between farmer, shopkeeper, farm-supplies merchant, and dealer in livestock – but in so far as sectarian loyalties played a part these men formed chains of co-religionists and thus, in a sense, restricted any tension that arose within these relationships to co-religionists. Finally because this was an area of net emigration there was a large stock of poor housing into which young couples could move cheaply so that even competition for houses was limited.

Positively, relationships were eased by the fact that Catholics and Protestants lived interspersed on farms that, not infrequently, had been several generations in the same families, so that Catholics and Protestants were commonly hereditary neighbours. There were even small groups of Protestant and Catholic farmers who regularly co-operated with one another. Clearly relationships in Ballybeg in the 1950s were poles apart from modern Belfast. For this very reason their degree of separation is instructive.

Religious membership separated them in many ways not immediately anticipated by an outsider just because so many secular activities were connected with churches. There was no non-sectarian meeting place in Ballybeg apart from public houses, which although partly defined by the religious affiliation of the publican were so normally run by Catholics that non-teetotal Protestants were bound to mix if they wanted a drink. By far the most important factor, however, was the rules of marriage already mentioned. Occasionally intermarriage occurred but this always led to the cutting off of ties with one set of relatives, so that biological relationships never led to recognised kinship. Sectarian ideals that stressed that marriage should occur only between members of the same religious group were vitally important just because ties to kin and affines in this area were very significant. The core of an individual's social network was constituted by kin, and the kin of kin met when visiting relations. Since married women scarcely visited those who were not kindred the significance of kinship for women was even greater than it was for the men.

The consequence was that most individuals operated within a *de facto* social framework that was sectarian, despite having some friendly links to neighbours on 'the other side'. This sectarian world was powerfully reinforced by the fact that the two religious groups had political aims so counterposed that they were in effect involved in a zero-sum game: one side's gain seemed obviously the other side's loss and as a result compromise was almost unthinkable. Neither side permitted open dissent within its own ranks. Catholics were nationalists, for whom the ideal of a united Ireland had so emotional an appeal that they spoke of a readiness to risk economic loss to achieve it. Protestants were Unionists (despite disliking Unionist politicians). For them to be ruled from Dublin would mean domination by the Catholic church, and this had no sort of appeal. To them it was sheer perversity of the Catholics to be willing 'to eat grass' for the sake of a united Ireland.

One of the most important results of this divergence of aim was that when Protestant and Catholic met, however friendly they were, they did not talk freely but spoke of their families and the weather and farming. The result was that Protestant and Catholic lived intermixed and in some cases and in some contexts had close and friendly contacts and yet for the most part managed to remain in almost complete ignorance concerning each other's beliefs.

A less obvious result was that because of such ignorance Protestants and Catholics could mix with each other quite freely and yet talk about each other in terms of harsh stereotypes. I want to stress that it would be truthful, but would nevertheless give a very false impression, to pick out prejudiced remarks and observations and say this was what people said when they were safely in their own group. It would be easy to make the people appear to be 'really' ignorant bigots. In fact their responses were complex and ambivalent, and it was possible to show this only by taking as examples particular individuals and, by building up a composite picture of their lives within their families and neigh-bourhoods, show the variety of their comments on different occasions, and the fact that prejudiced words might be offset by good-neighbourly acts.

How easy it was to misjudge local people was shown by Mary, the wife of a Protestant hill farmer. She was very ready to denounce Catholic priests, whom she believed to mislead their flock quite deliberately. She was emphatic, even against the arguments of some of her friends, that Catholics ought not to be given good jobs in the civil service, because she was sure they could not be politically trusted. On the subject of Catholics scrounging from the government she said acidly: 'There's not a Catholic in the country that hasn't got two pairs of spectacles and false teeth.' Yet I often heard her speak of her Catholic neighbours with respect, and sometimes with admiration; and her deeds belied her prejudiced speech. Having had some nursing training, she turned out regularly for a period of weeks to give unpaid help to a neighbouring Catholic woman who could not afford to pay for the nursing she needed. I saw her incur great displeasure from her husband's family by her insistence on giving warmth and food to a Catholic childhood friend and her child. This woman had broken all the local taboos: she had married a Protestant and their child had been baptised a Catholic; recently her husband had died and she had had him buried in the Catholic cemetery, thus in the eyes of his kin snatching him from them in death as in life. Now she was in great need and Mary, who had very little cash herself found work for her to do about the house as an excuse for sheltering her. To Mary they had been neighbours as children and she could not now abandon her. In terms of this present discussion it is relevant that Mary was both totally a member of her group and a devout Christian who herself linked her attitude to her neighbours with her concept of her religious duty.

Nevertheless it would be absurd to minimise the problem of prejudice. The respect and affection I retain for the people I knew on both sides in Ballybeg stems especially from the concern so many of them showed to be good neighbours to those on 'the other side'. At the same time it was painfully obvious that great potential existed for intercommunity violence. This potential existed be-cause, despite the people's genuine wish to be good neighbours, the lines between them were so sharp that they could change from seeing the members of 'the other side' as decent local people they knew well to seeing them as the enemy who might stab them in the back. They could easily, out of no particular malevolence, step into a kind of mythic world in which the neighbourhood was transformed and 'our fellows' became exclusively good and 'their fellows' were seen to be bad.

Such views are common when 'we' are separated from 'them' by a visible frontier. In Ulster, however, my close neighbour may be the one from whom I am separated by invisible barriers. Anthropological research has shown the strength of these social boundaries even when relations between Catholics and Protestants might justly be called good. Because of the invisible barriers the individual's sense of identity is shaped by growing up within a social network almost exclusively composed of co-religionists, and the carefully controlled patterns of communication in mixed religious company. It is possible, as John Whyte has put it, for each group to believe in myths about the others based on grotesque misinformaion, despite daily and friendly contact.[8]

I have here sketched the pattern of Catholic and Protestant relations in a situation in which there was little significant local competition between the two groups, and where there was the basis for at least a certain amount of friendly interaction between individuals in the two communities. It must be obvious that in urban environments where there is a history of economic competition and very little to bring people in the two groups together for any co-operative purpose, intergroup relations are likely to be far more strained. For this reason any discussion about Christian culture and violence in Ulster must relate to Belfast since it is here that violence has been at its worst. For this the two main sources will be the account by Frank Burton on the IRA,[9] and one by a political scientist, Sarah Nelson, on Protestant groups;[10] both are fine accounts of paramilitaries in the community.

The history of Belfast demography, going back to the middle of the last century, shows that in times of peaceful relationships the residential patterns of the working-class areas display interdigitation of Catholic and Protestant; but in periods of tension this changed rapidly, and religious divisions became clear-cut lines dividing the streets.[11] Relationships between neighbours of different faiths, therefore, could not have the same long-term basis as in Ballybeg; moreover even when they were neighbours, there were not the same practical reasons for co-operation that existed in the countryside, where mutual help with farm work was important. On the other hand the reasons for conflict that were specifically absent in Ballybeg were present to cause friction in Belfast, especially competition for jobs. There is no reason here to reiterate what is so well known.[12] The failure of Labour politicians (who were the only ones who might have secured the working-class vote on a non-sectarian basis) to capture the enthusiastic support of either group, let alone unite them on any issue except very temporarily, meant there was no sense of common political purpose in these areas, but only great potential for intercommunity hostility.

If we are to discuss Belfast since the 1960s in the context of this article, we cannot dismiss its violence as due to people alienated from religious groups. People in these areas had attachment to churches unusual for inner cities. However deprived, they were not socially disintegrated, but were very 'traditional' working class, with strong family ties, and many had considerable ties to their neighbourhoods, in which there were many links of friendship, kinship and marriage. Considering how much of the violence has been committed by young men, perhaps one of the problems we have to face is the fact that it was a society notable for the extent to which there was an absence of any youth culture stressing rebellion against parental values. Teenage boys, whether Catholic or Protestant, were seldom pious and voluntary attenders at their churches, but they were basically conformist.[13] It is important to stress this because, despite any deprivation that existed in economic terms, and Protestants as well as Catholics were by many standards deprived, violence cannot be dissociated from the majority of the adults by being blamed on alienated young men. Deviants turned out of their homes after quarrelling with their fathers or their mothers' boy friends and living rough with friends in a similar position may serve as the scapegoats for inner-city violence on the mainland, but not in Belfast.

In this kind of 'traditional' urban environment it is thus difficult to make out a case absolving decent local people from responsibility for events. In this situation things do not happen without people's knowledge, and up to a point their consent has to be assumed because of this. This is neatly illustrated by Bishop and

Mallie's comment that despite the ambition of the IRA leadership that the movement, like all efficient radically subversive organisations, should have a 'cell' structure that would protect it from betrayal, by keeping each member in ignorance of the identity of more than a few members, this could be only a vain hope. So many 'volunteers' knew one another already,[14] for example, because their families knew one another, and so many of the leaders were kin of past or present top men. Thus to repeat, one of the frightening paradoxes of the Ulster situation is just that it is the well socialised, and often dutiful, young men of Belfast who have been behind so much violence. They are so well integrated within traditional culture it must be implicated in the violence.

One escape from this conclusion would be to argue that the men of violence on each side were such terrorists that they simply intimidated local people to the extent that they were too frightened to take action against them. There is no doubt that there has been intimidation; there is every reason to believe that there was good reason for their fear. Recruits to all armies must to some extent dehumanise 'the enemy' and thus themselves. Paramilitaries, however, are almost always forced to define the enemy in such a way as to inflict greater brutalisation on themselves, because they either take no prisoners or singularly fail to treat them in accordance with the Geneva conventions. If the enemy is defined as the armed, dangerous man-in-uniform then the soldier may retain some compassion. (I vividly remember as a child having to rethink my perception of 'Germans' when I heard how a schoolfriend's brother, wounded in the retreat to Dunkirk, had been tended by a passing German soldier because, he said, he had two sons the same age.) If the uniformed enemy is still regarded as a legitimate target even when badly wounded; if the enemy is defined as a man who sometimes wears a uniform, and is a target when off duty; if the enemy is one who wore a uniform some years ago; if the enemy is the man not in uniform but one who is known to be/is believed to be/just possibly might be a member of the opposed paramilitary group; or one who might perhaps give aid and comfort to those who support it, then there is little room for any compassion. The paramilitary recruit, if he stays in his group, will be socialised until finally he 'sees' as *unmensch* anyone called 'the enemy'. The evidence of self-brutalisation seems to be shown most clearly when idealists end by being willing to kill even those of their own side if they become competitors in a power struggle. And both Protestant and Catholic paramilitaries have fought savage internecine battles.[15] It may take a lot of courage to stand against them.

Both Burton and Nelson agree, however, that although fear played its part in keeping people quiet this was generally less significant than is commonly supposed by counter-insurgency theorists. The people's reasons for at least tacit toleration have been much more complex. The real problem is why the ordinary people let the paramilitary recruit get away with behaviour that is often brutal. It cannot be said in their defence that they are really ignorant either of what is going on or of who is responsible. For, as has already been argued, both the Catholic and the Protestant districts from which most of the activists operate, are tightly knit, traditional neighbourhoods. As Nelson argues: 'Despite their secretive organisation, the killers still needed silence or tolerance from their own communities in order to continue operating. Conversations will have been overheard, cars will have been seen speeding back through Protestant areas, and families must have their suspicions.'[16]

In the first place the straightforward values of being a good neighbour in a tightly knit neighbourhood may make for great ambivalence and uncertainty as to the proper course of action. X may have done a bad act, but he may be the son of a good local family, the friend of someone in my family, and known as a decent lad until the Troubles. Is it right to tell the police of what may be only a suspicion? Second, most people in the neighbourhood share automatic attachment to one side in Ulster's divided society. Individuals may want only peaceful relations but almost inevitably they will identify with one side. In other words they are vulnerable to the 'Us'/'Them' view of the world that leads inexorably to a readiness to believe in the good intentions and probity of 'our lads' as against theirs. No one expresses this view with more sensitivity than Sarah Nelson, herself a Catholic, writing of the Protestant areas:

> In districts like Shankill and Sandy Row, they usually knew the people who were arrested on terrorist charges. Like the Ardoyne Catholics in Burton's book, they judged them on who they were, almost more than on what they had done . . . This is not quite the

same as saying that local people made excuses for or justified terrorism. Most felt you had to hit back at the IRA and wanted to believe their side would know who the IRA were. After killings of uninvolved civilians, community myths would often circulate which gave 'inside information' that the victim was really in the IRA . . . So they wished to believe the best about their own militants, the kind of people who were arrested, or whom they knew to be active. They knew, saw, and accepted – as counter-insurgency theorists, many politicians and outside observers did not – that many militants were not psychopaths or sectarian fanatics. If good boys (or their own boys) were involved they must have behaved honourably in a just cause. Thus many people were not prepared to condemn or inform on them even if militant groups also contained men they distrusted or disliked.[17]

Nelson points out that so far as these people were concerned it was the IRA who shot people in the back and blew up babies: 'It was not at all congenial to confront the fact that Protestant militants behaved as brutally as the IRA, and against innocent people; and so they refused to believe.'[18]

Refusal to believe gave leeway to the killers; so did denial that innocent people rather than the IRA were being attacked. Ironically, these mechanisms were almost as effective as outright support for the killers in permitting the campaign to continue. Most of the Protestant population were not ghoulish or vindictive cheerleaders in the assassinations. But if there were lessons about their own community's behaviour to be learned from the campaign, they were largely unwilling or unable to confront them.[19]

Nelson is here referring to the 1972-3 period. At this time there was great political and social upheaval:

it was no cliché to say the normal fabric of society had broken down. In that situation . . . more lawless, bullying or extreme elements often pushed their way into strong positions in the [Ulster Defence Association] . . . That this was more related to the times than to some naturally large percentage of virulent anti-Catholics is suggested by the fact that all kinds of nastiness were also unleashed by Protestants on Protestants . . . Disoriented and demoralised communities were ill-equipped to put restraints on the paramilitaries . . . People in loyalist areas would recall how the . . . fights, the hooded bodies in alleys made them feel paralysed, fearful and quite without power to control the situation.

When the normal relations with the army and the police were soured and normal law and order disrupted, sadistic killers had 'the luxury of being able to torture their victims all night in lock-up garages. . .'. Nelson comments that this 'complex, even messy' picture of loyalist areas in the early 1970s is the only accurate way of depicting the factors behind the sectarian killings of the period. Burton in his book on the Catholic Ardoyne discusses the attitudes of the Catholic population not directly involved in IRA activities, and they seem to have been as complex and probably as messy as those Nelson describes.[20]

Nelson's account of the loyalist areas at their lowest moral ebb can usefully be contrasted with events in 1975 when she shows how the population turned against a different loyalist group, the Ulster Volunteer Force. This had initially 'attracted the better class of terrorist'[21] as the UDA had gained a reputation for brutality and racketeering, but Nelson shows that its membership varied greatly in their opinions from some who espoused a new, anti-unionist socialism to more traditional hard-liners. With many of the details she gives for its rapid decline I am not here concerned, but it is relevant that one factor was the rejection of its violence by many of the loyalists. She writes that '1975 was not like 1972 in terms of violence, of Protestant alienation, or of fears about their constitutional future. Toleration of counter-terror was far more uneasy now . . . It was not just that the UVF carried out savage killings (like the Miami Showband murders) which shocked many people, but that it actually boasted about them.' Because of this, because the UVF was involved in a bloody power conflict with the UDA, and because the UVF was generally inept, 'The sea in which the fish swam started to turn sour . . . Information began to flow from the public to the authorities about unpopular UVF figures. Many were arrested . . .'[22] Even back in 1972 Protestants had been shocked by the sectarian killings and the fact that many tried to hide from themselves what was happening is some evidence for their abhorrence of the idea of such deeds.

It is, of course, much more unlikely that the Catholics of Burton's study would ever express their abhorrence of IRA actions by giving information to the security forces since their degree of alienation is much greater. Nevertheless it is clear that they were prepared to tolerate these actions for the most part only because they believed them to be essentially defensive.[23]

Summarising all that has been said about violence in Belfast the main points to emerge from the accounts of both Burton and Nelson are the confusion and the complexity of conflicting emotions faced by both sets of people studied. What has been done in their names has been quite horrifying, but these writers each show how the people have been engulfed in situations where, given the deep division of the society, their perplexity as to what they ought, or what they could, do is wholly understandable.

Is this all that can be said, however, about the impact of Ulster's Christian culture on behaviour during the Troubles? It seems entirely negative to say that the moral confusion of Belfast's working-class populations is understandable. Perhaps I should point out, of course, that I have chosen to focus this discussion on these areas because they have been exposed to the greatest violence. Obviously there is a great deal that could be said about the efforts of many groups in Ulster's population who have, explicitly on a Christian basis, tried to build bridges between the two religious communities. With their efforts I am simply not concerned in this article. What I do want to raise, however, is the question of whether there were any points at which Belfast's working-class population ever drew a line and said to the paramilitaries 'thus far and no further; certain acts will not be tolerated'. In one sense there is no evidence for this – it seems as if the men of violence have been able, within broad limits, to do anything they wished to do. Yet I want to go on to argue that it is perfectly possible to imagine further horrors they might have committed but from which they have refrained. Some would themselves have found such deeds abhorrent but, given the evidence of the extreme nastiness of others, it may be they were restrained only by a tacit recognition that some acts would not have been tolerated. Nelson's description of some killings clearly shows the existence in the Protestant areas of sadists. Burton's account of Tom, an IRA man in the Ardoyne, suggests something similar: 'He projected a fiercely militant personality which would stun people into silence, particularly during his accounts of certain acts and his portrayal of personal views: "You just put the hood on, shoot them, and watch them shudder. That's it. All this talk of conscience is a lot of shit the Catholic church try to put into you." ' Apparently Burton concluded in the end that Tom's real opinions were more complex than such utterances suggested, but it is clear that locally Tom was considered by some to be 'inherently evil', and it is easy to understatd that assessment.[24]

Such men, it seems safe to assume, would have done anything that could, at whatever Machiavellian level, have served their cause. No holds, it seems were barred. And yet . . . compare Ulster with the Punjab or with Sri Lanka, and it becomes possible to note what has not happened. No one, terrorist, paramilitary, freedom-fighter – whatever term you like to apply – has held up a bus, forced the passengers out, and then shot everyone, men women and children because they belonged to 'the other side'. There have been dreadful cases in which bus drivers or particular passengers have been killed. There was the notorious case, in July 1975, of the Miami Showband – an Irish dance band – whose minibus was blown up by Protestant paramilitaries who then mowed down the survivors, apparently because of a conviction that such groups might be used to smuggle explosives and weapons across the border. That was an act that was greeted with revulsion, but even so it was a different type of violence from that recorded in the poem at the beginning of this article.

That poem and a forthcoming book by Bruce Kapferer dealing with Sinhalese and Australian nationalism[25] lie behind the argument of this article. Kapferer is concerned with 'the great forces, both of enormous human suffering and of human liberation, which nationalism and the claims of identity have unleashed'. However, it is his comments on Sinhalese Buddhist nationalism and the ideology on which it is based that concerns our present discussion. The book deals in great detail and subtlety with beliefs that lie behind the present ethnicide in Sri Lanka, and it is quite impossible here even to sketch the case that Kapferer presents. However, he deals with the paradox that Buddhism in Sri Lanka is at one level one of the most peaceful of the world religions and yet at the same time it is linked indissolubly to violence, manifested particularly in Sinhalese reactions to sorcery. The link is formed by concepts of evil. As we saw earlier, Mbembe ideas of evil are bound to explanations of the world in which God and the ancestors provide a benevolent or neutral environment for human life, and all undeserved evils stem from human malevolence. Christian doctrine explicitly asserts total divine control of the universe, prohibits the ascription of misfortune to capricious powers, and sees evil as in the self, something to be transformed by good.

Against this, Sinhalese Buddhism proclaims the independent power of evil in the world, especially manifested in sorcery, which much be violently attacked. This attitude is shown, Kapferer argues, in the violence associated with rites at sorcery shrines, an essential part of Sinhalese life. He quotes the case of a priest appealing to 'Sidda Suniyam, king of the gods' on behalf of a woman whose husband had deserted her and was thought to be attacking her with sorcery. The priest prays: 'take hold of this evil husband, squeeze the breath from his body, crush his windpipe. Give him up as a sacrifice to the Blood Demon . . . Oh God, infect him with disease . . . smallpox, eczema, leprosy . . . Make this woman's heart full of happiness by meting out this punishment'.[26]

It is the same understanding of the nature of evil, and the equation of Tamils as the source of evil that would attack the Buddhist Sinhalese state, that Kapferer sees as lying behind the attacks on the Tamils. He acknowledges that there were complex economic and class factors that fuelled the resentment of the Sinhalese at the prosperity of the Tamil immigrants. The ferocity of the attacks, however, he links to their fundamental understanding of the world. Kapferer writes of the carnage: 'Gangs of Sinhalese thugs roamed the streets with lists of Tamil houses, buildings and businesses [lists which, he makes clear, were in part compiled for them by Buddhist monks], systematically burning them and slaughtering their inhabitants. Added to this horror was the sight of large gatherings of ordinary Sinhalese who looked on while, in some cases, Tamil victims were burned alive. By the end of July [1983] most of the 300,000 Tamil population of Colombo had fled the city or were in refugee camps . . . The Sri Lankan Government admits that something in the region of 350 Tamils having been killed. The numbers are certainly far greater . . . [no Sinhalese were killed] . . . for two or three days the Government and its agents took no preventative action while the killing continued . . . '[27]

Some, Kapferer says, have argued that the Sinhalese 'forgot' their Buddhism, but against this he cites the involvement of the monks in the making of the lists of Tamils, and 'groups of monks have been seen leading the public clamour for bloody vengeance'. He concludes that Tamils were for a while engulfed by the flames of a passionate Sinhalese Buddhist violence. 'While most Sinhalese did not participate in the killings in July 1983 many

nonetheless watched, and without acting, while Tamils burned . . .
Even those who sheltered Tamils said "they [the Tamils] got what
they deserved".'[28] By contrast Nelson records that Protestants
who described to her the burning of the Catholic occupied houses
in Bombay Street in 1969 stressed when talking about the people
that 'none of them was touched', and she notes defensive myths
had been fabricated that said that the Catholics had set fire to their
own street. Given the brutality of some of those involved in
Ulster's Troubles I think we have to assume that it is because they
have to reckon with a public opinion moulded by an ideology
different from that of Sri Lanka that, willing enough as the hit men
are to gun down a man out with his wife and children, Belfast
murderers very seldom deliberately kill the wife and children also.
In many cultures they would, but in Ulster the gunmen on both
sides have to take account of public opinion antagonistic to such
cruelty.

Nevertheless it must be apparent that despite the apparent
theological differences between Christianity and Sinhalese
Buddhism there has been too much in common in the behaviour of
the people for us to ignore the similarities. This, I would suggest, is
not surprising since at one level people in Ulster and Sri Lanka
share related religions, the religions of 'ethnic nationalism'. I use
inverted commas because I argue that Ulster Protestants also are
nationalistic in the sense in which I am using the term.[29] By
'religion' I am referring not specifically to beliefs about God but to
fundamental concepts about the nature of the world, and
especially to sources of evil in the world that threaten the person.
To the Mbembe, witches and sorcerers were an essential part of
'religious' belief because they explained misfortunes – and
witches, the embodiment of evil, were the only members of society
who might properly be killed by non-kinsmen. To the Sinhalese
Buddhist, sorcerers threaten evil to the individual and fury against
them is religiously licensed; but Kapferer, as we have seen, goes
on to argue that the Tamils are regarded as the source of evil
threatening the Sri Lankan Buddhist state, and state fury is
therefore justified against them. He further suggests that through
ethnic nationalism the well-being of the Sinhalese individual is
identified with the well-being of the Buddhist state – thus the
Tamils, by their political demands, which threaten that state, also
threaten the identity of the individual Sinhalese. Thus the fury

justified against the sorcerer is also justified against the Tamil. Kapferer is at pains to point out all the manifold economic and class factors that were blended into the relationships of Tamils and Sinhalese, but argues that the consequences of these cannot be understood without understanding how the religion of ethnic nationalism, and its concepts of the very identity of the person, shaped the impact of those factors.

The parallels in Ulster are striking. Of course there were economic interests that attached the working-class Protestant to the 'Orange' state and much has been made of the 'cross-class alliance' by which the bourgeoisie manipulated the Protestant workers. That is not an issue I am debating. If we assume, however, that an ethnic nationalistic religion is operating, things difficult to understand in other terms become more easily explicable. If we turn again to a consideration of religion as being concerned with the source of evil in the world, then it is apparent that one strain of fundamentalist preaching to which working-class Protestants are exposed more than most is that which pictures the Catholic church and the pope as 'Babylon', the very symbol of evil. Individual Catholics may be perceived as dupes but even if unwitting, they may be agents of an evil enterprise, or indeed of evil itself. And this is manifested in their attacks on the existence of Protestant Ulster, with which the identity of the Protestant workers was linked subjectively in ways that went beyond mere economic interests. Threats to its existence were threats to their personal identity. If this were true it would explain the events leading up to the outbreaks of rioting in Belfast. Clearly in 1969, Catholics in Belfast posed no threats to the Protestants of the Shankill and Sandy Row – but in Derry there was rioting in the Bogside. For some Protestants, I argue, this could be interpreted only as an uprising by evil forces that threatened the personal identities of Protestants. The forces of evil are not contained in one place, and a 'defensive' attack on Belfast Catholics could seem both necessary and virtuous.

If we look at the ethnic nationalist religion of the Ardoyne as Burton and others have depicted it we see something similar. Here the source of evil in the world is not Protestantism but the British, or sometimes specifically the English, comparable with Ayatollah Khomeini's concept of the United States as 'the Great Satan'. Not merely have England and the English been the source of particular ills for Ireland but in terms of this ethnic religion it pollutes, and those associated with the British themselves become sources of evil in the world, and to eradicate them is wholly moral. Bishop and Mallie comment that 'IRA men often talk in the language of religious conversion' when describing their recruitment into the movement, and say that the political education they received had this in common with religious instruction, that it caused the recruits to see the world in a new way.[30] If the British were the root of every evil then it was moral to kill not only British troops but all those minions of evil who supported them – and nothing could justify any retaliatory measures they might take – for evil, if thwarted at one moment by the good, does not for that reason become morally entitled to make retaliatory attacks on the good. If witches are poisoned no one is entitled to avenge them.

So I come back to the verse at the beginning of this article. Those who adhere to the religions of ethnic nationalism have something in common despite the great cultural differences between them. The Sikh shoots Hindus without distinction of sex or age, because they are all in his eyes agents of evil that must be eradicated. The young men in the Maze would not do that, but they can sever 'so-called legs and so-called arms' because those to whom they belong are, as themselves agents of evil, only 'so-called' humans; since they embody evil killing them entails no guilt. It is this implicit assumption that the outsider is the source of identity-threatening evil that distinguishes ethnic religion as a sub-species of 'civic religion'.

To some the words Catholic and Protestant stand for religious beliefs that, despite all the economic and social factors that separate people, are the main incentive for often valiant attempts to build bridges across the chasms dividing communities in Ulster. To others the labels are equally important but they are shorthand indications for adherence to very different beliefs which, whatever their formal ideas about God, imply beliefs about the nature of evil that are certainly not Christian. Within each religious community labelled 'Catholic' and 'Protestant' there is enormous tension between very different systems of belief.[31]

So where does this leave the question with which this essay started, the relationship between Christianity and Ulster groups? Undoubtedly the social group normally seeks religious support for its own identity and the churches lend themselves to this, sometimes unwittingly, sometimes feeding on the 'ethnic consciousness' of their adherents – but it is an error to assume that 'the church' is simply reducible to 'the group'. Worldwide, given a choice, groups at enmity with each other will attach themselves to different cults; if totemic groups exist the greatest significance of being a 'Crow' is being different from 'Eaglehawks'. Christian sectarianism in Africa is due not only to missionaries. The Mbembe had been sufficiently in contact with missionaries for almost every village to be linked to either the Roman Catholic or the Church of Scotland mission; initially I thought this had created new, sectarian, divisions but there was a deep, pre-existing cleavage and enemies would not join the same church. Indeed, a village at odds with both the other groups had even sent to a Lutheran missionary fifty miles away urging him to come to establish a third church amongst them. If no choice is possible, as in England at the time of the Norman conquest, then religion may ultimately help to unify different ethnic groups. Macauley notes that after 1066 the only Norman opposition to William's 'racist' attacks on the Saxons came from the clerics who denied his right to eject Saxon clergy from their positions. Where choice exists, however, such intergroup divisions will have ethnic – religious manifestations. Ireland's divisions were exacerbated because the major impact of settlement from England and Scotland came at the time of the Reformation. Competition led both to a new kind of loyalty to Roman Catholicism on the part of the Irish and an intense Protestant enthusiasm by the incomers. Nobody can deny the secular input into religious devotion in Ireland. Equally clear are the secular results of religious injunctions that lead to social separation: where kinship is so important clerical injunctions to marry within the faith have enormous social consequences. Nevertheless the identity of ethnic and church values is not total. Insofar as the churches, Catholic and Protestant, have continued to preach the central command to love God and to show this by loving 'neighbours', a potential threat is injected into the heart of the most inward-looking congregation, the seed of disruption, a breaking of the boundaries that is dangerous to that social purity that the secular group demands. Congregations may insulate themselves from this threat by various strategies: Catholics must attend mass but men commonly walk out before the sermon. Protestants seldom do this but they need not attend church at all and in fact the great majority of men especially the working-class men do not. Here perhaps is a role of the Orange Order that is often overlooked: membership of the Lodge allows the Protestant male to assert his religious loyalty without the inconvenience of any Christian religious observance.[32] Indeed the Orange Order is perhaps best understood as the ultimate manifestation of Protestant ethnic religion. Some clerics are notoriously committed to the cause of this religion; for them 'god-to-group co-ordination' is total. However, those religious leaders who fail to conform to the norms of ethnic religion and reiterate the gospel pose the ultimate threat to groups who define themselves on the basis of Christian denominational adherence – this threat is the conversion of good ethnics into heretics who assert that true Christianity transcends group boundaries. It is the central paradox of the Ulster situation that amongst the strongest opponents of Christian sectarian identity are so often those who want to refer to themselves as 'Christians'.[33] It is very unDurkheimian. It is this complexity that makes the Ulster situation theoretically fascinating as well as tragic.

## NOTES

1. Published in *The Spectator*, 16 May 1987, p. 29. Reprinted with permission.
2. Ogletree, Thomas W., *The Use of the Bible in Christian Ethics* (Oxford: Basil Blackwell, 1983), p. 197.
3. Martin, David, *The Dilemmas of Contemporary Religion* (Oxford: Blackwell, 1978), pp. 1–2.
4. See, e.g., Horton, Robin, 'A Definition of Religion and its Uses', *Journal of Royal Anthropological Society*, vol. 90 (1960), pp. 201–26.
5. Harris, Rosemary, *The Political Organisation of the Mbembe of Southeast Nigeria* (London: HMSO, 1965), chap. 2 for a discussion of Mbembe cosmology.
6. Burton, Frank, *The Politics of Legitimacy: Struggles in a Belfast Community* (London: Routledge & Kegan Paul, 1978), pp. 119–20.
7. See Harris, Rosemary, *Prejudice and Tolerance in Ulster: Neighbours and 'Strangers' in a Border Community* (Manchester: Manchester University Press, 1972).
8. Whyte, John, 'Interpretations of the Northern Ireland Problem: an Appraisal', *Economic and Social Review*, vol. 9, no. 4 (1978), pp. 257–82 (p. 81).
9. See Burton, ibid.

10. Nelson, Sarah, *Ulster's Uncertain Defenders: Loyalists and the Northern Ireland Conflict* (Belfast: Appletree Press, 1984).
11. See, e.g., Boal, Frederick W., 'Segregation and Mixing: Space and Residence in Belfast', Boal, F.W. and J. Neville H. Douglas (eds.), *Integration and Division: Geographical Perspectives on the Northern Ireland Problem* (London: Academic Press, 1982).
12. See, e.g., Reid, Alastair, 'Skilled Workers in the Shipbuilding Industry, 1880–1920', Morgan, Austen and Bob Purdie (eds.), *Ireland, Divided Nation Divided Class* (London: Ink Links, 1980).
13. See Nelson, ibid., p. 43.
14. Bishop, Patrick, and Eamon Mallie, *The Provisional IRA* (London: Heinemann, 1987), p. 256.
15. Ibid., pp. 220–2; and Nelson, ibid., p. 126.
16. Nelson, ibid., p. 121, and Burton, ibid., p. 109.
17. Nelson, ibid., pp. 122–3.
18. Idem.
19. Nelson, ibid., pp. 126–7.
20. Burton, ibid., pp. 88–94.
21. Nelson, ibid., p. 171.
22. Nelson, ibid., pp. 189–91.
23. Burton, ibid., pp. 125–6.
24. Burton, ibid., p. 101.
25. Kapferer, Bruce, *Legends of People – Myths of State: Violence, Intolerance, and Political Culture in Sri Lanka and Australia* (Washington and London: Smithsonian Institute Press, 1988).
26. Ibid., pp. 31–3.
27. Ibid., p. 29.
28. Ibid., p. 33.
29. For the argument that Ulster's Protestants are inherently not nationalist see David W. Miller, *The Queen's Rebels* (Pittsburg: University of Pittsburg Press, 1976). But he is here using the normal meaning of the term.
30. Bishop and Mallie, ibid., p. 260.
31. Burton, ibid., pp. 85–103 records an intense battle between a parish priest and the leaders of the PIRA for the hearts and minds of the people of the Ardoyne.
32. For a discussion of this issue see Harris, ibid.
33. See Barnes, Trevor, *The Wounded City: Hope and Healing in Belfast* (London: Fount Paperbacks, 1987) for a remarkable collection of biographical sketches of Protestants and Catholics making this kind of statement.

# 4 · A DISCREDITED CAUSE? THE IRA AND SUPPORT FOR POLITICAL VIOLENCE

## TERRORISM: DILEMMAS OF DEFINITION

The terrorist, folk devil of the late twentieth century, masked and armed with an ubiquitous self-loading rifle, is entrenched in popular consciousness as a potent threat to democracy and western civilisation. The threat is made all the more potent by coupling it with that perennial source of all evil: Soviet communism.

The argument that terms such as 'violence', 'protest', 'disturbance' and particularly 'terror' do not represent coherent social realities but rather designate the ideological stance of the user is borne out by the indiscriminate usage of the concept of terror. The narrow focus of many commentators on particular actions, generally violent actions, of actors obscures analysis of the aims, objectives and composition of collectivities.[1] Until the emergence, from the late 1960s onwards, of widespread social unrest in the western world, the remit of the term terror was restricted to a limited number of historical situations and groups such as the Narodnaya Volya of nineteenth-century Russia and the practices of the Nazi regime in Germany. The application of the term has now become so diverse and widespread that it is applied to collective action of extraordinary diversity and variety – often the only common denominator would seem to be opposition to established modes of domination and control. Indeed, the term terrorist can be used to stigmatise opposition groups far removed, in ideology and practice, from the use of bombs and bullets, thus delegitimising a complete spectrum of opposition. The British prime minister, Mrs Thatcher, comes very close to this position in a speech made in 1984:

> At one end of the spectrum are the terrorist gangs within our boundaries and the terrorist states which finance and arm them. At the other end are the hard left operating within our system, conspiring to use union power and the apparatus of local government to break, defy and subvert the laws.[2]

This statement encapsulates an important aspect of the response of the state to dissent: by branding it as illegitimate – or even illegal – and by reducing all forms of opposition and dissident collective action to conspiracy and subversion, the need to analyse and confront the socio-economic roots of conflict is negated. The way is then open to the reflex actions of authoritarianism in dealing with dissidents. However, it is also important for the state, while stressing the threat posed by dissent, to downplay the importance of collective action by portraying such action as being the work of a small minority of 'evil', 'unbalanced' or 'misled' individuals. In the event of widespread civil unrest the participants are often branded as criminals, set upon personal gain through looting or indulging in their criminal tendencies through attacks on the police or destruction of property. This was the offical position taken in the wake of urban unrest in England in 1980 and succeeding years.[3] Even in the case of widespread unrest, not directly attributable to local conditions, such as bad housing, or to small groups, it is possible to introduce explanations based on the alleged manipulation or intimidation of large groups of people by professional agitators. This tactic is particularly relevant to the situation in Northern Ireland. While the state has been successful in establishing an image of the IRA as a terrorist organisation, embarrassment is often caused by expressions of popular support for the IRA, for example, during the hunger strikes of 1980–1 and more generally at funerals and commemorations of IRA members.

Such expressions of support – which often involve violent confrontations with the security forces – are generally explained away as resulting from manipulation or intimidation. A recent example of this approach was the response of the chief constable of the Royal Ulster Constabulary, Sir John Hermon, to the large attendances at the funerals of eight IRA members shot during an abortive raid on a police post in May 1987:

In such an atmosphere [that engendered by republican funerals] the Provisional IRA will seek to manipulate young people, poison and pervert their minds and induce them into the ranks of terrorism . . . the godfathers behind all this are not interested in your welfare, they have not the slightest compunction about using you to serve their own purpose.[4]

The response of the British state to the conflict in Ireland is structured by a complex of considerations ranging from the international and strategic consequences of an unstable Ireland on the western flank of NATO to the need to show resolve in Ireland when faced with the possibility of serious dissent at home. The fact that Northern Ireland is not a faraway colony but a part of the United Kingdom makes both sudden disengagement or out-and-out repression non-viable options. By presenting the problem as one of terrorism the complexities of the situation are disguised and the option of a military solution is kept on the agenda. It is understandable that governments should react in this fashion to dissent within their borders, but it is the function of academic writing to divorce itself from political considerations (or, at least, openly partisan positions) and attempt a considered analysis of the problems involved. In the area of contemporary collective action, and with Ireland in particular, it would appear that the social sciences have hardly acquitted themselves with honour.[5]

The literature on the topic of terrorism, by now grown to vast dimensions, is dogged by the apparently insoluble problem of definition. Some writers evade the problem by not offering a definition but assuming a broad ideological consensus among their readers. Other commentators are unapologetic in defining terrorism simply as anti-state activity. One such commentator is Richard Clutterbuck, who writes: 'Terrorism aims by the use of violence or the threat of violence to coerce governments, authorities or populations by inducing fear.'[6] Others begin by including state violence (totally ignored by Clutterbuck) but then proceed to deal with the problem as though such violence does not exist. Paul Wilkinson, for instance, writes: 'Terrorism can be defined as the systematic use of murder, injury and destruction or threat of same to publicise a cause and to intimidate a wider target into conceding the terrorist's aims.'[7] Despite the all-embracing nature of this definition – which would include within its ambit the bombing of German cities by the RAF and the USAF during World War II –

in his more specific writings, on Ireland, for instance, Wilkinson makes no reference to the use of terror by the state and, indeed, specifically excludes it from his considerations.[8] Other attempts at definition make specific reference to the use of terror by the state, as in the case of Grant Wardlaw:

> Political terrorism is the use, or threat of use, of violence by any individual or group, whether acting for, or in opposition to, established authority when such action is designed to create extreme anxiety and or fear inducing effects in a target group larger than the immediate victims for the purpose of coercing that group into acceding to the demands of the perpetrators.[8]

The very broadness of this definition embodies its weakness. As Charles Townshend has pointed out, the distinction between the general concept of war and the particular act of terrorism is blurred. Townshend attempts to rectify this confusion by restricting terrorism to acts against non-combatants: 'The systematic use of violence by armed people to put unarmed people into fear, in the belief that this will deliver political results.'[9] This position is even more sharply stated by Eqbal Ahmad: 'Terrorism does not refer to the mutual fear of armed adversaries but only to the acts of intimidating and injuring unarmed, presumably innocent, civilians.'[10]

These latter definitions have the advantage of clearly limiting the scope of the term to violent acts against innocent civilians and non-combatants. However, the distinction between war and terror is somewhat artificial in the context of the twentieth century. While there is a clear analytical distinction in practice, the boundary has become progressively blurred. World War II and large-scale warfare since have been distinguished by the use of a strategy that directly involves civilian populations. Contemporary conventional warfare is dependent for its effectiveness on the mobilisation of total populations behind the war effort, particularly in the sphere of technological innovation and industrial production. The dividing line between combatant and non-combatant has become increasingly indistinct.

The various strategies of nuclear war – from mutually agreed destruction (MAD) to limited nuclear war – accept horrific loss of human life as inevitable. For politicians and military commanders the use of terror is a tactical question and not one of morality.[11] The use of terror as a tactic has been firmly established since the

American Civil War – the first real war of attrition – and has become a common feature of insurgency and counter-insurgency in this century. It is ludicrous to suggest, as do many commentators on the contemporary situation in Ireland,[12] that there is a clear distinction to be found between the IRA of the 1920s and the present-day version; the latter being terrorist while the former was a popular anti-colonial movement. The reality is, however, that the IRA of the 1920s did use terror (intimidation, shooting of suspected informers, etc.) to neutralise that section of the population, a considerable one, which did not wholeheartedly support its objectives and methods. Ernie O'Malley, one of the most experienced IRA leaders of the period, casually writes of a local shopkeeper who was less than enthusiastic about the IRA boycott of the police:

> Flannery had been previously warned by the IRA of the consequences that would attend a continuation of his help to the RIC. Horses belonging to him and a relation of his had been shot, and lack of a necessary animal kept him within the limits of Republican law.[13]

The shooting of a horse may appear to us to be of little consequence but in the 1920s in rural Ireland it was as devastating a blow to a person's livelihood to lose an animal as a car bomb in a business district would be to a businessman today. The level of technological development and the availability of such technology are clearly crucial factors in the way in which violent confrontations are structured and develop. Indeed the application of technological developments, by either party to a conflict, are a reflection of the means available to achieve a particular end rather than of the moral depravity of the participants. Ahmad puts this point succinctly:

> Oppression and injustice have existed for millennia. Why then this scourge of international terrorism now? Part of the answer lies in modern technology and its proliferation. Technology provides the physical elements of contemporary terrorism – transportation, coercion and communication. The airplane is a speedy, vulnerable and exceptionally manipulable means of transportation. Compact and formidable modern handguns can be deadlier than most 19th-century artillery. And the electronic media offers an instant means of communication with the entire world. When hijackers put the three elements together they arrange a global hearing. The American Indians never had such an opportunity. Technology has

rendered obsolete the means by which history's wars are kept secret.[14]

But there is a further dimension to this problem. The use of terror as a tactic is linked to the options open to the group in question and to the extent and nature of its support. The absence or otherwise of alternative strategies for bringing about change structures attitudes towards the use of violence. The lifespan and success of groups committed to change through violent means is dependent upon, at least, the tacit support of a significant reference group and the ability to call upon collective action when necessary. Organisations such as the Baader-Meinhof group and the Red Brigades failed to find such a broad level of support for their actions. Persistence in the face of a narrow and even declining basis of support, coupled with increasing pressure from the state, produces isolation and an ever-increasing spiral of violence and repression, thus alienating support even further. The very nature of multinational capitalism, its lack of a visible and vulnerable head and heart, the peripheral nature of even its most visible agents makes it invulnerable to terrorist attack, indeed, as Umberto Eco has pointed out, terrorism and multinational capitalism exist in a symbiotic relationship: 'Terrorism is not the enemy of the great systems; on the contrary it is their natural counterweight, accepted, programmed.'[15]

Where the conflict is one involving national or ethnic minorities, the situations can be different. Usually, the parameters of conflict are both structured and visible and open to some political negotiation. The participants in the conflict are not small, isolated opposition groups or an anonymous, multinational capitalism, but clearly distinguishable actors and their agents, identifiable within the context of a given socio-economic reality. In such situations there is usually a political space that allows the emergence of groups intent on social change by constitutional and legal means. It is only when the political system fails to deliver necessary reforms that support for more violent means of attaining change beings to grow.

The promiscuous use of the term terror and the crucial role it has come to play in the ideological discourse of contemporary western society makes the critical analysis of social conflicts particularly difficult. The distinctions between different types of conflict, ethnic, nationalist, etc., are rendered invisible as all types of collective action are subsumed under the label of terror.

# CONCEPTUALISING THE IRA

The Irish conflict is perhaps the most persistent and historically rooted conflict in western Europe. Politically motivated violence has been an integral part of the conflict for over a century, although this has always been balanced by a strong constitutional and peaceful strand of Irish nationalism. The relationship between the two strands is an uneasy one, and the strength of both fluctuates in response to British policy towards Ireland. Currently, militant nationalism is strong and in the form of the Provisional IRA has carried out a protracted and bloody war since the early 1970s. The activities of the IRA are a matter of great moral revulsion for many observers, and this moral revulsion, coupled with a somewhat uncritical acceptance of the dogma of terrorism, forms the basis of much commentary.

## The liberal approach

The recent writings of the historian E. P. Thompson have focused attention on the question of civil liberties and the rule of law.[16] It is Thompson's contention that the equation, commonly accepted by Marxists, law equals class power is incorrect and that the law is not simply, as most of the left assumes, an instrument of class power and oppression. His study of the Black Act, enacted in England in 1723, leads him to this conclusion, and in the final part of his study[17] he makes a powerful and convincing case for generalising the specific case of this Act and its background and effects to the status of law in general.

His target is 'a sophisticated, but [ultimately] highly schematic marxism' that reduces law to a superstructural phenomenon totally subservient to an infrastructure of productive relations – in short, a tool of the ruling class:

> From this standpoint the law is, perhaps more clearly than any other cultural or institutional artifact, by definition a part of a 'superstructure' adapting itself to the necessities of an infrastructure of productive forces and productive relations. As such, it is clearly an

instrument of the *de facto* ruling class: it both defines and defends these rulers' claims upon resources and labour power – it says what shall be property and what shall be crime – and it mediates class relations with a set of appropriate rules and sanctions, all of which, ultimately, confirm and consolidate existing class power. Hence the rule of law is only another mask for the rule of class.[19]

Against this, Thompson is at pains to stress the independent logic of the law, which, fortunately for those excluded from the ranks of the ruling class, is not directly linked to the class whims of one clique or another. The effectiveness of the law as an instrument of hegemony and its role in the process of legitimation would be undermined if it was the exclusive property of the ruling class. The continuation of this effectiveness could be guaranteed only if the law itself imposed some sort of inhibitions on the power of the rulers: 'The forms and rhetoric of law acquire a distinct identity which may, on occasion, inhibit power and afford some protection to the powerless.'[20]

In a series of impassioned and brilliantly polemic articles, written at the end of the last decade,[21] Thompson applies this argument to the contemporary situation in Britain and points to the dangers inherent in the gradual erosion of civil liberties through the medium of a piecemeal extension of state power and the emergence of what he calls the 'Secret State' and which elsewhere has been characterised as the strong state, or the security state.[22] His call for a greater concern for the preservation of civil liberties and his attempts to expose and constrain the activities of the state are timely and apposite. However, his position has come in for some criticism, and one line of criticism in particular is germane to the concerns of this article. Perry Anderson has made the point that there are severe difficulties inherent in making global generalisations about the 'law' from the narrow and specific example of English law: 'What Thompson has done is to conflate the historically very specific – and unusual – case of English law in the eighteenth century with law in general.'[23] The danger here lies in seeing the law as a 'homogeneous unity' with its own internal logic. Anderson illustrates this point with reference to the legal system of the Mongol empire, but it is hardly necessary to call upon such arcane examples; nor, it will be argued, is it necessary to leave the orbit of English law itself.

By the beginning of the eighteenth century, English rule in Ireland, mediated via a Protestant land-owning ascendency, was well on the way to consolidation. The Irish land system, and the social structure built upon it, had been eradicated: the traditional legal system, the Brehon laws, were but a memory. English soldiers upheld English laws and an English parliament ruled through its puppet Irish counterpart. Yet English law as applied to Ireland was radically different from the one in England itself: while vocal complaints were made at the suspension (in 1722) of habeas corpus in England, the fact that this cornerstone of English law did not even apply in Ireland was not a matter for concern. It may well be true, as Thompson contends, that

> [English] law was imbricated within the very basis of productive relations, which would have been inoperable without this law. And, in the second place, this law, as definitions or as rules . . . was endorsed by norms tenaciously transmitted through the community. There were alternative norms; that is a matter of course; this was a place not of consensus, but of conflict. But we cannot then simply separate all law off as ideology, and assimilate this also to the state apparatus of the ruling class.[24]

But this is English law as developed and applied in England. In Ireland the era of the Black Act was one of unparalleled oppression. The penal laws, enacted in 1704, were explicitly aimed at the suppression of the culture and customs of the majority population of Ireland: the native Irish. In effect, the law, as applied to Ireland, distinguished between different classes of men and women defined by their religion. The law in Ireland, its theory and practice, flatly contradicts Thompson's conception: 'The law, in its forms and traditions, entailed principles of equity and universality which, perforce, had to be extended to all sorts and degrees of men.'[25]

It is not necessary to rehearse the subsequent application of law in Ireland: it is sufficient to note that between 1800 and 1921 Westminster enacted 105 separate Coercion Acts dealing with Ireland. In the first fifty years after the Act of Union in 1800, Ireland was ruled by ordinary law for a mere five years.[26] It is indeed strange that it was possible with regard to Ireland to filter out precisely those elements of the law that Thompson regards as crucial. The renewal of interest in questions of civil liberties and the expansion of the power of the police and other security agencies is in part a response to events in Ireland. Ireland has been a training ground for both the military and the police. The army has perfected the tactics of 'low intensity operations' while the police have developed expertise in riot control, intelligence gathering and undercover operations. Experiences gained in Northern Ireland have been invaluable for mainland police forces in dealing both with urban unrest and terrorist incidents. The passing of the Prevention of Terrorism Act in 1974 gave the police wide emergency powers, which have been used to develop a sophisticated apparatus of surveillance in Britain itself. Under this Act some 59,481 people were detained and questioned in Britain in 1986, although out of this number a mere thirteen were charged under the provisions of the Act.[27]

A central tenet of the civil libertarian position when faced with the reality of state power in contemporary Britain is a condemnation of terrorism and an insistence that opposition to repressive legislation does not lead to support for terrorism. Indeed, as the National Council for Civil Liberties is at pains to point out:'NCCL opposes terrorism not only because terrorists threaten the lives of citizens, but because their activities provide the apparent justification for drastic curtailment of civil liberties.'[28] Thompson takes a similar position: 'Terrorism, kidnapping, bombing, etc., are abhorrent to me as they are to most of the left',[29] and he draws similar conclusions as to the link between terrorism and state power: 'Above all they [terrorist groups] provide in superfluity, the perfect pretexts for authoritarianism to rehearse its methods and enlarge its repertoire.'[30]

From the civil libertarian point of view both sides are to blame for the situation in Ireland and the consequent curtailment of traditional freedoms on the mainland. The British state was slow to implement reforms in Northern Ireland in the late 1960s, reforms which, had they been implemented, would have defused the situation. Equally, the IRA is to blame by denying the possibility of reform and by its violent activities making any reform impossible and forcing the state to adopt repressive measures. Importantly, however, the weight of condemnation is towards those organisations engaged in violence for the achievement of political ends. The civil libertarian argument is that the state is responding to terrorism; it may well be overreacting, and tending towards excess, but this is an understandable – if not justifiable –

reaction to the undeniable evil of terrorism. Central to this argument is a set of assumptions about the role of Britain in the Irish conflict and the nature of that conflict. There is a striking similarity between the analysis presented by spokespersons of the British state and those of the civil libertarians. Both see the role of Britain as essentially neutral – an unwilling participant in an internal conflict between two communities or two 'working classes'.[31] The focus of state action is the eradication of political violence, i.e. the Provisional IRA and other republican groups: only after their suppression does a political solution become possible. While the civil libertarians see grave dangers in the extension of state power, which is deemed necessary to combat subversion in Northern Ireland, they share the view that an internal solution is impossible as long as terrorism exists.

A considerable section of the nationalist minority in Northern Ireland might have a more jaundiced view of Britain's role and objectives. In their view Britain, for whatever reasons, is determined to uphold the status quo in Ireland and has no interest in reform, if indeed any reform were possible. There is in Ireland a broad spectrum of opinion that would share the view that internal conflict in the North is a product of British rule.[32] The basic argument of the civil libertarians, that the law can be used to control the activities of the state, is rejected out of hand – the legacy of Irish history would suggest to many that the law is cynically manipulated by the state to serve its own political ends.

A central dilemma of the civil libertarian and reformist argument is the existence of armed resistance within Ireland to the British state. For both Thompson and the NCCL the presence of armed resistance forecloses the space available for peaceful agitation and organisation, and permits the state to develop and extend its repressive apparatus. This type of armed resistance is seen to exist in Ireland and, by its very nature, and by the fact that it closes off the option of peaceful agitation, is defined as terroristic.

## The response of the state

The initial response of the British state to the events of 1969, which triggered off the present conflict, was confused and reluctant. The collapse of the RUC left no option but to place internal security in the hands of the British army. Armies are at best a blunt weapon and the British army, with a post-war experience of retreat from empire through a succession of bloody wars, was hardly suited to its role as an ersatz police force. The army operated within the legal framework of the Civil Authorities (Special Powers) Act of 1922. The scope and operation of this Act prompted the NCCL to compare the practice of unionist politics in the North in 1936 with fascist rule in Germany and Italy.[33] The Act was an impressive piece of repressive legislation: it permitted the death penalty, flogging, detention without trial, arrest without warrant – and in case any provision of the Act proved to be inadequate it contained an elegantly drafted catch-all provision (Art. 2 (4)):

> If any person does any act of such a nature as to be calculated to be prejudicial to the preservation of peace or maintenance of order in Northern Ireland and not specifically provided for in the regulations, he shall be deemed guilty of an offence against the regulations.

Although the British army did not invoke the more extreme provisions of the Act – such as the death penalty and flogging – the search and arrest provisions and internment without trial were the mainstay of the counter-insurgency operation during the period to 1972. By the beginning of the 1970s it was becoming clear that civil unrest in the western democracies could not be dealt with by methods based on counter-insurgency experience gained in colonial wars. The Irish experience clearly demonstrated the counter-productive results of such tactics, leading to increased internal resistance and the odium of international opinion. The problem facing the British government, in dealing with civil unrest in the North, was one of finding a legal security system, capable of countering the IRA while also presenting a façade of normality to the outside observer. An important component of this system was modifications to the legal system that would allow those involved in political violence to be dealt with through the courts. Before this, however, it was necessary to define and isolate the characteristic features of political violence: it is at this juncture that the term terrorism achieves quasi-legal status and joins the ranks of other euphemisms such as disturbance, coercion and emergency.

Lord Diplock, given the task of formulating the parameters of leglislation to deal with political violence, defines terrorist acts as:

the use of threat of violence to achieve political ends and 'terrorist activities' as embracing the actual use or threat of violence, planning or agreeing to its use, and taking activist steps to promote its use or to hinder the discovery or apprehension of those who have threatened it.[34]

This definition, as it stands, could be applied to a multitude of activities from the actions of the British administration in Malaya and Kenya to the operations of the RAF and the Red Brigades and back to the current operation of US foreign policy in Central America. That terrorism, however defined, is not the private preserve of illegal groups but has been and still is used by governments is by now widely accepted.[35] Lord Diplock was fully aware of the problems inherent in this type of formal definition, particularly in the sphere of what constitutes 'terrorist' activities as opposed to ordinary 'criminal' activities. Terrorist actions are distinguished by the (political) motivation that lies behind them; but, the learned judge accepts: '. . . motive does not provide a practical criterion for defining the kinds of crime with which we need to deal'. So motive must be excluded. If terrorist crimes are carried out for a political motive, and if motive cannot be used as a criterion, what type of persons then are to be the target of the legislation designed to suppress terrorism? Lord Diplock offers this solution:

> We are driven therefore to classify the crimes to which our recommendations apply by reference to the legal definition of what constitutes a crime, and not by reference to the motives (which may be mixed) which led the offender to commit it. For this purpose we have taken those crimes which are commonly committed at the present time by members of terrorist organisations. Except when otherwise stated in later sections of this report our recommendations apply to those crimes even though they may have been committed by criminals not connected with any terrorist organisation.[36]

By dispensing with motivation (which is normally accepted as a component part of any action, criminal or otherwise) Diplock reduces terrorism to specific actions to be defined and, when necessary, redefined by the state. Terrorist actions are divorced from any socio-economic context and become open to interpretation and reinterpretation as the state sees fit and as the situation dictates. The justification for the introduction of special legislation – and other drastic measures – is the nature of the emergency in

Ireland, which is viewed essentially in terms of a terrorist threat. The question that is not addressed here concerns the reasons for the transformation of the peaceful agitation of the civil rights period in the 1960s into open confrontation between militant republicanism and the British state.

The political impact of the civil rights movement can, in no small measure, be attributed to the way in which the campaign universalised the grievances of the minority through the rhetoric of civil liberties and social democracy. The traditional avenue of resistance, that taken by militant republicanism, had borne little fruit in the decades since partition and indeed may well have assisted the internal cohesion of unionism.[37] By inserting the demands of the minority into the rhetoric of reformism, the civil rights movement ensured a sympathetic hearing from both British and international opinion. The institutional contradictions of the Stormont state were exposed to view: discrimination, electoral malpractices, special legislation and a paramilitary and sectarian police force were forced on the attention of a bemused British public. The British state, however, responded in a reluctant and hesitant manner, allowing its hand to be forced only after the collapse of the local security forces under the impact of street demonstrations in Derry and Belfast.

Once directly involved, the British government promised to implement a broad programme of reform, based not upon the creation of legally guaranteed rights, but upon the reform of existing institutions and the establishment of new state agencies. Progress was slow and a political vacuum developed, which was filled by increasing confrontation between the British army and sections of the population. The classic dialectic of British intervention in Ireland began to reassert itself: constitutional nationalism (in the form of the civil rights movement) proved incapable of delivering sufficient concessions from the British, thus opening the way to the re-emergence of militant nationalism in the virulent form of the Provisional IRA.

## THE IRA: NATURE AND EXTENT OF SUPPORT

The problem facing counter-insurgency theorists, most of whom display an inbuilt support for the status quo, is that the nature of their analysis of social conflict, involving systematic and sustained violence, precludes the possibility of more than marginal support for the objectives and methods of those directly involved in anti-state violence.

This problem is shared, to a lesser degree, by commentators of a more liberal persuasion. When it becomes obvious that the maintenance of a high level of resistance to the state necessitates the support, tacit and active, of a considerable section of the population, this is attributed to intimidation and manipulation. This approach runs through the main body of established writings on the Irish conflict and finds consistent expression in the writings of Frank Kitson, Paul Wilkinson, Maurice Tugwell and Edgar O'Ballance.[38] In more overt ideological form it is the staple diet of a large section of the media and speeches of politicians. However, the official understanding of a social situation that involves a negative labelling process can often lead to policy decisions which, being based upon false assumptions as to the level of support for political violence, can have unpredictable outcomes. This was clearly so during the republican hunger strikes of 1980–1. The policy of the British government at the time was the military defeat of the IRA, which was seen as possible on the basis of an assumption of negligible support for the 'discredited cause'[39] of republicanism. The apparent inability to understand the social and historical support enjoyed by nationalism and republicanism allowed the state to embark upon a policy of confrontation – the outcome of which was the strengthening of the IRA and the emergence of Sinn Fein as a significant political and electoral force.

Contemporary Irish nationalism is a complex and often contradictory phenomenon with deep cultural, historical, economic and social roots.[40] All major Irish political parties, with the exception of the Unionist Party, play at least lip-service to nationalism, and few politicians would openly contradict the received truths about the necessity for, and benefits of, national independence or the correctness of waging war to attain independence from Britain. The reality of being a citizen of the Irish Republic, or a member of the nationalist community in the North, involves a positive attitude towards national independence. While there is a general, if diffuse, commitment to nationalism as a less than specific reality, attitudes towards the concrete expression of nationalist aims and objectives are profoundly ambivalent. A central locus of this ambivalence is attitudes towards the role of violence in the achievement of political ends. The majority of the population would prefer political solutions of a constitutional nature without the use of violence, but are nonetheless ambivalent towards the use of violence under particular circumstances. It is this grudging acceptance of violence in politics – characteristic of Irish society since the eighteenth century – which has been the despair of many commentators. It has been argued that this use of violence as a means of communicating discontent is a characteristic of pre-modern societies that declined during the early nineteenth century under the impact of industrialisation and democratisation. It was the failure of Ireland to modernise during this period that led to the extensive use of violence as a means of political communication during (and after) the last century.[41] This is a somewhat circular argument. Political modernisation in Britain was based upon a broad consensus on political values – nationality, democracy and the rule of law – and a belief that conflicts could be resolved within this consensus, despite the odd violent confrontation. No such consensus or legitimacy could emerge in Ireland in the context of a colonial situation where two competing ideologies of legitimacy were in conflict. The very structure of political rule in Ireland reflected this lack of legitimacy and incipient conflict. The subsequent history of the Stormont state follows a similar pattern. Although replete with the trappings of modern democracy, Northern Ireland rested upon the sands of dissent and sullen rejection from a third of its population. For a significant minority of republicans constitutional methods were a waste of time and violence the only currency of Irish politics. The trappings of political modernisation were not only inadequate in the face of the complexities of the Irish situation but, as the experience of the North has shown, could be moulded to exacerbate an already unstable situation.

A strange paradox lies at the heart of most writings on the IRA, a paradox which arises from the fact that the Irish Republic, universally recognised as a legitimate state, was spearheaded by the IRA when the country emerged from armed conflict with Britain. At the time, the conflict and the part played by the IRA was subject to the condemnation of the Roman Catholic church, much of the media and most of the Irish middle classes. Few contemporary commentators go as far as Conor Cruise O'Brien and condemn the struggle for independence as an unnecessary and irrelevant bloodletting – most fall back on a position that attempts to draw a distinction between the IRA of the 1920s and its present-day manifestation. Michael Laffan admirably expresses this paradoxical position in the following passage:

> However brutal and politically blind the Provisional IRA may be, however far removed its members are from the self-sacrifice of Pearse or the pragmatism of Collins, they remain unworthy heirs to an unbroken tradition going back to the mid-nineteenth century.[42]

As this article has argued, it is virtually impossible to draw any clear and concise distinctions between the tactics of the IRA in the 1920s and those of the IRA today, when the inevitable influence of technological change on the military options open to both sides has been allowed for. It is equally erroneous to dismiss the IRA as just another terrorist organisation linked into an alleged international conspiracy to destroy western democracy. An important point of contention in discussion issues such as these is the problem of the level and type of support enjoyed by the IRA. The question of measurement of support for political organisations, parties and indeed regimes is a vexed one in the social sciences. The inadequacy of the Marxist notion of false consciousness has been well documented but, as the debate on the 'dominant ideology' thesis has shown, the level of support for any regime is notoriously difficult to assess.[43] As far as the measurement of support for anti-state organisations is concerned it can be safely said that survey evidence is likely seriously to understate the level of support both in terms of actually identifying hard-core support and getting straight answers from the more ambivalent. Support for the IRA in the North stretches through a broad spectrum from the deeply committed – whether through ideological commitment or family tradition – to a much larger penumbra of those willing to supply safe houses, information, assistance during elections or even simply a vote for Sinn Fein.

The only large-scale attempt to quantify support for the IRA was carried out in the mid-1970s and published in 1978 at a time when the Provisionals were at a particularly low ebb in terms of their military campaign.[44] Separate surveys were carried out north and south of the border and both showed a significant level of support for the IRA. The compiler of the survey in the North is careful not to give a clear quantitative answer as to the level of support but he does conclude:

> In sum I have argued that PIRA is not simply a terrorist movement in the accepted sense of the term. Its longevity, its history and its goals suggest that it is deeply rooted in the society in which it operates . . . Unlike the Baader-Meinhof gang, the Brigate Rosse, and other terrorist groups, PIRA's aims are feasible, internally consistent and find some measure of support amongst the wider population. In essence, PIRA represents the 'cutting edge' of a movement which finds roots in the frustration of relative deprivation experienced by a section of the Catholic community in Northern Ireland.[45]

Since this survey was carried out much has changed in Ireland. The hunger strikes of 1981–2 acted as a catalyst for the emergence of Sinn Fein as a political force, and the abandonment of the traditional republican policy of abstention from the Dublin parliament opened the way to political activity in the South and marked a new emphasis on politics as opposed to a simple armed struggle. With the participation of Sinn Fein in elections since the hunger strikes, the extent of their support has become visible and cannot be explained away as an emotional response to the events of 1980–1.

The participation of Sinn Fein in elections – during the course of the present conflict – began with the by-election in Fermanagh-South Tyrone during the hunger strikes, but it was not until the Assembly elections of 1982 that the real measure of their support could be gauged. In the four elections since then, Sinn Fein have secured between 10 and 13 per cent of the total vote and have shown themselves to be an electoral force to be reckoned with. (See Table 4.1.) The use of electoral statistics as research data is fraught with difficulties. There are many factors which can influence voting behaviour and this is particularly true of voting patterns within the two communities in the North. The large vote for the DUP and the SDLP in the European Parliament Election of 1983 can be attributed to the high profile of the two sitting members, Ian Paisley and John Hume, while other factors, such as tactical voting, have effected the outcome of other elections. It must also be stressed that there is no direct and obvious relationship between support for political violence and electoral support. In the 1956 general election Sinn Fein polled a total of

**Table 4.1** Voting patterns in Northern Ireland, 1979–87 (percentage of total vote)

|          | 1979    | 1981    | 1982     | 1983   | 1984    | 1985    | 1987    |
|----------|---------|---------|----------|--------|---------|---------|---------|
|          | General | Council | Assembly | Europ. | Council | Council | General |
| Off. U   | 36.6    | 16.5    | 29.7     | 34     | 21.5    | 29.8    | 37.8    |
| DUP      | 10.2    | 26.6    | 23       | 20     | 33.6    | 26.2    | 11.7    |
| SDLP     | 18.2    | 17.5    | 16.6     | 17.9   | 22.1    | 16.4    | 21.1    |
| SF       | —       | —       | 10.1     | 13.4   | 13.3    | 10.6    | 11.4    |
| Alliance | 11.9    | 8.9     | 9.3      | 8      | 4.8     | 6.9     | 9.9     |

*Source:* Irish Information Partnership

152,431 votes – against 83,000 in 1987 – yet support for the IRA campaign launched in December 1957 was patchy to say the least.[46] None the less, in the current situation of protracted violence, political stalemate and economic hopelessness, it is reasonable to assume that those voting for Sinn Fein do so in the clear knowledge that they are supporting the IRA. It is also significant that Sinn Fein support is strongest among the urban working-class of Belfast and Derry. Support for Sinn Fein in the South differs from the North in that it tends to be of an emotional and transient nature when expressed in voting behaviour. The central hindrance to the development of Sinn Fein as a political force there is its identification in the eyes of the voters as a party more concerned with the North and the objective of a united Ireland than with day-to-day political and economic issues. Therefore there is considerable difficulty in transforming support for nationalist objectives into electoral success. In the context of the general acceptance of the legitimacy of the Republic and the commitment of the main political parties to nationalist ideology, Sinn Fein has little space in which to manoeuvre. Gerry Adams, the president of Sinn Fein, shows an awareness of this problem when he writes:

> As a leading member of the Fianna Fail front bench recently observed to Martin McGuinness, the relationship between Sinn Fein and Fianna Fail is that of 'second cousins' . . . It is a remark which illustrates as well as any lengthy thesis how Fianna Fail got its electoral support and how to this day it retains a dominance over the political life of nationalist Ireland. It appeals to national sentiment and republican instincts.[47]

Unlike in the North, there is in the Republic no clear correlation between support for the objectives of the IRA and electoral support. The survey published by Davis and Sinnott in 1978[48] showed a considerable reservoir of support for the IRA, although most of the respondents made a clear distinction between objectives and methods. The survey concluded that some 42 per cent supported the motives of the IRA while 21 per cent supported their activities. However, of the latter figure 13 per cent were slightly supportive while 8 per cent were moderate to strong in their support. It is only in periods of heightened nationalist emotion that this latent support becomes manifest as in the aftermath of the killing of thirteen civilians in Derry by British paratroopers (when there was a massive demonstration in Dublin, culminating in the burning of the British embassy) and during the hunger strikes when two candidates on hunger strike were elected to the Dublin parliament and some 40,000 first-preference votes were cast for them and other prisoner candidates. This vote denied Fianna Fail an overall majority in the Dail. Such events, however, only serve to underline the success with which Fianna Fail has managed to occupy the high moral ground of nationalism and republicanism by welding nationalist ideology to a clientist party machine and efficient grass-roots organisation. Whereas in the North the nationalist minority see poverty and deprivation as having their roots in the political system, this link was uncoupled in the South after independence. Since the beginning of this decade Sinn Fein have managed (however uneasily) to merge radical social, and economic policy with militant republicanism in the North but have had a distinct lack of success in the South. On the other hand, as long as political instability persists in the North the possibility of destabilising effects in the South as a consequence cannot be discounted.

## CONCLUSIONS

Despite the best efforts of the British and Irish governments, the IRA remains a potent guerrilla force capable of tying down large numbers of police and troops at considerable cost to the state in lives and money. The measure of support for the IRA is not quantifiable but it is considerable in the nationalist community and sufficient to ensure that their defeat is far from imminent. The Anglo-Irish Agreement, formulated to strengthen the hand of constitutional nationalism, would seem to have had limited success, and in the absence of concrete reforms may well prove to be of little long-term consequence. All the indications are that there is little real understanding in London of the dynamic of Irish nationalism and the current strength of its militant element. The tendency to act as though the problem is simply one of suppressing the IRA and Sinn Fein is strong, and the indications are that this tendency is once again predominating[49] in the thinking of British politicians.

## NOTES

1. See Tilly, C., 'European Violence and Collective Action since 1700', *Soc. Res.* 53, 1 (1986).
2. Carlton Club Speech, 'Why Democracy will Last', 26.11.84. See *The Times*, 27.11.84 for text of speech.
3. For a discussion of the way in which social conflict was dealt with during this period, see Hall, S. and M. Jacques, *The Politics of Thatcherism* (London: Lawrence and Wishart, 1983).
4. *Irish Times*, 16.5.87.
5. There are some notable exceptions to this. See, for instance, Townshend, C., *Political Violence in Ireland* (Oxford: OUP, 1983) for an excellent discussion of the nineteenth century.
6. Clutterbuck, R., *Guerrillas and Terrorists* (London: Faber, 1977), p. 21.
7. Wilkinson, P., 'Fighting the Hydra', in O'Sullivan, N., *Terrorism, Ideology and Revolution* (Hemel Hempstead: Harvester Wheatsheaf, 1986), p. 208.
8. Wardlaw, G., *Political Terrorism* (Cambridge: CUP, 1982), p. 10.
9. Townshend, C., in O'Sullivan, op. cit. p. 89.
10. Ahmad, E., 'Comprehending Terror' in *Middle East Reports*, May/June 1986.
11. For a discussion of the moral questions surrounding terror see Harris, J., 'The Morality of Terrorism,' in *Radical Philosophy* 33 (Spring 1983).
12. See, for example, Laffan, M., 'Violence and Terror in Twentieth Century Ireland' in Mommsen, W. J., and G. Hirschfeld (eds.) *Social Protest and Terror in Nineteenth and Twentieth Century Europe* (New York: St Martins Press, 1982).
13. O'Malley, E., *Raids and Rallies* (Dublin: Anvil, 1982), p. 50.
14. Ahmed, E., op. cit. p. 5.
15. Eco, U., *Travels in Hyperreality* (London: Picador, 1987), p. 116.

122 THE DYNAMICS AND LIMITS OF TERRORISM

16. Thompson, E. P., *Whigs and Hunters, The Origin of the Black Act* (Harmondsworth: Peregrine, 1975). See also, *Writing by Candlelight* (London: Merlin, 1980).
17. *Whigs and Hunters*, ch.10.
18. *Ibid.*, p. 259.
19. *Ibid.*, p. 259.
20. *Ibid.*, p. 266.
21. The major essays are collected in *Writing by Candlelight*.
22. See Hirsch, J., *Der sicherheitsstaat* (Frankfurt: EVA, 1980) for a discussion of the situation in the Federal Republic of Germany.
23. Anderson, P., *Arguments Within English Marxism.* (London: Verso, 1980), p. 198.
24. *Whigs and Hunters*, p. 261.
25. *Ibid.*, p. 264.
26. See Mulloy, E., *Dynasties of Coercion* (Field Day Pamphlet 10, Derry 1986).
27. See Annual reports of the Chief Inspector of Constabulary, Home Office, London 1976–86. See also the *Guardian* 24.9.87 (Hugo Young, '59,481 Reasons to Challenge this Act'). According to a report of the Irish Commission for prisoners overseas – sponsored by the Irish conference of Catholic Bishops – 6,249 Irish people have been detained under the Act, of which less than 3 per cent have been charged. In all, over 500,000 Irish people have been stopped and questioned under the Act. See *Irish Times*, 8.10.87.
28. Scorer, C. and P. Hewitt, *The Prevention of Terrorism Act* (London: NCCL, 1981), p. 5.
29. *Writing by Candlelight*, p. 170.
30. *Ibid.*, p. 171.
31. *Ibid.*, p. 172. See also Boyle K. and P. Hillyard, 'The Diplock Court Strategy: Some reflections on the law and the politics of law' in Kelly, M., *et al.*, *Power, Conflict and Inequality.* (Dublin: Turoe Press, 1982).
32. See Davis E. and R. Sinnott, *Attitudes in the Republic of Ireland relevant to the Northern Ireland Problem*, vol. 1 (Dublin: ESRI, 1979).
33. Report of a Commission of Inquiry appointed to examine the Purpose and Effect of the Civil Authorities (Special Powers) Acts (Northern Ireland) 1922 and 1933 (London: NCCL, 1936), p. 38ff.
34. Report of the Commission to consider Legal Procedure to deal with Terrorist Activities in Ireland (CMD 5185, HMSO, 1982). (Diplock Report)
35. The conceptual and practical problems confronting governments attempting to exclude their own actions from the accusation of terrorism are discussed in: Herman, E., *The Real Terror Network* (Boston: West End Press, 1982). Wardlaw, G., op. cit., Schlesinger, P., 'On the Shape and Scope of Counter Insurgency Thought', in Littlejohn, G. *et.al.*, *Power and the State* (London: Croom Helm, 1978). Halliday, F., *Beyond Irangate, The Regan Doctrine and the Third World* (Amsterdam: TNI, 1987).

36. Diplock, Para. 6.
37. See Farrell, M., *The Orange State* (London: Pluto, 1974). Bishop P., and E. Mallie, *The Provisional IRA* (London: Heinemann, 1987). For a discussion of the emergence of the Civil Rights Movement, see Smyth, J., *Dysfunctional Reform: The Welfare State in Northern Ireland*. ECPR (Goteborg), 1982.
38. Kitson, F., *Low Intensity Operations* (London: Faber, 1971). Tugwell, M., 'Politics and Propaganda of the Provisional IRA' in *Terrorism*, vol. 5, no. 1–2, 1981. O'Ballance, E., 'IRA Leadership Problems', in *Terrorism*, vol. 5, no. 1–2, 1981. Wilkinson, P., 'The Provisional IRA: An Assessment in the wake of the 1981 Hunger Strike' in *Government and Opposition*, vol. 17, no. 2, 1982.
39. M. Thatcher, quoted in *Irish Times*, 28.5.81.
40. For a discussion of Irish nationalism, see Cronin, S., *Irish Nationalism* (London: Pluto, 1980).
41. This position is taken by O'Farrell, P., *England and Ireland since 1800* (Oxford: OUP, 1975).
42. Laffan, M., op. cit., p. 172.
43. For a discussion of this problem see Held, D., 'Power and legitimacy in modern Britain' in Mclellean, G., *et al., State and Society in Modern Britain* (Oxford: Martin Robertson, 1984).
44. Davis, E., and R. Sinnott, op. cit.
45. Moxon-Browne, E., 'The Water and the Fish' in Wilkinson, P., *British Perspectives on Terrorism* (London: Allen and Unwin), p. 69.
46. See Bishop, P. and E. Mallie, op. cit., ch. 3.
47. Adams, G., *Politics of Irish Freedom* (Dingle: Brandon, 1986), p. 48.
48. Davis E., and R. Sinnott, op. cit.
49. Events during 1988 would seem to reinforce this argument. The response to the 'security crisis' brought about by an upsurge in IRA activity has been a purely military one: increased use of the SAS and other undercover units, the promise of legislation to seize terrorist funds, threats to take legal action against journalists interviewing members of the IRA, etc.

# PART II

# REACTIONS TO TERRORISM

# 5 · THE INEVITABILITY OF POLITICS: RESPONSES TO TERRORISM IN NORTHERN IRELAND

In terms of its challenge to the very basis of a constitutional state, the political violence in Northern Ireland since 1969 has been unique among the European states in recent decades. The suspension of the Northern Ireland parliament in 1972 seems now to be irrevocable. Any future constitutional polity must be established on a basis different from that which operated from Stormont between 1922 and 1972, a condition recognised by the Anglo-Irish Agreement in 1985. The forces which have produced this situation are inadequately described by terms such as insurgency, civil war, or terrorism, though elements of all three have been present in the eighteen years of conflict. What has been common to them all is the constraints they have placed on political options. Attention will be paid here to governmental responses to this political violence, especially to those which have involved the legal system in Northern Ireland. Predictably enough, such responses have varied over time, to such a point of inconsistency in some areas that they could appropriately be described as iatrogenic.

The relation between violence and political claims is a notable example. For a decade now the British government's policy (regardless of which party was in power) has been to treat all convicted prisoners in Northern Ireland as ordinary criminals, i.e. without recognising political motivation as meriting a special status. It held to this determination even in the face of the hunger-strike deaths of 1981. Yet simultaneously both administrative and legislative provisions existed which constituted a recognition of the political character of violence in Northern Ireland. For one thing there were still large numbers of prisoners who possessed the special category status afforded them between 1972 and 1976. Secondly, the anti-terrorist statutes in force in both Northern Ireland and the United Kingdom defined 'terrorism' as the 'use of violence for political ends'.[1] In the light of these contradictions, the government's stand on its principles over the status of prisoners is probably to be explained more by domestic (UK) considerations than by serious calculation of its effects in Northern Ireland. In the outcome, the most notable result of the hunger strikes and the Thatcher government's visible intransigence was an escalation in positive political support for Provisional Sinn Fein, the political wing of the republican movement.

Regardless of the security, penal, juridical or other objectives that such a policy of 'criminalisation' puts in place, it has also been evident that in a context where the violence has such tenacious historical and geo-political links, the necessity of political resolutions recurs constantly in public debate. In the most recent of numerous official inquiries into aspects of the 'emergency', Sir George Baker explicitly addressed the problem 'as similar to the chicken and the egg: the political process has no real chance of developing until terrorism is eliminated, but terrorism cannot be eliminated until there is a political solution.[2] This formulation expresses the dilemma precisely. It also acknowledges the political dimensions of the violence in a manner that is frequently absent from the public declarations of British authorities.

While there is a constantly shifting boundary between the political and the security responses to violence in Northern Ireland, there have also been significant shifts in the disposition of antagonistic forces. Predominantly of course the conflict has been one between the Provisional IRA and the security forces, particularly the British army. In 1969, however, the initial commitment of British troops was made to guarantee the safety of the Catholic minority against Protestant violence, exercised in part through the predominantly Protestant local police, the RUC. If at times the conflict has come to seem (as it is represented in republican terms) a war of national self-determination against an occupying foreign army, there have also been periods when it bore more the character of a civil war, with communitarian violence, expulsions, and sectarian killings the predominant mode. The complexity of the situation has more recently been given another twist. At some key moments, principally when British political initiatives threatened the prerogatives exercised by the dominant community, as represented in the various shades of unionist opinion, the antagonists have been the Protestant political and paramilitary forces and the security forces comprising the British army and the R'JC. In the period since the signing of the Anglo-Irish Agreement in November 1985 this last dimension of the conflict has been particularly apparent. At the time of writing its ultimate outcome must still be regarded as uncertain.

In the light of these introductory comments it will be apparent that an account of 'responses to terrorism' in Northern Ireland cannot presume the stability of the term 'terrorism' nor the simple disposition of two opposing forces, the government and the people on one side, a terrorist sect on the other. The analysis which follows will attempt first of all to specify the relation between terrorism and political history in Ireland, noting the relative familiarity of political violence and its context of coercive government. Secondly, we will examine some of the major features of the legal and political responses to the armed violence in Northern Ireland since 1969.

The first thing to note about contemporary violence in Ireland is its historical depth and continuity. This has important effects in validating current struggles and political dispositions. The slogan of peace activists in Belfast in 1976, '7 years is enough', could be readily amended by Provo graffitists to read '700 years is enough'. More pertinent to the organisation of contemporary armed forces, both legitimate and illegal, are the historical continuities of the period since the Act of Union of Great Britain and Ireland in 1801. Oliver MacDonagh has mapped out the peculiar status of Ireland within the Union in the nineteenth century and after. Government was more interventionist in Ireland and more continuously coercive. The striking evidence of Ireland's difference from mainland Britain was that the usual condition of Ireland in the nineteenth century was its administration through coercion. For example, MacDonagh notes, if normality is thought of as the preservation of the rule of law, the right of habeas corpus and so on as in Britain, then Ireland was normal in only sixteen of the one hundred years of the nineteenth century. In only one year of the second half of the century, 1872, was Ireland free from special coercive provisions, ranging from suspension of habeas corpus to the Peace Preservation Act.[3] The intention of this system of legal coercion was to deal effectively with a range of forces which challenged the legitimacy of the social and political order in Ireland. There were three types of challenge: firstly, agrarian violence, frequently organised through secret societies but increasingly politicised through the nineteenth century; secondly, nationalist revolutionary violence, rarely of significant strategic threat to the authority of Westminster but of enormous political significance; and lastly, sectarian violence, mostly restricted to the north and particularly Belfast, and capable of determining political directions, as in the defeat of the first Home Rule Bill in 1886. Coercion was not the only response to violence: at different times political resolutions accomplished a reduction in the incidence of both agrarian and sectarian violence – in the first case by a protracted renegotiation of property rights in land from 1849 to 1903; in the second case as a consequence of the reorganisation of British Conservative politics around a commitment to the Union of Britain and Ireland. Only nationalist revolutionary violence appeared not directly amenable to political solutions within the framework of the British political system. Its separatist rationale limited the capacity of the political arena to respond to it. At the same time, prior to 1916 the appeal of physical force nationalism was many times diminished by its failure to achieve substantial gains. The ignominious failures of the 1848 and 1867 rebellions in Ireland were followed by long periods of constitutional political reorganisation in Irish politics. The Fenian bombing campaigns on the British mainland in the 1880s helped to consolidate the spectre of terrorism as the very essence of Fenianism.[4] But its challenge to social and political order in Ireland was limited, given the dominance of agrarian issues and 'Home Rule' politics during this period.

In applying coercive measures to control agrarian or terrorist violence in these years, the British government employed a number of techniques. These ranged from more intensive policing through to now familiar modifications of the judicial system, especially in the suspension of trial by jury, the introduction of a system of internment (through arrest on suspicion and detention without trial or right of habeas corpus) and extended powers of investigation and jurisdiction granted to magistrates.[5] The vigour of government response to agitation and political violence in nineteenth-century Ireland is unquestionable. But such responses, however understandable in particular crises, also perpetuated the cycle of violence. Charles Townshend had summarised the dynamic bluntly: 'this account is restricted to violent relationships, to the reciprocal effect of government in Ireland and resistance to it'.[6]

In these brief comments on the nineteenth-century background, one other feature of response is worth noting in view of its relevance for recent events. This concerns the status of prisoners convicted or detained under the various coercive or emergency measures. The concept of 'political prisoner' is not of recent invention and the indeterminate status of those imprisoned under the nineteenth-century coercion acts was a matter of dispute and confusion at the highest levels. Townshend has identified significant debate between the prime minister, Gladstone and the lord lieutenant of Ireland, Earl Spencer, over the status and treatment of the Fenian prisoners in 1869–70. Both acknowledged the distinction between political and other crime, Spencer asserting it 'mere prudery to say that we cannot admit of the distinction between political and ordinary crime'. What was in dispute was whether this distinction warranted different conditions within prison or early release, the latter being Gladstone's preference. In the 1880s the same confusion was evident with the (Liberal) government at the start of the decade reopening Kilmainham gaol for the reception of such notable political prisoners as Charles Stewart Parnell; and the (Conservative) government towards the end of the same decade refusing to admit the distinction.[7] Under any administration, however, the status of political prisoner was rarely accorded to those convicted of violent crimes, as witnessed by the grim memoirs of Michael Davitt and Jeremiah O'Donovan Rossa. Davitt was more comfortable once he had reverted to a more purely political role after 1879, being accorded a quasi-political status in 1881 by the Liberal administration, even though he had been on a 'ticket-of-leave' after his earlier release.[8] As in recent years, political status in the nineteenth century was an unstable category, an acknowledgement determined by a wider set of political calculations of the contexts of crime or illegality. Similarly in the 1920s the British government on a number of occasions responded to the problem of IRA prisoners with a recognition of the political motivation for criminal acts, in some cases leading to early release. In each case the government acted out of a desire to speed the process of normalising the relationship between Ireland and Britain after partition.[9]

For most of the later nineteenth century the response of Westminster to any style of resistance in Ireland was typically coercive. This did not imply the absence of measures to diminish the occasion for resistance, particularly through political reforms of local government, through land and social legislation and (whenever the Liberals were in power) through moves towards home rule. These parallel measures, however, effectively came to naught after the 1916 Easter Rising. In the five years following, violence on the side of both government and the republican movement intensified. After partition in 1921, the coercive norm continued in the new 'statelet' of Northern Ireland. In order to deal with republican resistance to the new state a Civil Authorities (Special Powers) Act of 1922 provided for arbitrary arrest and detention of suspects. Although initially a temporary Act it was renewed annually until 1933, then made permanent.[10] If the preservation of coercion through the Special Powers Act was a symptom of the new state's level of insecurity, the use of it by successive unionist governments was itself productive of the very conditions which affirmed that insecurity. Not surprisingly, a major provision of the Act, internment or detention without trial, was used almost exclusively against republican militants, for example, during IRA bombing and military campaigns in 1938–9 and 1956–62, and for a week during the royal visit in 1951. In the 1920s some Protestant militants were interned, only to be subsequently recruited into the special constabulary.[11] Hence, however justified its use in such circumstances, the Special Powers Act became symbolic of the sectarian nature of the unionist state. In the words of Richard Rose, political scientist and analyst of the Stormont regime in its dying days, the Act was one of the 'institutions of discord' which signified the regime's insecurity and lack of legitimacy.[12]

Besides such legislative bulwarks of the Northern Ireland state other features of the unionist regime exacerbated social divisions on communitarian lines. The first was the sectarian nature of the security apparatuses in Northern Ireland, both in the police force, the RUC, and in the notorious, exclusively Protestant auxiliary force, the 'B' Specials. Fifty years of experience and expectations on both sides of the political and communitarian fence has made the control of the security forces a critical issue for the development of a legal and political response to violence in the 1970s and 1980s. Secondly, political remedies for social grievances of the disaffected nationalist minority under Stormont rule were almost entirely absent. Consequently the political status of the minority after partition was considerably worse and their outlook bleaker than it had been for the half-century or more preceding partition. The tacit endorsement of social and economic discrimination by Westminster up till at least 1968 must be regarded as a further impediment to the mounting of an effective response to the sustained violence of the early 1970s, which was aimed at ensuring the unionist state would not be restored.

Against this background we can see what is distinctive about contemporary violence in Ireland and about responses to it. In the first place it is worth noting the range of sources of violence in the last eighteen years to indicate the complexity of the situation confronting the legal and political systems. The origins of the present Troubles lay not in the mounting of a renewed republican bombing campaign but in the increasingly violent response of the Northern Ireland security forces to civil rights campaigners in the late 1960s. Consequently from the outset the question of state violence has tended to be a central issue in the political struggles. This is particularly relevant for considering the adequacy of legal responses since the failure to guarantee effective remedies against excessive or unjustified state violence became in turn a major grievance. As the nature of state response receives fuller treatment later we may briefly look at other sources of violence.

Characteristic of the entire period has been the incidence of street or public demonstrations. These have ranged from the sorts of activities familiar to other western societies since the 1960s – marches and meetings advancing various sorts of political claims or protests. From an early stage, however, these became 'sectarianised', with civil rights demonstrations being seen by many in the Protestant communities as direct challenges to their privileges in the unionist state. Consequently marching, on both sides, regained the territorial or symbolic significance it had possessed since the nineteenth century. Historical memories are continually reproduced in Northern Ireland through celebratory or memorial marching, commemorating the victories or grievances of the Catholic or Protestant communities. These occasions have frequently led to violent clashes between both sides, or with the security forces. In the early 1970s the most serious of these tended to involve nationalist and republican marches, with particularly disastrous occasions like the British army shooting of 13 civilians in the Bloody Sunday march in Derry in 1972. The changing political circumstances and security policies of the mid-1980s have seen the more serious street clashes involving loyalist or Orange marches in clashes with the Ulster police.

The major violence, however, has arisen from the activities of the paramilitary forces of both republican and loyalist sides. Although the bulk of the literature on Irish terrorism concentrates on the Provisional IRA, the Protestant paramilitaries have also been responsible for a large number of the sectarian killings and bombings. Members of the Protestant paramilitary forces have comprised up to one third of those convicted for violent crime associated with the Troubles. When one adds to these numbers the incidents involving sectarian violence on the part of the overwhelmingly Protestant army reserve, the Ulster Defence Regiment, the extent of loyalist violence has been considerable. On the other hand it is not difficult to understand why the actions of the Provisional IRA constitute the most conspicuous evidence of the intensity of conflict in Northern Ireland. They have long constituted the major and most effective paramilitary force on the nationalist or republican side. In spite of elaborate security and intelligence operations, they have continually shown themselves capable of striking at the most prominent public targets, notably representatives of the British state. In contrast to the loyalist forces, which have only rarely acted outside the North, the IRA has at various times taken the battle to the British mainland and even occasionally to Europe. This broader profile has gained it something of a reputation as one of many international terrorist organisations. Occasionally there have been charges that the IRA was part of an international network, but, in spite of some evidence of Libyan funding, it is clear that its concerns are overwhelmingly local and nationalist.[13]

Finally, in this brief review of the sources and variety of violence in Northern Ireland, how costly has been the violence? For nearly ten years now there has been a decline in the level of violence.

This has been a result of a general decrease in the sectarian tensions and street warfare following the conditions of virtual civil war in the years 1971–6; in part it may be a consequence of increasing reliance on policing rather than military operations in security policy; most of all, however, it has resulted from a change in the activities or strategies of the various paramilitary groups. In place of the policy of the mid-1970s, which aimed to make Northern Ireland ungovernable by political or military means, the IRA has increasingly focused on security targets only. By mid-1985, the pattern of casualties, according to one analyst, indicated that 'the conflict appears to have stabilised into one between the PIRA and the security forces'.[14] Even so, the view of Kevin Boyle and Tom Hadden, that it is far more dangerous to live in an American city where the rate of violent death by murder is double that in Northern Ireland, is too sanguine. The level of violence remains notably high given the rarity of violent death from any source in Northern Ireland before 1968.[15] Yet the fact remains that the diminution of violence since the mid-1970s has been considerable. The economic costs attendant on the violence remain at a very high level. More than £1 billion has been paid out in compensation claims by the British government; while support for Northern Ireland 'in social security and other spheres and in security costs' currently runs at over £1,500 million a year.[16] Not surprisingly the impact of the conflict in social terms is equally momentous. The Troubles have provided the conditions for the continuing reproduction of inequality in the North. In a recent analysis, economist Bob Rowthorn has estimated the male Catholic unemployment rate at 38–40 per cent, compared with non-Catholic at 18–20 per cent. These compare with 1971 figures of 17.3 per cent and 6.6 per cent respectively. Since the major growth sector in the Northern Ireland economy has been in the security apparatuses, which are still largely Protestant, the impact on the Catholic minority is readily observed.[17] At the same time, the worsening economic situation for *both* communities, especially for the working class, has undoubtedly had its impact on political allegiances across the board. It has been persuasively argued by Moxon-Browne that the 'relative deprivation' of working-class Protestants compared to their better-off co-religionists has intensified 'intra-Protestant tensions'. Measures imposed from outside, i.e. Westminster, to redress the social and economic disadvantages of Catholics in Northern Ireland may be seen by the most disadvantaged of the Protestant majority community as a major threat.[18]

Given these conditions, what have been the political and legal responses to politically related violence, and have they exacerbated or alleviated the conditions of conflict? The historians of contemporary Ulster have not been kind to British policy or politicians since 1969. MacDonagh regards the major actions, such as the suspension of Stormont in 1972 and subsequent half-hearted attempts to establish a local power-sharing executive, as marked by irresponsibility, opportunism, even frivolity.[19] In the first sustained examination of state policy in the Ulster crisis, Paul Bew and Henry Patterson from a rather different perspective come to much the same conclusion, arguing that British policy has done much to exacerbate the conflict.[20] For both types of analysis, where the British government preferred solutions, they were usually based on a profound misunderstanding of the political realities of Ulster. Frequently they were for the appearance of something being done in an internationally embarrassing situation. Consequently, the responses to terrorist actions or political violence have as frequently worsened the condition of affairs as bettered them. This is not to say that effective response could always be clearly seen in advance. The dilemmas of political responses to the situation are illustrated by the hazards involved in formulating legal processes for the management of the crisis.

From before the fall of Stormont in 1972, the adequacy of the legal system to cope with the emergent situation in Northern Ireland was in question. In an early study discussing the principles that might organise the administration of justice, given the initial assumptions of a liberal state and rule of law, Boyle, Hadden and Hillyard posited the alternatives in 1975. The state could follow a 'due process' model, retaining the fundamental structures of trial by jury, rules of evidence, limited powers of arrest and interrogation as had been in place beforehand. Or it could develop an administration of justice as in effect part of a security policy for Ulster. In the outcome, the 'security' response has been characteristic.[21] That is, the judicial process has been modified with the intention of limiting the normal hurdles in the way of a successful conviction, such as the necessity to persuade a jury of the guilt of the accused and controls over the admissibility of certain types of evidence, such as unsworn statements of the defendant or uncorroborated evidence of an alleged accomplice. The danger of this sort of response, argued Boyle and his colleagues in 1975, was that it was more likely than the 'due process' model to generate a backlash by undermining public confidence in the administration of justice. This view was to some degree adopted at the same time by the Gardiner Committee reviewing the emergency powers 'which should be limited both in scope and duration . . . [T]hey can, if prolonged, damage the fabric of the community and they do not provide lasting solutions.'[22]

As mentioned earlier, the unionist state had always had in place the power to intern those threatening the security of the state. As recently as 1959 it had been used effectively against the IRA. In 1971, in one of the last actions of the failing unionist regime, there was a mass internment of republican and other agitators and activists. So widespread was the reaction to this event in the communities affected by it that it is commonly considered to be the critical turning-point, the beginning of the end of the Stormont regime. Ironically, the army, which had initially opposed internment,[23] subsequently used it as an overall approach to the gathering of intelligence and control, principally of the Catholic population, a process further alienating the latter. The provocative character of detention and interrogation procedures at this time was the object of critical comment by the Gardiner committee in 1975. While acknowledging 'the need for firm and decisive action on the part of the security forces', their report recalled that 'violence has in the past provoked a violent response'.[24]

Detention was an executive power – there was no judicial appeal against an order. Not until more than a year after the first internments was any review process set up. The Detention of Terrorists Order, proclaimed in November 1972, ended detention by executive order. Should the army or police want to hold anyone for longer than 28 days under the new arrangements, the detention had to be approved by a specially appointed judicial commissioner. The procedure of course was still administrative, rather than judicial. Internment under these arrangements continued for another three years, with more than 2,000 people being detained during the period, a very significant figure in a population of 1½ million, especially considering the army in 1971 had not considered more than 100 or 150 would have to be interned.

The argument for internment rested on its previous success in controlling IRA campaigns, on the evidence of increasing armed violence during 1971 and on the problems of the criminal justice system in such conditions. Consistent with its extension and refinement as a policing response, the British government moved in 1972 to examine the efficacy of the criminal justice system itself. There had been some evidence of intimidation of jurors and witnesses in criminal trials; more importantly, in Belfast the juries were frequently all Protestant, in part owing to the property qualification for jurors. An inquiry by Lord Diplock in 1972 recommended the abolition of jury trial for a range of offences involving violence against persons or property, but also including alleged possession of firearms and membership of proscribed organisations, such as the paramilitary forces. Diplock also moved to change the rules on admissibility of evidence, opening the way to the use of evidence obtained by force.[25] When the government implemented these recommendations in the Northern Ireland [Emergency Provisions] Act in 1973, the system of trial in what became known as Diplock courts was instituted. This has become the permanent mechanism for trial of the scheduled offences as outlined above. Trial is by a single judge and there are various restrictions on cross-examination. Other sections of the Emergency Provisions Act of 1973 'effectively abrogated the rule of law'.[26] In particular the army could detain people for up to 4 hours or arrest them for up to 72 hours without having to justify their actions before any tribunal.

For these few years of the mid-1970s, it is clear that security considerations governed legal innovation. The process was explicitly displayed in the reasoning of the Diplock Report. Appointed in the wake of the internment and during an escalation in sectarian violence, the inquiry had little time for critics of prior security policy since the broader threat of terrorism to public safety required little demonstration. Hence, at the same time as it moved to institute radical changes in the criminal justice system to meet the terrorist threat, it avowed that the problem of official violence or unlawful abuses were not a matter for review since such abuses were criminal offences which 'can be dealt with by criminal and civil proceedings in the courts against the offenders themselves'.[27] In spite of the abnormal conditions which prevailed at the time, with massive deployment of the army on the streets of Northern

Ireland, the Diplock Report here considered that the normal provisions of the criminal law sufficed to remedy official abuses. By contrast, abnormality was accepted as justifying continuing internment of 'members of terrorist organisations' who were *ipso facto* 'criminal'. Similarly, the security situation demanded re-organisation of established provisions of the criminal justice system, e.g. with regard to admissibility of evidence: here the Diplock Committee sought to limit the extent of this undermining of convention by regarding such provisions not as intrinsic to the criminal law itself but as technical procedures which 'lawyers, particularly English and Irish lawyers, were used to'.[28] The Diplock Report appeared to constitute the criminal justice system itself as culpable in the deterioration of the security situation.

Since the enactment of the Diplock recommendations, there have been two major reviews of the legal changes, one by the Gardiner Committee in 1975, the other by Sir George Baker in 1984. The Gardiner inquiry represented some shift in official attitudes to security questions since Diplock. With its requirement to assess counter-terrorist measures 'in the context of civil liberties and human rights', the committee took a broader method and perspective than had the Diplock inquiry. While continuing to acknowledge the security problems posed by terrorism and violence, the Gardiner Report was concerned with the longer-term impact of emergency provisions on political and social life in Northern Ireland. Hence it acknowledged violence and the social contexts which sustained it. 'In the present situation', it commented, 'there are neighbourhoods in Northern Ireland where natural social motivation is being deployed against lawful authority rather than in support of it.'[29] Emergency provisions were no substitute for measures to remove the causes of the emergency: 'a solution to the problem of Northern Ireland should be worked out in political terms, and must include further measures to promote social justice between classes and communities'.[30] More immediately, the report delivered a critical judgement on internment which, it said, had proved 'inimical to community life and had fanned a widespread sense of grievance and injustice'.[31] Nevertheless the inquiry was conducted at a time when violence was still at a level which the committee thought justified internment. But in the course of a year of attempted conciliation with the Provisional IRA, the Labour Northern Ireland secretary of state Merlyn Rees decided to phase out internment, and all remaining detainees were released over Christmas 1975.[32] By contrast the Diplock trial system remained in place, affirmed as integral to the counter-terrorist apparatus by the Gardiner Report. By delivering a greater certainty of conviction of suspected terrorists and para-military members, the Diplock system rendered one rationale of internment defunct. In the first major review of the much criticised Diplock courts since Gardiner, Sir George Baker in 1984 recommended retention of the non-jury trial system and delivered a lengthy justification of the use of uncorroborated accomplice evidence in terrorist trials, a controversial practice in recent years. Non-official reviews of the system's operation have not been so favourable. Boyle, Hadden and Hillyard concluded in 1980 that the Diplock court system had operated without discrimination and with efficiency. 'But this bureaucratic success', they added, had 'been achieved at a high cost in terms of public acceptability and confidence in the system of criminal justice.'[33] They were particularly critical in this regard of the great dependence of the courts on confessions 'obtained during prolonged interrogation'. Four years later, Sir George Baker considered public concern about interrogation practices sufficiently serious to recommend the introduction of taped interrogation at police stations.[34]

The implementation of the Diplock and later measures suggests the difficulty faced by a legal system altered to improve conviction rates, in a society which had been used to the characteristics of a 'due process' model including limited police powers. The introduction of the army to Northern Ireland and particularly the use, and abuse, of internment shattered those earlier norms. As has been mentioned earlier, the army tended to use detention as part of an intelligence-gathering exercise. During the period of quasi-judicial review of internment orders (1972–5), about one in three detainees were released on the order of the commissioner.[35] The fact that detention was aimed only at republicans or nationalists up till the beginning of 1973 was of course a major cause of grievance in Catholic communities. Moreover the policing of troublespots in Northern Ireland was in this period differentiated – for the most part the army operated in Catholic areas, using its detention powers vigorously. Protestant communities were subject to the more conventional police practices of the RUC.[36] The effect of this is evident in the figures on detention compared with conviction gathered by Boyle, Hadden and Hillyard. Where Protestants comprised one in three convicted terrorists by 1974, they numbered only one in ten of internees. Thus internment, a mechanism for managing the crisis of violence in 1971, in fact validated the view of detainees that they were 'prisoners of war', particularly as they were housed in camps.[37] However appealing the security justification of internment in the immediate term, the longer view of it suggests that it only contributed to the further alienation of the nationalist community.

In their detailed studies of the judicial system during the early years of the emergency the same researchers found substantial evidence of discrimination in the legal process. Bail was more frequently granted to Protestants than Catholics. In cases of equivalent behaviour, Catholics were more likely to face 'riotous behaviour' charges than Protestants, who were charged with the less serious offence of 'disorderly behaviour', and in cases involving possession of firearms, Catholics were more likely than Protestants to face the most serious of the available charges.[38] On the other hand, one effect of the Diplock system was at least to remove the sectarian bias that had been evident in earlier rates of conviction against republican prisoners by largely Protestant juries. But the Diplock system has had its own serious problems – there has been evidence of case hardening of judges; and the courts have tended to admit evidence that would be inadmissible or highly contestable under normal circumstances.[39] These problems in the system culminated in the so-called 'supergrass' trials of the early 1980s. There is some evidence that for a period there was an official police policy to grant immunity to terrorist suspects in return for their evidence against alleged accomplices. Normally judges in jury trials would advise the jury of the danger of conviction on uncorroborated evidence. As two critics of the system describe the procedure under Diplock, 'in Northern Ireland terrorist offences are tried by non-jury Diplock courts where, in supergrass trials, the danger warning has been ritualistically given by the judge to himself'.[40] In the first of these cases in Northern Ireland (involving Protestant defendants) the judge declared that the informer's evidence 'had a clear ring of truth in my ears' and convicted fourteen of the sixteen defendants – all convictions were subsequently overturned on appeal.[41] The disrepute occasioned to the police and the courts by the supergrass trials seems finally to have led to the end of this resort. Nevertheless, as in so many other aspects of the legal and judicial response in the emergency years, this happened only after public confidence in the legal system had already been seriously undermined. In spite of the Baker Review's sanguine estimate of the use of supergrass (or 'accomplice') evidence in the courts, other legal opinion was highly critical of the system. In an independent review for the Cobden Trust, Tony Gifford QC considered in 1984 that 'the supergrass trials have already caused a dangerous anger and alienation among a broad section of both Protestant and Catholic populations'.[42] Indeed, the success of the supergrass trials in arousing disillusion in *both* communities has arguably been a major reason for the experiment falling into disfavour.

Not surprisingly, the adjustment of the legal system has not been the only political response which exacerbated tensions and legitimised dissent from the political regime in Northern Ireland. Related to it is the question of the status of prisoners in Northern Ireland. The hunger strikes of 1981 were the ultimate outcome of decisions taken in 1971 and 1972 over the management of internees. In a step which many in government must have constantly regretted, a decision was made in June 1972 to grant 'special category status' to prisoners convicted of charges in connection with the troubles. The effect was that convicted prisoners, who were accepted by the paramilitary groups to which they claimed to belong, joined their fellows who were interned in the semi-autonomous compounds at the Long Kesh prison outside Belfast. The incarceration of large numbers of people by executive decree, together with the increasing numbers of special category prisoners, undoubtedly did much to legitimise the republican political position and Catholic alienation from direct rule by Westminster. The Gardiner Committee recommended an end to special category status, a recommendation taken up by Merlyn Rees simultaneously with the phasing out of internment. This represented an attempt to normalise the situation since, Rees believed, 'the full processes of the law were much more effective and more acceptable to the community than any emergency procedures and he was therefore determined that criminals should be brought to justice through the courts'.[43] Normalisation implied the criminalisation of all politically related incidents of violence;

but the appeal to the 'full processes of the law' was illusory from the outset because the Diplock system was so firmly in place and, as we have seen, that short-circuited the 'full processes'. We have to add to this fact the further observation of the virtual impunity of the security forces in the not infrequent killing of civilians. In such circumstances it is entirely understandable why the dramatic demonstration, through the hunger strikes, of the republican assertion of political status revitalised republican support in the North. Margaret Thatcher could assert that there was 'no political justification for murder or any other crime', but the experience of the previous decade showed that security justifications could constantly be invoked to excuse the excesses of the emergency.

Whatever the ethics or political wisdom of the Thatcher government's failure to negotiate the political status demand, its immediate costs were high. Sinn Fein made notable political gains in the three years after the hunger strikes, though these have been eroded somewhat in the most recent elections. The year 1981 also proved to be costly in terms of violence, with the number of incidents and deaths escalating, against the trend of decline since 1976. None the less, it is clear that the government's obduracy had some strategic justification in view of the attempts by both Labour and Tory governments to implement a key political aim, Ulsterisation of management of the conflict. This involved a major expansion of the role of the police with the intention of an eventual downgrading of the role of the army. The criminalisation of terrorism or political violence, of which the refusal to accord political status was part, was in conformity with the attempt to limit the war-like character of the emergency. The future of this policy has been under threat since 1985 as the major challenge to the police has often come not from Catholic communities or republican paramilitaries but from loyalist marches and street violence. In 1986, there were direct attacks on the houses and workplaces of police by loyalist paramilitaries.

This was the not unsurprising outcome of the Anglo-Irish Agreement of November 1985, the latest in a long line of previously unsuccessful British policy initiatives to provide an alternative to direct rule.[44] The difference of this latest initiative is that it admits the interest of the Irish government in any future arrangements in the North. Previous moves centred on an attempt to re-establish devolved government in the North under conditions that guaranteed an effective political role for the Catholic minority. By the establishment of an intergovernmental conference to meet in Belfast, the Westminster and Dublin governments avoided or evaded the problem of local consent to future political discussions. The significance of the Agreement here is its emphasis on security matters. An explicit object of the Agreement was the facilitation of the development of cross-border security operations and potentially of some type of interchangeable jurisdictions. The prominence of the security concerns in the communique and Agreement was confirmed in the early meetings of the intergovernmental conference. It is clear that a wide range of matters relating not only to co-operation between the security forces in Northern Ireland and the Republic, but also to prison conditions and the state of relations between the Northern security forces and the nationalist community are now open for discussion.

At the same time, while the Agreement has put in place a new set of political options which continue to generate both opposition and attempts to work up longer-term constitutional solutions to replace direct rule, the British government has continued a security policy on much the same lines as that prevailing since 1975. Criminalisation of political violence appears now to be firmly in place, strengthened paradoxically by the tendency of the conflict to revert to warfare between the paramilitaries and the security forces. While such a policy may contain the violence, the strategies of Thatcherism have not succeeded in diminishing the political fortunes of those forces in Northern Ireland which continue to provide a rationale for it. The political future of Sinn Fein was strengthened in the course of the hunger strikes, and the 1987 general elections suggest it is still a considerable force. Similarly, unionist intransigence seems if anything to have hardened in the wake of the Anglo-Irish Agreement. If the elimination of terrorism is dependent on political solutions, then prospects at the time of writing still seem poor.

In this context, current legal responses continue to be dominated by security considerations. In spite of continuing criticism of the Diplock trial procedures, the most recent amendments to the emergency powers failed to provide a return to jury trial. The implementation of some of Sir George Baker's 1984 review of the Northern Ireland (Emergency Provisions) Act 1978 has involved some review of those powers, including repeal of police powers of arrest without warrant under the Act (but leaving them to rely on similar provisions of the Prevention of Terrorism Act 1984), an attempt to tighten criteria of admissible evidence, and a widening of the attorney-general's discretion to certify some criminal cases as triable by jury rather than in the Diplock courts.[45] At the same time there is a tendency in recent policy to accommodate Northern Ireland to policing provisions that are more generally applicable in the United Kingdom. Hence the new Public Order provisions approved by the House of Commons in March 1987 repealed the 1954 Flags and Emblems (Display) Act (of Stormont origin), and extended to Northern Ireland a number of requirements of the 1986 Public Order Act which increased police controls over street marches and demonstrations.[46] Such a development appears to confirm the view that legal and policing responses to political violence in Northern Ireland have not been moulded simply by the particular circumstances of the Troubles but are more generally characteristic of contemporary capitalist state responses to protest and political dissent.[47] Earlier critiques of this process have suggested that this has merely occurred earlier in Northern Ireland. Yet by 1987 the Northern Ireland secretary of state explained the draft Public Order provisions by reference to the preceding implementation of new arrangements on mainland Britain.

## CONCLUSION

As the 'emergency' moves towards its third decade, violence remains characteristic of political struggles in Northern Ireland. Earlier in this chapter it has been shown that the political and legal responses which have characterised this emergency have many precedents in the longer-term history of the province and of Ireland in general since the nineteenth century. What is common to the history and to recent developments is the mutability of the categories of crime, legality and political order. The temptation to deal with the problem of violence through the simple remedy of criminalising all its forms and even, at times, all its potential practitioners (the rationale for internment) has long been charac-teristic of British policy in Ireland. The embedded character of political violence in Ireland, and in Northern Ireland today, shows the peculiar difficulty faced by any attempt to deal with the violence free of its political context. Sir George Baker's 'chicken and egg' dilemma was an unusually forthright acknowledgement of this from within the British State. The capacity of a governing power to admit the limits of its own role in perpetuating the conditions of violent political conflict has been severely tested and found wanting in Northern Ireland. Governing by emergency provisions, it is clear from the experience of the last two decades, reproduces and even exacerbates the conflict it seeks to remedy. It is certainly no substitute for political resolution.

## NOTES

1. The definition as used in the Northern Ireland (Emergency Provisions) Act 1978, c.5, s.31 and the Prevention of Terrorism (Temporary Provisions) Acts, 1974, c.56, s.9(1) and 1976, c.8, s.14(1); see Freestone, David, 'Legal Responses to Terrorism: Towards European Co-operation?', Lodge, J. (ed.), *Terrorism: A Challenge to the State* (New York: St Martin's Press, 1981), p. 217.
2. Review of the Operation of the Northern Ireland (Emergency Provisions) Act 1978, Cd.9222, HMSO (London), 1984 (Baker Review), par. 15.
3. MacDonagh, Oliver, *States of Mind: a Study of Anglo-Irish Conflict, 1780–1980* (London: George Allen and Unwin, 1985), p. 32; the authoritative study of these measures and their political contexts is Townshend, Charles, *Political Violence in Ireland: Government and Resistance since 1848* (Oxford: Clarendon Press, 1983).
4. Townshend, op. cit., 1983, pp. 158–66.
5. See, e.g., ibid., p. 63 (internment – 1871); pp. 172–3 (trial by jury abrogated – 1882); p. 209 (magisterial inquisition – 1887).
6. Ibid., p. vii.
7. Ibid., pp. 58–9 (p. 211).
8. Radzinowicz, L. and R. Hood, 'The Status of Political Prisoners in England: The Struggle for Recognition', *Virginia Law Review*, vol. 65 (1979), p. 1,454.
9. Farrell, Michael, *New Statesman*, 28 Aug. 1981.
10. Boyle, K., T. Hadden and P. Hillyard, *Law and State: The Case of Northern Ireland* (London: Cobden Trust, 1975), p. 7.
11. Buckland, P., *The Factory of Grievances: Devolved Government in Northern Ireland* (Dublin: Gill and Macmillan, 1979), pp. 216–18.
12. Rose, R., *Governing without Consensus: An Irish Perspective* (Boston: Beacon Press, 1971), p. 113 (p. 128ff.).
13. The 'international' connection has been examined in detail by Michael McKinley. See his sceptical conclusions in 'The International

Dimensions of Terrorism in Ireland', Alexander, Y. and A. O'Day (eds.), *Terrorism in Ireland* (London: Croom Helm, 1984) and '"Irish Mist": eight clouded views of the Provisional Irish Republican Army', *The Australian Quarterly* (Spring 1985), pp. 203–13.

14. Arnold, Hugo, *Fortnight,* no. 227 (21 Oct. 1985), p. 7.
15. Boyle, Kevin and Tom Hadden, *Ireland: A Positive Proposal* (London: Penguin, 1985), pp. 12–17; cf. Rose, 1971, pp. 424–5, showing the rate of violent death in the 1960s as lowest in Northern Ireland among eighteen western nations.
16. Boyle and Hadden, op. cit., 1985, pp. 13–15.
17. Rowthorn, Bob, *Fortnight,* no. 231 (16 Dec. 1985), pp. 4–5.
18. See Moxon-Browne, E., *Nation, Class and Creed* (Aldershot: Gower, 1983), pp. 169–71 (p. 178).
19. MacDonagh, op. cit., 1985, ch. 8.
20. Bew, Paul and Henry Patterson, *The British State and the Ulster Crisis: From Wilson to Thatcher* (London: Verso, 1985).
21. Boyle, Kevin, Tom Hadden and Paddy Hillyard, *Law and State* (London: Martin Robertson, 1975), p. 120.
22. Report of a Committee to consider, in the context of civil liberties and human rights, measures to deal with terrorism in Northern Ireland, Cd.5847, HMSO (London), 1975 (Gardiner Report), par. 21.
23. See *Sunday Times* Insight Team, *Ulster* (Harmondsworth: Penguin, 1972), pp. 258–67.
24. Gardiner Report, par. 20.
25. Report of the Commission to Consider Legal Procedures to Deal with Terrorist Activities in Northern Ireland, Cd.5185, HMSO (London), 1972 (Diplock Report).
26. Boyle *et al.,* 1975, pp. 39–40; and Hillyard, Paddy, 'Law and Order', Darby, J. (ed.), *Northern Ireland* (Belfast: Appletree Press, 1983), p. 40.
27. Diplock Report, par. 3.
28. Ibid., par. 28.
29. Gardiner Report, par. 18.
30. Ibid., par. 21.
31. Ibid., par. 148.
32. For a critical assessment of the context of this decision by Rees see Bew and Patterson, 1985, pp. 75–85.
33. Boyle, K., T. Hadden and P. Hillyard, *Ten Years On In Northern Ireland* (London: Cobden Trust, 1980), p. 86.
34. Baker Review, op. cit., par. 319.
35. Boyle *et al.,* 1975, pp. 62, 70; the procedures are reviewed in Gardiner Report, par. 121–38.
36. Gardiner Report, par. 84.
37. Boyle *et al.,* 1975, pp. 74–5.
38. Ibid., ch.6.
39. In addition to Boyle, Hadden and Hillyard (1975 and 1980) see also Greer, Stephen and Anthony White, 'The case for restoring jury trials to Northern Ireland', *Fortnight,* no. 237 (21 Apr. 1986), pp. 5–7.

40. Jennings, Tony and Stephen Greer, *Fortnight*, no. 232 (27 Jan. 1986), p. 8.
41. Gifford, Tony, *Supergrasses: The Use of Accomplice Evidence in Northern Ireland,* (London: Cobden Trust, 1984), p. 16. I am grateful to David Moss for this reference.
42. Ibid., p. 34.
43. *Survey of Current Affairs* (Nov. 1975).
44. See *Survey of Current Affairs* (Dec. 1985), for text of the agreement and the joint communique.
45. Northern Ireland (Emergency Provisions) Bill, 2nd reading, in *Hansard,* vol. 107, no. 24, 1077 (16 Dec. 1986).
46. *Survey of Current Affairs* (March 1987), p. 2 and Livingstone, Stephen and Steve McBride 'Authoritarian State Intact', *Fortnight*, no. 249 (Mar. 1987), pp. 10–11.
47. Hillyard, op. cit., 1983, pp. 58–60.

# 6 · THE AMBIGUOUS DYNAMICS OF THE ANGLO-IRISH AGREEMENT

The Agreement will lead the Irish Government into an impossible political situation in which they will find themselves assuming responsibility for actions and becoming involved in situations, particularly on the security field, over which they will have no control.

> Charles Haughey, Dail Debate, 19 November 1985

Although Mrs Thatcher has insisted that there is no transfer of sovereignty, the fact remains that a foreign Government has been given a say in the internal affairs of a part of the United Kingdom – without even being required to renounce its own claim to Northern Ireland.

> Bruce Anderson, *Sunday Telegraph*, 18 November 1987

The Anglo-Irish Agreement of November 1985 set up an intergovernmental conference which by Article 2 (Section B) committed the British government to make 'determined effort' to resolve any difference on Northern Ireland in political matters with the Irish government. The Agreement also institutionalised an Irish dimension by the establishment of a secretariat partly staffed by Irish officials in Maryfield, Co. Down. In the short term, the Agreement has been associated with an increase in communal tension and violence. Deaths arising from political violence rose in 1986 from 54 to 62, while civilian injuries rose dramatically from 468 to 734. During 1987 there were almost 100 deaths from political violence, double the figure for the last year of unalloyed direct rule. Economically as the CBI's January statement 1987 illustrates, it has been linked to a 'wobble' in local business confidence. Politically, it has failed to isolate Sinn Fein who, after some losses in the January 1986 mini-referendum, have largely retained their share of the vote. Internationally, and at the inter-state level the Agreement has been a considerable success, but it has not eliminated, as is so often claimed, megaphone diplomacy between Dublin and London. In 1986 there was a major row over RUC policy in Portadown; and in 1987 there occurred an even more explosive dispute over an alleged linkage between the 'reform' of the Diplock Court system and extradition. The British ambassador in Dublin has been publicly criticised by the Irish government. In the United States, the two governments do not stand together on the 'MacBride principles' campaign (sponsored by former IRA Chief-of-Staff Sean MacBride, these principles call explicitly for a quota system). The principal difficulty with the Agreement is that those involved in framing it on the Irish side, while being fully aware of the needs of constitutional nationalism, had a weaker understanding or comprehension of the traditions of northern Unionism or Republicanism. A similar absence of a profound grasp of modern Irish historical and political realities characterised those on the British side but there was perhaps a sharper awareness of British interests. To justify such a claim, however, it is necessary to look at the various ways in which it has been argued that the Agreement might contribute towards a benign resolution of the Northern Ireland conflict. In particular, three 'models' (among others) have been advanced and it is necessary to examine these:

## THE EQUALITY OF THE TWO TRADITIONS

It has been vigorously claimed that the Agreement might be an agency for the promotion of an equality of the two traditions in Northern Ireland. Article 5A states:

> The Conference shall concern itself with measures to accommodate the rights and identities of the two traditions in Northern Ireland, to protect human rights and to prevent discrimination. Matters to be considered in this area include measures to foster the cultural heritage of both traditions, changes in electoral arrangements, the use of flags and emblems, the

avoidance of economic and social discrimination and the advantages and disadvantages of a Bill of Rights in some form in Northern Ireland.

Some parts of this project have been completed. There has been new legislation to deal with the very minor problem of the 'I' registered voters (voters from the Irish Republic who were not previously allowed to vote in Westminster elections) and the repeal of the Flags and Emblems Act, which banned the flying of the tricolour of the Irish Republic. Other parts are dead – there seems, for example, to be little prospect of a Bill of Rights. Is there any good reason why the Conference should not be an agency for deepening the recognition of both traditions?

In a limited way this might indeed be the case. The present writer argued for the repeal of the Flags and Emblems Act in 1985.[1] However, few can point to anything the Conference has done to foster the cultural heritage of the unionist community. More profoundly, there is the dimension of the economic and social; in Northern Ireland today Catholics are two and a half times more likely to be unemployed than Protestants. It is this key group; urban unemployed working-class Catholics who have consistently provided the support for Sinn Fein and who continue to do so.[2] It is inadequate simply to strengthen the Fair Employment Agency, which surveys employers to ensure that neither Protestants nor Catholics are under-represented (desirable though that has long been in itself)[3] without a commitment to provide greater material resources to reduce mass unemployment. The malign possibility exists that the current rhetoric of the government and its agencies will merely heighten expectations which will not be satisfied by Thatcherism's economic policies – leading in the end to more ghetto support for Sinn Fein.

## A STIMULUS TO POWERSHARING?

Many people, including Mrs Thatcher herself, have spoken as if the Agreement was designed to encourage a powersharing experiment in Northern Ireland.[4] Those who support this perspective emphasised the debate within unionism since November 1985.[5] In fact, this debate has been notable mainly for its limited and incoherent nature. The Official Unionist Party contains a small and rather isolated wing (whose most prominent figure is Ken Maginnis, MP for Fermanagh), which is prepared to offer responsibility sharing or powersharing in exchange for the removal of the Agreement. Virtually nobody on the unionist side is interested in subordinate devolution within the framework of an Agreement which will continue to preserve Irish government influence in sensitive areas. The mainstream Social Democratic and Labour Party view, on the other hand, is that the 1974 powersharing failed not because the Irish dimension was too strong but because it was too weak; the SDLP can only contemplate a deal with unionists which is firmly within the context of the confirmation of the Agreement.[6]

The SDLP always has to be aware of the continued electoral threat of Sinn Fein. The electoral statistics are consistent with the view that Sinn Fein fell from a highpoint of 1983 (13.7 per cent of the vote) through to 1985; that this fall was further stimulated by the immediate impact of the Agreement as shown by a relatively weak Sinn Fein performance in the four by-elections of January 1986. However, by May 1986, two council by-elections in Magherafelt, in Sperrin and Erne East,[7] the tide seemed to turn as Sinn Fein stabilised. In the general election of 1987, Sinn Fein polled 11.4 per cent of the vote, as against 11.8 per cent in the local government election of 1985.[8] Some rural losses to SDLP were mainly, though by no means entirely, compensated for, by a very solid urban performance.

SDLP gains in Belfast seats appears to have been entirely at the expense of previous centre voters (Alliance or Gerry Fitt) rather than Sinn Fein. While SDLP generally did well in the 1987 elections, their leader John Hume actually polled fewer votes in 1983; whereas Sinn Fein president, Gerry Adams, actually polled more. In two West Belfast Council by-elections on the eve of the Remembrance Sunday tragedy at Enniskillen, Sinn Fein outpolled SDLP by almost two to one in Belfast, even though the Alliance vote collapsed into the SDLP. It is too early to say if Enniskillen and later, similar disasters, including the bombing of the Hanna families and Catholics in both the Bogside and Falls areas, will have a significant impact on Sinn Fein's level of electoral appeal; if it does not, because of its younger age profile, more committed support and the return of some tactical anti-unionist votes lost in Newry and Armagh and South Down, Sinn Fein is likely to do better in the 1989 local government elections than the 75,000 votes it polled in 1985.

The Sinn Fein leadership can feel that its greatest enemies – boredom, disillusionment and warweariness – have been temporarily, at least, dissipated by the post-Agreement mood of expectancy and instability. The fact that the so-called unionist veto on progess has been destroyed by the Agreement, is as much a comfort to them as it is to constitutional nationalists. Having moved away from a potentially debilitating ultra leftism on economic and social issues, Sinn Fein appears to have most to fear from self-inflicted military blunders like Enniskillen. It is doubtful though whether Sinn Fein ever at any point in the Republic had (or has) any electoral prospects worth speaking about and this must remain a weakness.

## STRENGTHENING THE UNION

Both the prime minister and the secretary of state for Northern Ireland, Mr Tom King, have argued that, presumably by reducing the degree of nationalist alienation, the Anglo-Irish Agreement will strengthen the union. Interestingly enough, the Irish signatory Garret FitzGerald has agreed. In his contribution to an Edinburgh document, *Northern Ireland – A Challenge to Theology,* Dr FitzGerald speaks of making the 'status quo work'. The Anglo-Irish Agreement was the document that signalled the end of Irish 'irredentism' – the means by which it could be recognised that Irish unity will not come about for two generations and then only by consent; FitzGerald has recanted of his previous more optimistic views on this point as unrealistic. Even more remarkably, in his Edinburgh text Dr FitzGerald acknowledged that the Irish government had responsibility without power in the North and in that sense 'nothing substantive had changed'.

Yet it remains difficult to see why Britain has any material interest in the strengthening of the union. A significant section of opinion in Whitehall sees the Agreement as the first step in a process of decoupling Northern Ireland from the rest of the United Kingdom, precisely because Northern Ireland is such a drain on the political and economic resources of the British state. The clear message is that Britain perceives itself – correctly or not – to have no quarrel with Irish constitutional nationalism (or the gradual and peaceful extension of its hegemony over the whole island of Ireland) but that it does have a quarrel with both revolutionary nationalism and Ulster unionism. Revolutionary nationalism it hopes to undermine by political means and security co-operation. Unionism it hopes to weaken by holding it at arm's length and keeping it in a reduced and demoralised condition. The union may well survive such a process but it is unlikely to be strengthened by it.

## CONCLUSION

Minimalists on the British side may be rather concerned about the fact that devolution – which is an aim of the Accord – appears at present to be an impossibility. Maximalists may be less worried; the Agreement has already been an international success and it sets up a structure that forcibly differentiates Ulster Protestants from the rest of the British community with which they identify and, it is hoped, it may therefore in time force them to reconsider their relationship to the rest of Ireland. Even if no mental shift occurs – and it seems rather unlikely – it may be hoped that economic and demographic changes will weaken unionism further. Unionism has after all been steadily weakening with respect to nationalism for at least three decades.[9] For this group, Britain has no significant political reason for staying in Ireland; indeed, Northern Ireland is a massive drain on resources (costing £1.7 billion per annum). The principal difficulty lies in the fact that Britain cannot be seen to be defeated by the IRA and, so far, the Agreement's role in ideologically and militarily neutralising the IRA has been minimal. The process of British disengagement has not been assisted by the economic vulnerability of the Irish Republic and its ideological rigidity. Garret FitzGerald's much vaunted liberal image has successfully contributed to the international isolation of the unionists, but it has not contributed a jot to the internal modernisation of Irish society as the dramatic sectarian referenda on abortion (1983) and divorce (1986) reveal. The Agreement itself has had as one of its entirely predictable ideological effects a growing conviction of the rightness of Irish nationalism's claim against Irish unionism.

Opinions that would once have been repressed are now expressed openly. The 'liberal' pro-Agreement *Irish Times,* for example, observed in a leader in September 1986: 'In matters of religion, the Protestant people of the north trail far behind their Catholic fellow-Irish in the observance of what most people see as the norm for democratic living together.'[10] In the aftermath of the Enniskillen bombing such a comment would have been strongly challenged in the newspaper's letter columns – but in mid-1986, when it appeared, it provoked no reaction at all.

However, the growing dislike for the – to many genuinely inexplicable – gyrations of unionism has not been accompanied by any increased willingness to make political, economic or ideological concessions to bring about Irish unity. Quite the opposite, Peter Mair's work[11] has shown a steadily decreasing commitment in the Republic to the sentimental ideal of Irish unity and this has been confirmed by the most recent MRBI poll. This is a process which may be accentuated when the last great truly 'green' figure of Irish politics, Charles Haughey, leaves the stage.

Such a *mélange* of inconsistent but also inflexible and unhelpful opinions raises a fundamental question about the Agreement; was Britain justified in taking such a huge gamble on constitutional nationalism? There clearly have been short term problems. The British government in Northern Ireland insists that everyone should wholeheartedly support the work of the security forces, while, at the same time, pursuing a policy which favours above all a party (the SDLP) which does not wholeheartedly support the security forces. The SDLP knows that while in 1985, 51.4 per cent of their voters gave the second preference to Alliance, some 34 per cent gave it to Sinn Fein. Equally, the British are deeply disappointed about the difficulties which have attended the Republic's accession to the European Convention on Terrorism. Mr Haughey knows also that a very significant proportion of his supporters in the South do not accept that Ulster unionists have any right to prevent Irish unity. The militant republicans have strong connections on this point with mainstream nationalist political culture and assumptions; they are not in this sense an isolated minority, as is so often said, and international co-operation against them has so far been a fraught process. (Much of the difficulty with extradition processes is caused by the nationalist perception that it may prove to be a back door method of granting legitimacy to partition.) Despite the disappointments of the first two years, British politicians are almost certain to take the view that the Agreement may achieve its objectives on a longer haul, even though there is, at present, no good reason to believe that this should be so. Because of the absence of a serious economic dimension to British strategy – partly, at least, because it is easier to massage the Irish identity than to transform material conditions – the initial phase of the Accord's life was probably the most promising. It, at least, had the bonus point for nationalists of unionist shock and dismay; this is now much less visible. It is not unreasonable to presume that the law of diminishing returns will affect the Agreement's operation on nationalist opinion. Nevertheless, British politicians are likely to assume – very reasonably in this instance – that any weakening of commitment to the Accord will significantly weaken the SDLP. A minimalist implementation ('progress will be slow', the British have told the Irish) of the Accord will be the order of the day.

Even within this framework, however, there still remains a strong case for attempting to reduce the communal tension in Ulster by reintroducing the border poll, opening up the processes of the intergovernmental conference and looking at ways in which the British community in Ulster might have a better access to the British state, now that the Irish nationalist community is guaranteed special rights of consultation. If the scope of conference was widened to deal with the Irish community in Britain it would shift the debate on to the phase of minority rights and away from that of nationalist irridentism.[12] It would presumably please both sides in Ireland. One crucial question for the future is not whether the Agreement (direct rule with a green tinge) continues to exist but a wider question of whether Britain is prepared to devote real resources (other than the most formalistic and rhetorical) to reassuring the large majority of Northern Ireland's citizens who wish to remain within the UK. The need is for the British state to adopt a self-critical mode instead of a stance of unreasoning and inflexible self-righteousness which mirrors the worst facets of the Ulster Protestant mentality. In particular, is Britain prepared to separate radically questions of internal reform from those of apparent creeping unification? The Accord has weakened the relative acceptability of direct rule which 57 per cent of Protestants and 50 per cent of Catholics (*Belfast Telegraph* poll, November 1984) found 'satisfactory'. The stable elements in the governance of Northern Ireland remain the predominant elements of governmental practice which, reflecting the province's administrative and economic integration within the UK, remain largely unchanged since 1985. Two years on, the Agreement looks less like the 'framework of the solution' (Hume) and more like just another shell for the expression of an intractable conflict. All the SDLP leader's favoured mystical medical metaphors – lancing the boil, treating the disease etc. – can hardly hide the fact that the 'healing process' (to use one of Hume's most attractive notions) has yet to begin.

Opinion on Northern Ireland is largely divided into two camps. One camp presumes that the Agreement is bound to be replaced by something better; according to taste, this will be either a more Unionist or Nationalist solution. The other camp believes that the Agreement will stay and will have a benign effect – leading to the emergence of a more pliable unionism and the retreat of Sinn Fein. Both camps are, on present showing, likely to be disappointed. But, at least, the widespread sense of economic dependence – which largely explains the weakness of the Unionist campaign against the Accord – means that there will not be independence.

## NOTES

1. Bew, P., and H. Patterson, *The British State and the Ulster Crisis* (London: Verso, 1985), p. 148.
2. Bew, P., P. Gibbon and H. Patterson, *The State in Northern Ireland 1921–72*, (Manchester and New York: Manchester UP and St Martin's Press, 1979), ch. 6.
3. For an exposition of the need for an attack on 'structural inequality' see Bew and Patterson, op. cit.
4. See Brendan O'Leary's contribution to Teague, P. (ed.), *Beyond the Rhetoric* (London: Lawrence and Wishart, 1987).
5. For a very much more low-key assessment of the significance of the Task Force Report (a devolutionist report with power-sharing undertones), see *Fortnight* (Nov. 1987), p. 11.
6. Meehan, Margaret, *The SDLP and the Anglo-Irish Agreement* (Queen's University, Belfast, MSSc thesis, 1987).

7. Magherafelt Sperrin 21 May 1986

Turnout 58.2% (80.6 1985)

| | | 1st Pref. | Percentage | 1985 |
|---|---|---|---|---|
| F. McKendry | SDLP | 2101 Elected | 44.8 | 40.5 |
| B. McMullan | SF | 1828 | 39.0 | 29.5 |
| F. Donnelly | WP | 760 | 16.2 | 3.9 |
| | | | | OUP/ |
| | | | | DUP 26.1 |

Fermanagh Erne East
Turnout 77.3%

| | | 1st Pref. | Percentage | 1985 |
|---|---|---|---|---|
| B. McCaffrey | SF | 3082 Elected | 40.8 | 37.4 |
| T. Johnson | OUP | 3210 | 42.5 | 31.6 |
| S. Rehill | SDLP | 1269 | 16.8 | 17.3 |

In Strabane in the autumn the SF vote fell from 13.2 to 13.1 per cent. On the general election, see my 'How Northern Ireland Really Voted', in *Irish Political Studies*, vol. 3 (1988).

8. For a useful discussion of Sinn Fein electoral support, see *Sunday Telegraph*, 15 Nov. 1987.
9. See Bew, Paul, 'The Unionists of Northern Ireland and the Anglo-Irish Relations', broadcast on Irish Radio and subsequently published in the *Belfast Newsletter* (4.1.87).
10. *Irish Times*, 18 Sept. 1986.
11. See his contribution to Teague (ed.), op. cit.
12. The role of Dublin would be along the lines of proposals we suggested long before the agreement was signed. These provided for improvement in relations between the two nations in the British Isles, which is not far different from what Charles Haughey referred to in his totality of relationships remarks.

In our new relationship, we would not make the same mistake as the Anglo-Irish agreement – singling out six little counties in the entire British Isles for special attention. This has defied all logic and has baffled people in Great Britain.

They are asking why it was necessary to have Dublin as a protecting power here in Northern Ireland to make certain that the British Government fairly treated Roman Catholics who lived in Belfast, but took no account of Irish Roman Catholics who lived in Birmingham.

If the British Government, which is responsible for the whole of the United Kingdom, is thought by the Dublin Government to be treating Roman Catholics unfairly because of their religion, then this criteria must apply to Roman Catholics in Great Britain, too.

The great mistake is to have this special arrangement for interfering in the administration of six counties out of the large number in the republic and Great Britain. That doesn't make sense and is a recipe for trouble-making.

Molyneaux, J., *B.N.L.*, 10 August 1987

# 7 · NORTHERN IRELAND: CORRUPT IDEOLOGIES AND THE FAILURE OF GOVERNMENT CAGEBUILDING

If a caretaker must deal with vicious dogs, he may devise a variety of restrictive cages into which the dogs may be placed. Some structures will no doubt hold better than others. But if in fact the dogs must hunt together in order that they and the caretaker may prosper, cagebuilding is no solution. The dogs will continue to tear and bite at each other no matter how cleverly their cages are constructed. Only when the dogs themselves have been civilised can they prosper. Admittedly, until the dogs are civilised, cages are necessary. But a caretaker who knows only how to build cages will always need them and will never be delivered from the poverty that is a consequence.

The partition of Ireland in 1921 is one of many cages and cages-within-cages which the British government has built in a centuries-old effort to master the Irish. But is it an illusory solution to a problem which cannot be abated by the construction of cages.

Many will object to this analogy because it neglects the fact that those who built the cage are not the benign and neutral caretakers the analogy seems to imply. It also ignores all the justifications they can cite for the vicious behaviour each has displayed toward the other. Our *Violence in Northern Ireland* details the many arguments which Northern Protestants use in justifying their hostility towards Irish Catholics.[1] American readers are also familiar with Irish Catholic grievances toward Protestant unionists, as reported in widely distributed tabloids such as *The Christian Science Monitor* and *USA Today*.[2] But notwithstanding the fact that each dog has its own justifications, the fact remains that their fighting is self-destructive. One largely neglected reason for the failure to eliminate this destruction is their caretaker's tendency to concentrate almost exclusively on cagebuilding: government has tended to seek ways of allowing uncivilised people to live together rather than to deal in a realistic way with the need to civilise them.

Partition is but one example. Many scenarios for structural changes in the government of Northern Ireland continue to be set forth. The Institute for the Study of Conflict (ISC) has reviewed seven constitutional options in its 1982 report,[3] and more recently has spoken in cautious but hopeful terms of the 1985 Anglo-Irish Agreement, calling it 'the most important single political development with regard to Northern Ireland since the Sunningdale Agreement of December 1973, which established a framework for a "power-sharing" devolved government'.[4]

But whether they be partition, direct rule, or some form of power-sharing, these efforts at restructuring Anglo-Irish and minority-majority relations have one thing in common: they are aimed at structurally containing rather than eliminating the readiness of one side to bite and tear at the other.

Even the best of cages is bound to fail if it is expected to reform its occupants. Yet often the assumption is made that some new form of government will transform people whose ideologies have succeeded in corrupting every form of political arrangement that has so far been devised. This assumption is hidden in the reply of the Rev. Sean McNanus in an interview published in *USA Today:*

> Peace can only come to Northern Ireland when there is justice, freedom, democracy, and national reconciliation, which can come once the British government withdraws. There can never be peace in my country while the Union Jack flies over it.[5]

McNanus, national director of the Irish National Caucus, an Irish nationalist lobbying group in Washington DC, implies that if only Northern Ireland were free of the British union, the conditions of peace would be established. But the true conditions of peace require that Catholic and Protestant communities will not despise one another – restructuring the cage will not change the dogs. It may make it easier or more difficult for one dog to abuse the other, but it is the tendency for one dog to abuse the other (the need for cages) that must be eliminated.

Sufficiently large numbers of unionists prefer violence over peace, if the peace means loss of the union or accommodating the Catholic community. Sufficiently large numbers of nationalists prefer violence, if peace means a failure to drive the British out. Too many on all sides would rather continue this self-defeating war even if it means the total destruction of the good life that they could otherwise lead.

The ISC has commented on the continued failure of institutional solutions (1986) to what is at bottom an irrational dogfight:

> Since the failure of [the Sunningdale Agreement] in May 1974, the British government has repeatedly tried to construct some internal institutional means through which the Northern Ireland people as a whole can democratically express their legitimate political aspirations. Each attempt has failed, either because it did not offer the minority nationalist community a sufficiently certain role in the decision-making process, or because it qualified the principle of simple majority rule to an extent unacceptable to the unionist community.[6]

Continued failure to achieve any semblance of peace raises the question of whether organisational changes alone are sufficient to overcome inbred hostilities of such magnitude. While the ISC assessment of the reasons for failure is appropriate in its specific terms, a more general problem is apparent. The mutually exclusive goals, distrust, and hostility which each side has for the other has rendered every attempt at balancing powers futile. Changes in the boundaries of their cages have been insufficient to overcome the intercommunal hostility that is an endemic part of being a member of each respective community. Irish Catholics and Irish Protestants must be changed in their values, goals, traditions and fundamental sense of morality before changes in their form of government will make a lasting difference in their lives. While it is unrealistic to argue that changes in governmental structures produce no change in the disposition of a people, it is equally unrealistic to imagine that organisational change inevitably leads to the changes in fundamental attitudes and values necessary to make any specific government form work.

The need for changing ideologies has been severely neglected by policymakers in the case of Northern Ireland. This neglect appears for two primary reasons. First, governments and politicians are predisposed to approach problems in organisational terms.

Changes in behaviour and in morality are generally sought through efforts at restructuring relationships. But in Northern Ireland, these efforts at restructuring have failed because (1) they have assumed that organisational change will automatically produce the desirable changes in communal predispositions even though the magnitude of communal differences makes such change unlikely, or (2) that organisational changes can succeed without the necessity for change in attitudes. Partition, a basic form of cagebuilding, gives the illusion of being an easy solution to fundamental political differences: put ideologically divided and bitterly hostile opponents in different cages and let their differences grow unchecked. Direct rule erects another cage in which it is hoped the opponents can be forced to coexist. Power-sharing is not directed at reducing one group's hostility towards the other but at giving each group enough power to defend itself against the abuses of the other.

Second, the government's neglect of the need to change community ideologies has been reinforced by a great unwillingness to face up to the religious dimensions of the conflict. In the course of our interviews with Protestant religious leaders, we were struck by the reluctance of many members of the clergy to acknowledge that religious or church-propagated ideology plays a primary role in the hostility.[7] Of equal concern is the reluctance among many church leaders publicly to challenge the Rev. Ian Paisley's brand of Protestant leadership. As a consequence, there has been little support either in the churches or in government for efforts to undermine the destructive ideologies that have succeeded in preventing peace.

Yet an historically informed assessment of communal mythologies leaves little room to doubt the durability of conflicting values, attitudes and rationalisations. After almost 400 years of entrenchment, communal hatred has been supported by antagonistic belief systems and rationalisations of the violence. These self-destructive ideologies have remained an unshakable obstacle to the implementation of economic and political solutions. Irish Protestants and Catholics have, since the Reformation, developed this hatred as keystones of their religions.

If there is any hope for peace, that hope has its chance only in efforts by the government, the schools, and the churches to teach a different view of history, a different morality, and opposition to the continued use of violence as a means of conflict resolution. Protestant children must no longer be taught that Catholics are their political enemies; they must not be taught, as some are, that Catholics are also their religious enemies. When Protestant clergy teach that the pope conspires to wipe out Protestantism or that the Protestant way of life cannot survive if Catholics are given an equal chance, this gives genuine religious motivation for acts of violence. Members of both communities must come to see the folly in celebrating the vicious circles of sectarian victories and defeats that mar the pages of Irish history. Terrorists must not be made into heroes. Catholics and Catholic institutions must recognise that it is possible to have a moral order without legislating a Catholic morality. People in both communities must learn a new hierarchy of values, one that emphasises that it is much less important which side wins than that the solution improves the living conditions of the Irish people. Their sense of justice needs to be redirected, with less emphasis on redressing past wrongs and more emphasis upon a clear-headed assessment of what will minimise the social damage done to present and future generations.

Instead of hiding behind the view that religious leaders should not engage in politics, the churches and clergymen of all faiths should renounce the behaviour which is so obviously contrary to Christian morality. Unfortunately, those who have claimed the role of moral leaders are, at best, reluctant to challenge the advocates of violence. At worst, we find the most eloquent champions of violence among them. In the course of their research during the summer of 1980, the authors found among the Protestant leadership many good men in difficult circumstances. Most insisted that Paisley does not speak for them or for Protestants in general. Indeed they expressed many views which depart significantly from the extremist stereotype. But they also painted a picture of themselves as prisoners of their followers or as being somehow unfit to enter the political arena as men of God. This understanding of their role and responsibility is unfortunate. Those who profess to be moral leaders can have no meaningful effect on their followers' moral life if they do not also have an effect on their political activities.

This truth is self-evident. But its consequences are nowhere more obvious than in the case of the peace movement in Northern

Ireland. In 1980, the Peace People, as they are called, suffered great divisions in leadership and support because their leaders could not agree on whether to engage the political process more directly.[8] The Protestant churches are divided in this same fashion, the most impotent among them being those who refuse to confront the political process directly and recognise that the value of their teachings must be found in their effect on human relations. Moral leaders must 'get in the way' of destructive and immoral ideologies. Those who are unwilling to 'get in the way' will remain ineffective.

If the Protestants of Northern Ireland are as insecure and maligned as they have indicated to us, if indeed they are also correct in claiming that Paisley does not enjoy the support that it appears to outsiders he does, then the time is ripe for these leaders to challenge the stereotypes they loathe by decisive and courageous public action. Roman Catholics must condemn the IRA and renounce their church's control of the government of the Republic. The burden of hundreds of years of negativistic socialisation is too great to expect that changes in governmental structures will work by themselves. The dogs must be changed if their cages are ever going to be more than impediments to their freedom and prosperity.


## A MODEST PROPOSAL

The question is, how are these changes to be brought about? Perhaps the answer can be found in an analysis of the Irish problem by Michael Heactor.[9] Heactor argues that Ireland has historically been economically exploited by England and this has created an economic dependence in Ireland and 'economic dependence is reinforced through juridicial, political, and military measures'.[10] The difference in economic and social development in Ireland, Heactor notes, creates a tendency to de-emphasise class conflict and in its place status group solidarity (such as religious groupings) assume greater significance. Thus to shift Ireland away from endless sectarian conflicts it is critical that some means be found to advance the long-suffering economy of Ireland and Northern Ireland and fully to integrate this economy into the more advanced English economic system, where sectarian conflict ended centuries ago and is unthinkable in the United Kingdom, where few citizens ever attend church services. Only with a modern economy can class conflict replace sectarian disputes.

Such a proposal will require enormous effort from Westminster and this is not at all likely, for the British government has a continuing tendency to show no signs of emphasising the economy of Northern Ireland and even neglects economic growth in Scotland and the north of England as well. Yet Heactor's point persists, that only through radical change in the material conditions of Ireland and Northern Ireland can the present conflict be resolved. The sectarian violence in Ireland and Northern Ireland can be brought to a close only by bringing the economy of the island at long last into the twentieth century. Only something amounting to a secular revolution has a genuine promise of peace among peoples adhering to such thoroughly corrupted religious traditions. This reasoning applies just as surely in the Middle East as in Ireland. Sectarian conflict can be curbed only if some way is found to make the competing ideologies appear irrelevant.

## NOTES

1. Galliher, John F. and Jerry L. DeGregory, *Violence in Northern Ireland: Understanding Protestant Perspective* (Dublin: Gill & Macmillan, 1985).
2. See, for example, Smith, Scott S., 'Misconceptions of nationalism prevent peace', *Christian Science Monitor*, 2 Apr. 1987; and McNanus, Sean, 'No Peace in Ireland under the Union Jack', *USA Today*, 17 March 1987.
3. Institute for the Study of Conflict, 'Northern Ireland: Problems and Perspectives', *Conflict Studies*, no. 135 (1982).
4. Institute for the Study of Conflict. 'Northern Ireland: An Anglo-Irish Dilemma?', *Conflict Studies* no. 185 (A Report compiled for the Institute for the Study of Conflict, 1986).
5. *USA Today*, 17 March 1987.
6. *Conflict Studies*, no. 185 (1986), op. cit.
7. Galliher and DeGregory, op. cit.
8. 'Northern Ireland; War in Peace', *Economist*, 16 Feb. 1980.
9. Heactor, Michael, *Internal Colonialism: The Celtic Fringe in British National Development, 1536-1966* (Berkeley: University of California Press, 1975).
10. Heactor, op. cit., p. 33.

# 8 · NORTHERN IRELAND: INTERNAL-CONFLICT ANALYSES

In a Stewart Parker play, shown on television in May 1987, a Protestant girl meets a Catholic boy for the first time. She complains about the system that creates such segregation. What is the point of Catholics looking towards a Dublin they hardly know, and Protestants to a London they distrust? The point was not only that Northern Ireland's two groups had different aspirations; but that the objects of their desires – Dublin and London – regarded them with a mixture somewhere between loathing and fear. 'Sure who the hell would have us?', says the Protestant girl.

## DEFINITION

The episode above implies some level of commonality, however reluctant. It may spring from their common rejection by outsiders; or there may be more positive reasons. Either way, their position reflects a view that the conflict is rooted within Northern Ireland, and that any resolution or improvement of it depends in the end on Protestants and Catholics reaching some form of agreement.

Academics who adopt what might be described as an internal-conflict approach to the conflict start with the same premise. It is doubtful if any of them take the purist position that the conflict can be explained without reference to external factors. Northern Ireland does not exist in a vacuum. It would be nonsense to deny the influence of events and policies in Britain and the Irish Republic, for example, on developments there. So the difference between this and other standpoints is rather one of emphasis. In essence it may be defined by two central characteristics. Either explicitly or implicitly, it looks to features within Northern Ireland both for an explanation of the conflict and for the means of its resolution: for analysis and prescription.

The shared analysis has both an historical and a theoretical dimension. Historically many of its advocates look back to the pattern established by the Plantation of Ulster in the early seventeenth century, and modified since then – a pattern where two hostile groups lived cheek by jowl in what A. T. Q. Stewart later called the same 'narrow ground'. This pattern was distinctive to Ulster and did not apply in other parts of Ireland. It established, or rather reinforced, the distinctiveness of Ulster. In particular it came to reflect the reality that the kernel of the conflict was the northern part of the island. Constitutional changes such as partition or the European Economic Community left it remarkably unaffected, like the eye of a hurricane.

In theoretical terms this has important implications. Essentially it challenges the central importance of economic factors – whether a more prosperous Irish Republic would woo unionists towards unity, or whether nationalists would reject unity if it threatened welfare provision – in explaining the conflict. Instead it implies an ethnic analysis which points to a consciousness of collective identity as the prime moving force in Irish history. Ethnic conflicts are more intractable than class conflicts. They are about group membership and identity.

The internal-conflict view is not defined simply by a shared analysis. It also prescribes how the conflict might be contained or resolved. Economic policies are unlikely to affect matters radically, unless they are targeted towards specific aims, such as the removal of inequalities in employment. At its most extreme expression, the broader constitutional framework is also largely irrelevant. Whether they are within a United Kingdom, a united Ireland, an independent Ulster or the present proconsular set-up, Catholics and Protestants will still live in the same areas and their relationship with each other will ensure that the conflict continues. This argument would maintain that the Anglo-Irish Agreement, however useful in other respects, simply does not address the central issue. Instead it may be more important to encourage and support developments within Northern Ireland which have kept the violence within bounds.

## ACADEMIC APPROACHES

How does all this translate into practice? Six academic approaches to the Irish conflict, each of which adopted an internal-conflict analysis, were suggested by John Whyte in 1978. These were:

1. The 'no-nation' theory, which was essentially David Millar's explanation of unionist 'contractarianism' – the conditional loyalism to Britain which often confuses outsiders.
2. The investigation of historical precedents. The essence of this approach was that current behaviour by both Catholics and Protestants was determined by an 'inherited folk memory' (Stewart, 185) of grievance and mutual distrust.
3. The study of self-segregation – the view that the two communities lived, to a large extent, self-contained lives, and that the high level of segregation between Catholics and Protestants was at least partly voluntary. The writings of Rosemary Harris and Barritt and Carter were considered to belong to this category.
4. The social-psychological approach. Whyte considered that the psychological explanations of conflict, despite the work of Fraser and others, had been underrated. Issues such as prejudice, ethnic identity and attitudes and stereotyping remain unexplained.
5. The search for a model. Referring briefly to Lijphart's attempt to construct a model for describing the conflict in Northern Ireland, Whyte plumped for Jackson's 'double-minority' model as the most satisfactory.
6. The study of intra-ethnic tensions. Here Whyte drew attention to analysts who emphasised tensions within the Protestant and Catholic communities as well as those between them.

## A PRESCRIPTIVE FRAMEWORK

These six approaches fell short of a theory. As Whyte put it, 'each is a contribution to an explanation, rather than an attempt at a complete explanation'.

Today, more than ten years later, there is still no model within which we can locate research strengths and weaknesses. Indeed few would argue that internal analyses can provide a comprehensive explanation of the conflict. But a more modest framework may be constructed around the internal analysts' approach to the question of policy options. The question here is, what sort of approaches have been suggested by writers from the 'internal conflict' school to ameliorate the persistent violence in Northern Ireland, and how can their suggestions be classified?

Studies of the conflict have adopted four main approaches, sometimes overlapping:

1. Political or constitutional initiatives.
2. The operation of security strategies and the restraint of violence.
3. The implementation of internal reforms.
4. The encouragement of reconciliation.

Not all internal analyses give equal weight to all four approaches; indeed some of them, notably some of those which emphasise security, may have no sympathy for any of the others. It should also be noted that none of these approaches include such radical analyses as those of O'Dowd, Rolston and Tomlinson, who argue that Northern Ireland is irreformable; consequently attempts to improve human rights, however well intentioned, are doomed to failure.

If this framework is accepted, it has policy and strategic implications. It suggests the need for a much broader approach to policy options. Hence, when one avenue for improving affairs is blocked, emphasis should be shifted to another. Most obviously the current political stalemate, rather than being regarded negatively, should allow more attention to be paid to the removal of disparities in employment and other internal inequalities.

The framework also provides a basis for examining patterns in recent research and for identifying gaps. What is clear is that there has been a great variety in the level and pattern of research activity within the four categories.

## 1. Political or constitutional initiatives

Recent approaches to conflict research by political scientists have become more diffused, even disjointed. Padraig O'Malley's superb book, *The Uncivil Wars,* is a major contribution to the literature, and places the politics of the conflict in a broader context. This apart, it is hard to discern a strong pattern. Miller's concept of contractarianism, which so impressed John Whyte, has excited little subsequent interest.

Since Rose's depressing 1976 book there have been two main directions in political-constitutional writings. The first, which has been towards closer historical studies, is by Bew, Gibbon and Patterson; the other has been towards constitutional formulas, such as that suggested in 1986 by Boyle and Hadden – neither of them political scientists. Only the first of these has theoretical ambitions, that is, aims to develop a body of political theory upon which others can build.

## 2. The operation of security strategies and the restraint of violence

Recent years have seen a shift of interest from the causes of conflict to the operation of violence. This includes many works which are politically neutral. Demographers such as Michael Poole, F. W. Boal and Russell Murray have carried out important studies into current patterns of violence (see Boal and Douglas 1982 for a useful collection of these views), and Townshend's fascinating examination of the tradition of violence in Ireland adds an historical dimension to this. The first important book specifically dealing with the Provisional IRA may lead to further analyses of paramilitary activities (Bishop and Maillie, 1987).

Most of these works are relatively non-ideological. On the more contentious question of security, two schools, often diametrically opposed, dominate. One, the counter-insurgency approach used by Kitson, Clutterbuck and others, is concerned primarily with the military conduct of the anti-terrorism campaign; this often advocates a more rigorous and efficient application of 'law-and-order' policies. The other school, notably Boyle, Hadden and Hillyard, is concerned with the threat to democracy and human rights posed by military operations. In the main, however, academics have shied away from examining the difficult and dangerous issues involved in the balance between the demands of human rights and personal security.

## 3. The implementation of internal reforms

There has also been a significant growth of research into inequalities of opportunity, especially since the early 1980s. The research sponsored by the Fair Employment Agency, an official watchdog organisation in Northern Ireland, and work by Cormack, Osborne and others, have added a level of objectivity to an area remarkable for its polemics. A major investigation by the London Policy Studies Institute (PSI), sponsored by the Standing Advisory Commission on Human Rights, further enables some assessment of the progress of reform (PSI, 1987).

One major gap in this research landscape is the failure of economists to make their necessary contribution to our understanding of the conflict. There is no shortage of economic analyses by sociologists, including a number of important contributions by Marxists. But most professional economists have carefully avoided issues relating to the conflict in the community. As a result it is still difficult to estimate the mutual relationship between conflict and the economy, the economic cost of violence and the economic implications of constitutional change.

Perhaps the most urgent need, however, is the creation of an objective basis for measuring majority-minority conditions, operating across a broad front. The continuing imbalance in employment against Catholics is the major cause for concern. There is evidence, however, that improvements in housing have effectively removed one of the major grievances of Catholics in the civil rights years. Indeed the PSI survey indicates that Protestants now feel that they are discriminated against in the allocation of public housing. This may be the consequence of the levelling out of disadvantage, but it must be examined seriously. It is inconsistent to feel concern about Catholic grievances in 1969 and ignore Protestant grievances some twenty years later. At present it is difficult to examine this issue objectively, and this will continue until a regularly monitored data base is established.

## 4. The encouragement of reconciliation

In quantitative terms the greatest current increase in research activity is into relationships between Catholics and Protestants. Research into institutions and conflict has flourished across a broad field – schools (Murray, Dunn, Darby); housing (Brett); the churches and religion (Gallagher and Worrall, Hickey, and two books on Paisley). The activity of social psychologists in the conflict has also increased, with important books by Heskin and the Harbisons and recent questioning of the contact hypothesis – the theory that greater contact between the protagonists tends to reduce hostility and prejudice – by Trew and others; it is clear, however, that they have not taken up the central research role that Whyte hoped for.

In local studies the earlier imbalance against Protestant communities has been reduced by Nelson and a number of current research projects. There has been more systematic examination of violence at local level, suggesting that local relationships may control violence as well as perpetuate conflict. A number of these studies have also examined intra-ethnic tensions, and in particular the importance of divisions between different Protestant denominations.

The importance of local studies is not simply academic. They hold the key to one of the most difficult and unexplored paradoxes in the Northern Irish conflict. This paradox concerns the strong tendency throughout the world for community conflicts to expand towards unqualified violence between the participants. In such conflicts, in Coleman's term, a 'Gresham's law of conflict' often takes over, by which 'the harmful and dangerous elements drive out those which keep the conflict within bounds' (Coleman, 1957). In Northern Ireland, however, there is strong evidence that community violence has diminished rather than risen in intensity at both provincial and local levels since 1969. To take the most obvious example, the annual casualty figures, having reached a peak of 468 deaths in 1972, declined steadily between then and 1987; higher levels during the hunger strikes and following the Anglo-Irish Agreement are still subsidiary to this underlying decline. The question is: why has it developed in this way rather than drawn the two communities into more violent confrontation?

Shibutani and Kwan believed that the most important factors in determining the course of each conflict were the peculiar interrelations between the combatants: 'What each side does is a response to the actual or anticipated moves of its opponents; thus the course of events is built up by social interaction' (Shibutani and Kwan, 1965, 135). This process often intensifies the conflict by creating a spiral towards unrestrained violence. In Northern

Ireland, however, the same reciprocal process has controlled rather than stimulated the spread of violence.

The long duration of the conflict between Catholics and Protestants over three centuries has led to the evolution of social mechanisms which regulate and control their relationships. These were the consequence of two hostile groups inhabiting what Stewart calls the same 'narrow ground'; unable to remove each other and unwilling to assimilate, they gradually evolved forms of relationships which regulated rather than resolved their antagonisms. The mechanisms were each appropriate to particular settings, varying between urban and rural conditions, and in accordance with the religious ratio peculiar to each locality. In a relatively small number of areas Catholics and Protestants have effectively avoided conflict by avoiding each other. In most places it is possible for members of the two groups to develop relationships without abandoning their separate basic allegiances – drinking in the same pubs, using the same shops, working together, belonging to the same clubs. There is also plenty of evidence that common economic or social interests shared by Protestants and Catholics can overcome sectarian suspicion.

All these mechanisms, which operate to a greater or lesser degree in all localities in Northern Ireland, act as restraints on the conduct of the two conflicting communities. Rather than presenting a single model which applies to Northern Ireland as a unit, they demonstrate that intergroup relationships should be regarded as a spectrum. At one end is a highly polarised, potentially violent relationship; at the other a high level of co-operation and interaction. Different communities throughout Northern Ireland can be found at every point. Individuals too do not take a consistent position within the spectrum; rather their position may vary with the setting or situation in which the cross-group contact takes place. Nor is the spectrum itself static; it has altered through time, and the alterations have accelerated most dramatically in times of community violence.

The main function of the mechanisms is to reduce and manage community violence at local levels. Obviously they are more successful in some areas than in others. But the cumulative effect of so great a variety of micro-controls also constitutes a macro-control. In effect they are obstacles to absolute group cohesion for both communities, and therefore to a more extreme and genocidal form of conflict.

Local research holds the key to identifying and understanding the operation of these controls. Their identification raises another dilemma. If the local controls are effective in controlling the effects of violence, it seems sensible to encourage them as a matter of policy. On the other hand the more efficient the controls, the less the incentive to confront the problem and seek a 'solution', however that is defined. Some republicans may argue that the problem will not be resolved until the British leave, and some loyalists that it will continue until the paramilitaries have been eliminated by military action. If people become accustomed to 'an acceptable level of violence' they will become increasingly willing to settle for such a limited objective.

This implies that a more complete solution is attainable. Richard Rose suggested that it is not: 'Many talk about a solution to Ulster's political problem but few are prepared to say what the problem is. The reason is simple. The problem is that there is no solution' (Rose 1976, 139). This gloomy analysis has a positive as well as a negative side. If it is accepted, the consequence is that it may be more sensible to seek to improve, rather than to 'solve', the problem. The emphasis should be shifted, at least in the short term, away from a vain search for a political solution towards more concrete, and perhaps more realisable objectives. How might those mechanisms be supported which have preserved for most people a relatively normal life despite the persistence of violence? How can the economic and social inequalities which led to the outbreak of violence in the 1960s be removed? Is it important to support the new integrated schools which have developed so rapidly since 1980? In other words, given apparent political stalemate, is there not a strong case for introducing internal reforms which will remove minority – and majority – grievances?

The researcher may not be able to resolve these questions. But they will not be resolved unless they are first identified and explored through research.

## ACADEMICS AND CONFLICT RESEARCH

This process is obstructed by some current aspects of conflict research. A major obstacle is the tendency for conflict researchers – never naturally co-operative – to remain within separate disciplinary islands. Does the problem even go beyond this? There is evidence that different disciplines are attracted to different elements in the conflict, and under-estimate others. Consequently they produce significantly different views.

Imagine a stranger wandering into the internal-conflict literature on the Northern Ireland conflict, innocent and without a guide. His view of what is going on will depend predominantly on which disciplinary tradition he happens to stumble on first. In general the predominant themes emphasised by historians and political scientists are division, violence and dysfunction. The sociologists, anthropologists and psychologists whose work is based on community studies often present a distinctly different theme. Here the emphasis is on the relatively low influence of the conflict on day-to-day living; it is generally more optimistic. Harris, Leyton, Heskin, Donnan and McFarlane, for example, while acknowledging the centrality of the conflict, emphasise the ability of people to construct relatively normal lives despite it.

Two major characteristics mark out the conflict in Northern Ireland from other violent ethnic conflicts. They are its persistence and its relatively low level of violence. These two phenomena help to define that it is essentially a limited and controlled conflict, one which is unlikely to be eliminated and unlikely to become significantly worse. The reason why the two sets of disciplinary groups – the political scientists and historians who work mainly on a province-wide or broader stage, on the one hand; the sociologists and anthropologists who work more often in local communities, on the other – produce different pictures is that they do not describe the same image. The former set is more interested in the persistence of violence; the latter in the control of violence. The scenes they describe are fashioned by the interests of the observer and by the academic prism through which it is viewed. They are both distorted images.

The only way to integrate and broaden the two images is for conflict research to become more interdisciplinary. If research is problem-led, as conflict research often is, researchers soon find themselves straining against the borders of their disciplines. Social historians, psychologists, sociologists, demographers, anthropologists, without abandoning their original training, need each other more and more.

# REFERENCES

Barritt, D. and C. Carter, *The Northern Ireland Problem* (OUP, 1962).

Bew, P., P. Gibbon and H. Patterson, *The State in Northern Ireland* (Manchester University Press, 1979).

Bishop, P. and E. Mallie, *The Provisional IRA* (Heinemann, 1987).

Boal, F. W. and J. Douglas (eds.), *Integration and Division* (Academic Press, 1982).

Boyle, K. and T. Hadden, *Ireland: A Positive Proposal* (Penguin, 1986).

Boyle, K., T. Hadden and P. Hillyard, *Law and state* (Martin Robertson, 1975).

Brett, C. *Housing a Divided Society* (IPI, 1986).

Clutterbuck, R., *Protest and the Urban Guerrilla* (Cassells, 1974).

Coleman, J., 'The dynamics of conflict' (1957), in Marx, G. (ed.) *Racial Conflict* (Little, Brown, 1971).

Cormack R. and R. Osborne, *Employment in Northern Ireland* (Appletree, 1982).

Darby, J., *Conflict in Northern Ireland* (Gill and Macmillan, 1976).

Darby, J. (ed.), *Northern Ireland: the Background to the Conflict* (Appletree, 1983).

Darby, J., *Violence and the Control of Conflict in Northern Ireland* (Gill and Macmillan, 1986).

Darby, J. and S. Dunn, 'Segregated Schools: the research evidence', in Osborne, R., R. Cormack and R. Miller (eds.), *Education & Policy in Northern Ireland* (PRI, 1987).

Darby, J., D. Murray, D. Batts, S. Dunn, S. Farren and J. Harris, *Schools Apart?* (NUU, 1977).

Donnan, H. and G. McFarlane, 'Informal social organisation', in Darby, J. (ed.), *Northern Ireland: the Background to the Conflict* (Appletree, 1983).

Dunn, S., J. Darby and K. Mullan, *Schools Together?* (Coleraine: University of Ulster, Centre for the Study of Conflict, 1985).

Fraser, M., *Children in Conflict* (Secker and Warburg, 1973).

Gallagher, E. and F. Worrell, *Christians in Ulster* (Oxford University Press, 1982).

Harbison, J. and J., *A Society under Stress* (Open Books, 1980).

Harbison, J., *Children of the Troubles* (Stranmillis College, 1983).

Harris, R., *Prejudice and Tolerance in Ulster* (Manchester University Press, 1972).

Heskin, K., *Northern Ireland: A Psychological Analysis* (Gill and Macmillan, 1980).

Hickey, J., *Religion and the Northern Ireland Problem* (Gill and Macmillan, 1984).

Jackson, H., *The Two Irelands: A Dual Study of Intergroup Tension* (Minority Rights Group, 1971).

Kitson, F., *Low Intensity Operations* (Faber and Faber, 1971).

Leyton, E., *The One Blood: Kinship and Class in an Irish Village* (Memorial University, Social & Economic Studies, 1975).

Lijphart, A., 'The Northern Ireland problem, theories and solutions', *British Journal of Political Science,* vol. 5 (1975).

Miller, D., *Queen's Rebels* (Gill and Macmillan, 1978).

Murray, D., *Worlds Apart: Segregated Schools in Northern Ireland* (Appletree Press).

Murray, R. 'Political violence in Northern Ireland', in Boal, F. W. and J. Douglas (eds.), *Integration and Division* (Academic Press, 1982).

Nelson, S., *Ulster's Uncertain Defenders* (Appletree, 1984).

O'Dowd, L., B. Rolston and M. Tomlinson, *Between Civil Rights and Civil War* (CSE Books, 1980).

O'Malley, P., *The Uncivil Wars: Ireland Today* (Blackstaff, 1983).

Policy Studies Institute, *Equality and Inequality in Northern Ireland* (three volumes) (PSI, 1987).

Poole, M., 'The demography of violence', in Darby, J. (ed.), *Northern Ireland: the Background to the Conflict* (Appletree, 1983).

Poole, M. and F. W. Boal, 'Religious residential segregation in Belfast in mid-1969', in Clark, B. D. and M. B. Gleave, *Social Patterns in Cities* (1973).

Rose, R., *Governing without Consensus* (Faber, 1971)

Rose, R., *Northern Ireland, a Time for Choice* (Macmillan, 1976).

Shibutani, T. and K. Kwan, 'Changes in life conditions conducive to interracial conflict', in Marx, G. (ed.), *Racial Conflict* (Little, Brown, 1971).

Stewart, A. T. Q., *The Narrow Ground: Aspects of Ulster* (Faber and Faber, 1977).

Townshend, P., *Political Violence in Ireland* (Oxford University Press, 1983).

Trew, K., 'Contact between Protestants and Catholics in Northern Ireland', in N. Hewstone and R. Brown (eds.), *Contact and Conflict in Intergroup Encounters* (Blackwell, 1986).

Whyte, J., 'Interpretations of the Northern Ireland problem: an appraisal', *Economic & Social Review,* 9, 4 (1978).

# 9 · TERRORISED INTO TERRORIST: 'PETE THE PARA' STRIKES AGAIN

Peter Gabriel John McMullen, also known as 'Pete the Para', served in the British army, and, in 1972, defected to the Provisional IRA (PIRA). Today he is an inmate of Otisville Federal Prison, New York State, awaiting extradition hearings. He is a fugitive both from British law and from a PIRA Army Council execution order. As a man who has been terrorised and describes himself as a 'terrorist', he straddles the issues of several definitions. In a parallel fashion, his birthplace, Magherafelt in Northern Ireland, straddles the fence of national definition. These six northeastern counties of Ireland are actually a province in the United Kingdom. His split national identity, together with his having come of age in a time of terror, typifies the psychodynamics of millions of children who are growing up in intercommunal violence today. Many of them, like McMullen's own four, are children of other children who grew up in violence. They are the second generation of terrorised children who become terrorists. Peter is the son of a former NCO in the British army and grew up on military bases in England and on the Continent. His personal experience of violence and prejudice are integral to his present circumstances.

Peter McMullen is both the archetype and the focus of this psychological study. His motivation and perspective illuminate the phenomenon of the victim of violence and prejudice who expiates his victimisation through the victimisation of others.

We shall consider some theories articulated by psychologists and psychiatrists who have attempted to analyse and explain the psychology of terrorism by considering the microcosm – the

individuals who commit these acts. Finally, we shall consider
McMullen and his contemporaries, who are members of paramilitary organisations in Ireland, the Middle East and southern
Africa, through the findings of twenty years of psychological
testing of more than a thousand individuals growing up under
conditions of violence and prejudice. We shall consider the
relationship between the data on the cognitive and affective
development of these children aged from six to fifteen as it relates
to psychological evaluations of adult members in the paramilitary
organisations identified with their respective 'community'. But the
microcosmic view is, by its very nature, incomplete. The social and
political milieu catalyses and directs the behaviours that bring the
individual into a like-minded group and determine the objectives
and behaviour of the group in the larger arena.


## A MATTER OF DEFINITIONS

Terrorism is as subjectively defined as the experience of terrorisation is subjectively experienced. Terrorists and terrorised are
inextricably bound with each other and neither can be defined
apart from the experience of the other.

Terrorisation of large groups of people can and has been
effected by governments; by guerrilla organisations; by lone,
deranged individuals; by military forces; by paramilitary organisations and even by entertainers (for instance, the famous Martian
landing broadcast by Orson Welles on 30th October 1938).

The process of terrorisation is the exertion of irresistible
strength threatening annihilation. It is accompanied by unpre-
dictability and received with the physical and psychological shock
of any severe trauma. Terrorisation is the application of force such
as to overwhelm the victims' capacity for choosing their behaviour.

There are four basic threats that induce traumatic stress
response, and these are all present in the situation of terrorisation.
They are: threat to life; threat to bodily integrity; threat to
security; and threat to self-image. There seems to be a consensus
among laboratory and field researchers that when a stimulus is
appraised by an individual as one of these kinds of threats, there
is a stress reaction that is measurable both physically and
psychologically.

Response to the threat and its series of emotional consequences (sequelae) comprise the coping mechanisms, and are a product of ameliorating and exacerbating factors in the individual's social environment. This includes their bio-psychological and social past, present and anticipations of future being. Coping styles include physiological responses such as psychosomatic disorders; immobility; channelled activity; stereotyping or scapegoating; capacity for and orientation towards intimate relationships.

It is hard to determine, in some cases, from what direction terrorism is initiated. A British White Paper of May 1948 referred to an 'irresistible wave of terrorism' sweeping the then Palestine mandate and 'defying the force of 80,000 troops'. There is documented evidence that the civilian population of that country had been terrorised by the sudden and unprovoked attacks of military forces ostensibly searching for 'illegals' in their midst throughout the previous eight years and more. Two years earlier, in an incident similar to and parallel with their action in Derry, Northern Ireland, in 1972, the British Parachute Regiment fired at random in the main thoroughfare of Tel Aviv, wounding and killing passers-by and shopkeepers. In Palestine and Northern Ireland (and perhaps other places as well) terrorisation of the civilian population by military and other organs of government predated the organisation of guerrilla groups and also antedated their utilisation of terror tactics against the civilian population even after the groups were formed.

Given this history, it is not surprising that the several individuals in the compendium of psychological studies of members of paramilitary organisations who identified themselves as 'terrorists' were former members of the British army!

Common sense and experience tell us that people who are badly treated and/or unjustly punished will seek revenge. It should not be surprising then that young adolescents who have themselves been terrorised become terrorists, and that in a situation in which they are afforded a kind of sanction by their compatriots, because of the actions of an unjust government, their resort to terror tactics becomes a way of life.

One of the main differences between a military or guerrilla operation and the actions of relatively isolated and fringe type 'terror squads' or criminal groups like bank robbers who take hostages or kidnappers derives from the idiosyncratic targetting characteristic of the latter kind of group. The military or guerrilla terrorist attacks an unsuspecting civilian population in order to exert maximal force immediately and takes prisoners or hostages secondarily (bombing or shooting immediately). Also, the military or guerrilla group takes prisoners or hostages for purposes other than bargaining, although bargaining or negotiating may ensue. These 'wear' tactics are undertaken for the purpose of demoralising the larger target population. The criminal or deviant kind of small group has as its objective taking a particular kind of prisoner for purposes of vengeance on a specific part of the larger society or polity. These gradations and subtleties sometimes make a difference in the kind of threat posed to the terrorised and consequently the sequelae may also differ. One significant aspect of these differences in definition has to do with the obliteration of the distinction between 'political' and 'criminal' offences in Northern Ireland and, consequently, in the 1986 extradition treaty between the United States and the United Kingdom. If, in fact, the offences of which McMullen is accused were criminal offences, there would not have been so much 'bang' without human casualties or some kind of material benefit sought or effected.

On the other hand, if terrorism is to be ascribed to the enforcement agencies of the state (army and police), then the data on violence and threat presented in Tables 9.1 to 9.29, is a quantified compendium of the level of threat imposed on the civilian population and the ascribed retaliation by the para-militaries, which of course, exacerbates the terrorisation of the civilian population.

The psychosomatic consequences of their terrorisation are evidenced in the statistics on birth defects (see Table 9.30), alcoholism and suicide for this population during the years of escalating violence. Some of the birth defects may be attributable to the consequences of CS-gas residue, which may well have been ingested by pregnant Catholic women in the areas of greatest contamination – the urban ghettos.


# WHO CALLS HIMSELF A TERRORIST

If we look at the Provisional IRA, the Ulster Defence Association (UDA), the Irish National Liberation Army (INLA), the Official IRA, the Ulster Freedom Fighters (UFF) and groups in other parts of the world, who have been psychologically evaluated

**Table 9.1** Shooting incidents in Northern Ireland, July 1972–December 1976

|      | Jan. | Feb. | Mar. | Apr. | May | June | July | Aug. | Sept. | Oct. | Nov. | Dec. |
|------|------|------|------|------|-----|------|------|------|-------|------|------|------|
| 1972 |      |      |      |      |     |      | 2778 | 640  | 747   | 812  | 634  | 729  |
| 1973 | 678  | 695  | 799  | 477  | 369 | 303  | 283  | 239  | 266   | 298  | 312  | 299  |
| 1974 | 297  | 229  | 292  | 329  | 353 | 227  | 240  | 317  | 222   | 266  | 280  | 154  |
| 1975 | 110  | 112  | 141  | 199  | 121 | 139  | 126  | 244  | 175   | 183  | 180  | 73   |
| 1976 | 124  | 208  | 110  | 154  | 157 | 137  | 171  | 266  | 138   | 167  | 149  | 127  |

**Table 9.2** Number of explosions in Northern Ireland, July 1972–December 1976

|      | Jan. | Feb. | Mar. | Apr. | May | June | July | Aug. | Sept. | Oct. | Nov. | Dec. |
|------|------|------|------|------|-----|------|------|------|-------|------|------|------|
| 1972 |      |      |      |      |     |      | 184  | 126  | 87    | 98   | 82   | 57   |
| 1973 | 57   | 73   | 104  | 65   | 104 | 110  | 67   | 79   | 64    | 79   | 118  | 58   |
| 1974 | 63   | 90   | 111  | 44   | 64  | 69   | 55   | 42   | 28    | 32   | 49   | 38   |
| 1975 | 24   | 46   | 19   | 26   | 17  | 25   | 26   | 25   | 47    | 72   | 37   | 35   |
| 1976 | 47   | 82   | 78   | 83   | 50  | 48   | 83   | 79   | 56    | 82   | 33   | 45   |

**Table 9.3** Assassinations of Protestants in Northern Ireland, July 1972–December 1976

|      | Jan. | Feb. | Mar. | Apr. | May | June | July | Aug. | Sept. | Oct. | Nov. | Dec. |
|------|------|------|------|------|-----|------|------|------|-------|------|------|------|
| 1972 |      |      |      |      |     |      | 18   | 5    | 4     | 2    | 0    | 6    |
| 1973 | 2    | 5    | 2    | 3    | 1   | 8    | 2    | 4    | 2     | 1    | 0    | 2    |
| 1974 | 4    | 0    | 3    | 3    | 1   | 2    | 3    | 1    | 3     | 3    | 13   | 1    |
| 1975 | 0    | 3    | 5    | 6    | 2   | 9    | 3    | 6    | 8     | 3    | 2    | 2    |
| 1976 | 12   | 2    | 3    | 1    | 4   | 5    | 0    | 1    | 0     | 1    | 2    | 0    |

**Table 9.4** Assassinations of Catholics in Northern Ireland, July 1972–December 1976

| | Jan. | Feb. | Mar. | Apr. | May | June | July | Aug. | Sept. | Oct. | Nov. | Dec. |
|---|---|---|---|---|---|---|---|---|---|---|---|---|
| 1972 | | | | | | | 18 | 9 | 6 | 10 | 8 | 12 |
| 1973 | 6 | 7 | 7 | 0 | 7 | 6 | 3 | 9 | 3 | 1 | 3 | 1 |
| 1974 | 5 | 7 | 4 | 2 | 9 | 2 | 2 | 1 | 4 | 7 | 13 | 2 |
| 1975 | 1 | 12 | 3 | 12 | 4 | 7 | 3 | 3 | 3 | 10 | 6 | 0 |
| 1976 | 10 | 4 | 2 | 0 | 0 | 2 | 0 | 0 | 0 | 5 | 5 | 0 |

**Table 9.5** Terrorists killed in Northern Ireland, July 1972–December 1976

| | Jan. | Feb. | Mar. | Apr. | May | June | July | Aug. | Sept. | Oct. | Nov. | Dec. |
|---|---|---|---|---|---|---|---|---|---|---|---|---|
| 1972 | | | | | | | 6 | 9 | 10 | 7 | 3 | 3 |
| 1973 | 1 | 11 | 3 | 4 | 5 | 4 | 2 | 6 | 2 | 0 | 4 | 4 |
| 1974 | | 2 | 2 | 2 | 4 | 2 | 0 | 3 | 1 | 3 | 2 | 2 |
| 1975 | 3 | 0 | 1 | 2 | 0 | 3 | 3 | 0 | 1 | 4 | 0 | 4 |
| 1976 | 2 | 5 | 0 | 2 | 0 | 1 | 2 | 1 | 0 | 3 | 0 | 0 |

**Table 9.6** Civilians killed in Northern Ireland, June 1970–December 1974

| | Jan. | Feb. | Mar. | Apr. | May | June | July | Aug. | Sept. | Oct. | Nov. | Dec. |
|---|---|---|---|---|---|---|---|---|---|---|---|---|
| 1970 | | | | | | 11 | 6 | 0 | 2 | 0 | 3 | 1 |
| 1971 | 1 | 8 | 2 | 0 | 2 | 0 | 2 | 28 | 11 | 17 | 10 | 33 |
| 1972 | 18 | 15 | 27 | 14 | 31 | 16 | 75 | 35 | 27 | 30 | 11 | 25 |
| 1973 | 12 | 27 | 14 | 9 | 17 | 26 | 11 | 18 | 8 | 4 | 16 | 9 |
| 1974 | 13 | 14 | 17 | 10 | 22 | 10 | 8 | 10 | 11 | 15 | 28 | 8 |

**Table 9.7** Army personnel wounded in Northern Ireland, July 1972–December 1976

|  | Jan. | Feb. | Mar. | Apr. | May | June | July | Aug. | Sept. | Oct. | Nov. | Dec. |
|---|---|---|---|---|---|---|---|---|---|---|---|---|
| 1972 |  |  |  |  |  |  | 77 | 66 | 45 | 35 | 31 | 34 |
| 1973 | 13 | 32 | 34 | 50 | 25 | 19 | 21 | 24 | 9 | 15 | 16 | 22 |
| 1974 | 21 | 27 | 19 | 17 | 14 | 9 | 5 | 18 | 7 | 52 | 13 | 3 |
| 1975 | 2 | 0 | 0 | 2 | 2 | 0 | 3 | 1 | 6 | 13 | 6 | 11 |
| 1976 | 3 | 12 | 17 | 7 | 7 | 13 | 9 | 26 | 1 | 34 | 1 | 6 |

**Table 9.8** Weapons recovered from Protestants in Northern Ireland, July 1972–December 1976

|  | Jan. | Feb. | Mar. | Apr. | May | June | July | Aug. | Sept. | Oct. | Nov. | Dec. |
|---|---|---|---|---|---|---|---|---|---|---|---|---|
| 1972 |  |  |  |  |  |  | 12 | 32 | 18 | 63 | 20 | 50 |
| 1973 | 26 | 53 | 87 | 75 | 32 | 44 | 40 | 50 | 265 | 67 | 65 | 34 |
| 1974 | 41 | 93 | 52 | 90 | 27 | 97 | 48 | 37 | 29 | 33 | 23 | 21 |
| 1975 | 5 | 36 | 46 | 49 | 35 | 53 | 20 | 30 | 35 | 41 | 41 | 21 |
| 1976 | 18 | 16 | 23 | 26 | 28 | 25 | 11 | 11 | 26 | 15 | 17 | 16 |

**Table 9.9** Weapons recovered from Catholics in Northern Ireland, July 1972–December 1976

|  | Jan. | Feb. | Mar. | Apr. | May | June | July | Aug. | Sept. | Oct. | Nov. | Dec. |
|---|---|---|---|---|---|---|---|---|---|---|---|---|
| 1972 |  |  |  |  |  |  | 89 | 221 | 98 | 62 | 73 | 45 |
| 1973 | 51 | 66 | 97 | 84 | 67 | 56 | 57 | 73 | 49 | 55 | 60 | 42 |
| 1974 | 75 | 42 | 62 | 84 | 79 | 63 | 47 | 45 | 43 | 50 | 38 | 41 |
| 1975 | 18 | 24 | 34 | 42 | 36 | 31 | 22 | 25 | 31 | 45 | 72 | 33 |
| 1976 | 27 | 45 | 58 | 80 | 60 | 36 | 36 | 43 | 62 | 58 | 39 | 55 |

**Table 9.10** Total number of kneecappings in Northern Ireland, January 1973–December 1976

|      | Jan. | Feb. | Mar. | Apr. | May | June | July | Aug. | Sept. | Oct. | Nov. | Dec. |
|------|------|------|------|------|-----|------|------|------|-------|------|------|------|
| 1973 | 8    | 10   | 10   | 6    | 5   | 0    | 3    | 10   | 6     | 5    | 7    | 4    |
| 1974 | 8    | 19   | 7    | 16   | 8   | 10   | 16   | 13   | 11    | 6    | 8    | 6    |
| 1975 | 11   | 18   | 12   | 19   | 13  | 10   | 10   | 25   | 12    | 43   | 12   | 3    |
| 1976 | 10   | 3    | 2    | 6    | 6   | 7    | 15   | 19   | 8     | 6    | 7    | 9    |

**Table 9.11** Ammunition recovered from Protestants in Northern Ireland, July 1972–December 1976

|      | Jan. | Feb.  | Mar. | Apr.  | May   | June  | July | Aug.  | Sept. | Oct.  | Nov. | Dec.  |
|------|------|-------|------|-------|-------|-------|------|-------|-------|-------|------|-------|
| 1972 |      |       |      |       |       |       | 1101 | 3298  | 5984  | 5256  | 899  | 7805  |
| 1973 | 3231 | 4257  | 9362 | 7803  | 16910 | 5936  | 4330 | 34286 | 2903  | 11139 | 8205 | 10990 |
| 1974 | 2950 | 18987 | 6444 | 18036 | 3826  | 11444 | 8314 | 8595  | 1708  | 2065  | 1160 | 1404  |
| 1975 | 98   | 3181  | 5472 | 3068  | 9758  | 1496  | 2228 | 2350  | 6271  | 4121  | 2526 | 2167  |
| 1976 | 1260 | 1632  | 3074 | 2236  | 2943  | 1186  | 450  | 6300  | 2905  | 652   | 714  | 3892  |

**Table 9.12** Ammunition recovered from Catholics in Northern Ireland, July 1972–December 1976

|      | Jan. | Feb. | Mar. | Apr. | May  | June | July  | Aug.  | Sept. | Oct. | Nov.  | Dec.  |
|------|------|------|------|------|------|------|-------|-------|-------|------|-------|-------|
| 1972 |      |      |      |      |      |      | 12811 | 30966 | 11317 | 7786 | 11270 | 12016 |
| 1973 | 3236 | 3661 | 9904 | 7209 | 3930 | 6448 | 3147  | 7361  | 9015  | 6831 | 3508  | 3817  |
| 1974 | 5686 | 6961 | 3625 | 5511 | 7540 | 6936 | 4707  | 3491  | 2463  | 5874 | 6350  | 3118  |
| 1975 | 1178 | 1546 | 1487 | 1795 | 1522 | 1082 | 524   | 7565  | 4189  | 2387 | 4427  | 3166  |
| 1976 | 2442 | 4624 | 5830 | 4792 | 6305 | 3419 | 2742  | 1254  | 3096  | 5436 | 1942  | 1180  |

**Table 9.13** Protestant terrorists out of action

| | Jan. | Feb. | Mar. | Apr. | May | June | July | Aug. | Sept. | Oct. | Nov. | Dec. |
|---|---|---|---|---|---|---|---|---|---|---|---|---|
| 1973 | 257 | 97 | 116 | 116 | 151 | 174 | 185 | 195 | 195 | 215 | 238 | 249 |
| 1974 | 447 | 277 | 308 | 334 | 370 | 354 | 346 | 342 | 352 | 388 | 393 | 420 |
| 1975 | | 461 | 479 | 481 | 491 | 530 | 512 | 517 | 527 | 583 | 586 | 593 |

Catholic terrorists out of action

| | Jan. | Feb. | Mar. | Apr. | May | June | July | Aug. | Sept. | Oct. | Nov. | Dec. |
|---|---|---|---|---|---|---|---|---|---|---|---|---|
| 1973 | 1082 | 687 | 752 | 818 | 884 | 981 | 1035 | 1070 | 1095 | 1123 | 1148 | 1094 |
| 1974 | | 1112 | 1079 | 1111 | 1131 | 1120 | 1279 | 1255 | 1275 | 1278 | 1343 | 1347 |

**Table 9.14** Internment figures for Republicans in Northern Ireland, August 1971–December 1975

| | Jan. | Feb. | Mar. | Apr. | May | June | July | Aug. | Sept. | Oct. | Nov. | Dec. |
|---|---|---|---|---|---|---|---|---|---|---|---|---|
| 1971 | | | | | | | | 240 | 290 | 372 | 503 | 651 |
| 1972 | 758 | 809 | 913 | 760 | 553 | 372 | 346 | 239 | 248 | 273 | 293 | 294 |
| 1973 | 303 | 338 | 372 | 409 | 459 | 508 | 557 | 576 | 600 | 619 | 620 | 547 |
| 1974 | 536 | 534 | 531 | 581 | 577 | 573 | 540 | 529 | 502 | 504 | 516 | 517 |
| 1975 | 488 | 472 | 571 | 319 | 304 | 270 | 241 | 216 | 191 | 172 | 93 | 0 |

**Table 9.15** Internment figures for Loyalists in Northern Ireland, February 1973–February 1975

| | Jan. | Feb. | Mar. | Apr. | May | June | July | Aug. | Sept. | Oct. | Nov. | Dec. |
|---|---|---|---|---|---|---|---|---|---|---|---|---|
| 1973 | | 9 | 22 | 23 | 21 | 27 | 33 | 33 | 38 | 39 | 49 | 47 |
| 1974 | 47 | 49 | 51 | 48 | 70 | 59 | 49 | 44 | 37 | 31 | 24 | 25 |
| 1975 | 15 | 4 | | | | | | | | | | |

**Table 9.16** Rubber bullets fired in Northern Ireland, August 1970–December 1975

| | Jan. | Feb. | Mar. | Apr. | May | June | July | Aug. | Sept. | Oct. | Nov. | Dec. |
|---|---|---|---|---|---|---|---|---|---|---|---|---|
| 1970 | | | | | | | | 12 | 27 | 199 | 0 | 0 |
| 1971 | 259 | 1033 | 255 | 243 | 50 | 27 | 1718 | 2975 | 3292 | 3419 | 1554 | 1927 |
| 1972 | 1563 | 3813 | 1588 | 2170 | 2588 | 1560 | 3480 | 2545 | 1429 | 1649 | 573 | 405 |
| 1973 | 1416 | 2248 | 1032 | 2013 | 1151 | 1507 | 1843 | 847 | 314 | 219 | 75 | 58 |
| 1974 | 92 | 210 | 170 | 457 | 265 | 105 | 32 | 152 | 20 | 1054 | 95 | 0 |
| 1975 | 0 | 17 | 0 | 0 | 0 | 1 | 9 | 70 | 12 | 10 | 3 | 0 |

**Table 9.17** Plastic bullets fired in Northern Ireland, October 1975–December 1976

| | Jan. | Feb. | Mar. | Apr. | May | June | July | Aug. | Sept. | Oct. | Nov. | Dec. |
|---|---|---|---|---|---|---|---|---|---|---|---|---|
| 1974 | | | | | | | | | | 175 | 39 | 2 |
| 1975 | 0 | 0 | 4 | 303 | 97 | 144 | 41 | 2313 | 561 | 16 | 38 | 39 |
| 1976 | 7 | 541 | 49 | 108 | 66 | 192 | 171 | 2137 | 63 | 71 | 22 | 37 |

**Table 9.18** CS gas grenades fired in Northern Ireland, April 1970–December 1974

| | Jan. | Feb. | Mar. | Apr. | May | June | July | Aug. | Sept. | Oct. | Nov. | Dec. |
|---|---|---|---|---|---|---|---|---|---|---|---|---|
| 1970 | | | | 13 | 159 | 406 | 267 | 75 | 186 | 44 | 0 | 0 |
| 1971 | 0 | 1 | 0 | 0 | 0 | 8 | 69 | 239 | 388 | 469 | 170 | 762 |
| 1972 | 420 | 407 | 167 | 18 | 10 | 0 | 94 | 6 | 15 | 7 | 10 | 48 |
| 1973 | 22 | 2 | 10 | 41 | 9 | 30 | 85 | 13 | 31 | 24 | 3 | 0 |
| 1974 | 5 | 2 | 1 | 2 | 26 | 1 | 3 | 1 | 1 | 578 | 10 | 0 |

**Table 9.19** Occupied houses searched in Northern Ireland, March 1970–December 1976

| | Jan. | Feb. | Mar. | Apr. | May | June | July | Aug. | Sept. | Oct. | Nov. | Dec. |
|---|---|---|---|---|---|---|---|---|---|---|---|---|
| 1970 | | | 4 | 2 | 6 | 21 | 599 | 71 | 20 | 11 | 9 | 6 |
| 1971 | 21 | 179 | 173 | 150 | 252 | 333 | 335 | 145 | 349 | 1353 | 2579 | 1385 |
| 1972 | 1514 | 916 | 627 | 117 | 196 | 857 | 764 | 1572 | 1933 | 218 | 1829 | 822 |
| 1973 | 801 | 1570 | 1910 | 1539 | 1280 | 856 | 1215 | 1005 | 1504 | 1075 | 988 | 598 |
| 1974 | 1159 | 888 | 1890 | 1776 | 993 | 1032 | 1431 | 1573 | 2738 | 2257 | 2110 | 1749 |
| 1975 | 173 | 198 | 72 | 138 | 605 | 138 | 199 | 124 | 417 | 972 | 581 | 290 |
| 1976 | 431 | 568 | 694 | 915 | 1038 | 976 | 1314 | 1317 | 843 | 964 | 922 | 767 |

**Table 9.20** Vehicles searched in Northern Ireland, May 1970–December 1976 (in 100s)

| | Jan. | Feb. | Mar. | Apr. | May | June | July | Aug. | Sept. | Oct. | Nov. | Dec. |
|---|---|---|---|---|---|---|---|---|---|---|---|---|
| 1970 | | | | | 10 | 63 | 299 | 194 | 192 | 209 | 266 | 234 |
| 1971 | 225 | 219 | 640 | 898 | 698 | 596 | 655 | 883 | 752 | 1489 | 1055 | 1082 |
| 1972 | 734 | 889 | 1014 | 1321 | 1507 | 1340 | 1083 | 2430 | 2410 | 6088 | 5691 | 6022 |
| 1973 | 4590 | 1704 | 1975 | 2024 | 2223 | 2769 | 4594 | 4356 | 4559 | 4712 | 3761 | 2250 |
| 1974 | 2409 | 2743 | 4504 | 6040 | 6072 | 7129 | 7441 | 7340 | 7024 | 7410 | 5994 | 5376 |
| 1975 | 5307 | 4479 | 5391 | 6667 | 5031 | 2816 | 2745 | 3171 | 3821 | 4310 | 3568 | 3732 |
| 1976 | 3610 | 3267 | 3393 | 3662 | 3422 | 3618 | 3098 | 2491 | 2500 | 2038 | 1672 | 1634 |

**Table 9.21** Military deaths in Northern Ireland, January 1972–December 1976

| | Jan. | Feb. | Mar. | Apr. | May | June | July | Aug. | Sept. | Oct. | Nov. | Dec. |
|---|---|---|---|---|---|---|---|---|---|---|---|---|
| 1972 | 4 | 7 | 8 | 8 | 9 | 18 | 18 | 20 | 13 | 7 | 7 | 7 |
| 1973 | 2 | 8 | 15 | 7 | 13 | 3 | 6 | 2 | 2 | 2 | 4 | 2 |
| 1974 | 4 | 1 | 6 | 3 | 1 | 2 | 4 | 3 | 0 | 3 | 6 | 2 |
| 1975 | 0 | 1 | 0 | 0 | 0 | 1 | 4 | 2 | 0 | 2 | 8 | 2 |
| 1976 | 2 | 1 | 5 | 4 | 0 | 1 | 3 | 2 | 0 | 3 | 7 | 1 |

**Table 9.22** CS gas cartridges fired in Northern Ireland, April 1970–August 1975

| | Jan. | Feb. | Mar. | Apr. | May | June | July | Aug. | Sept. | Oct. | Nov. | Dec. |
|---|---|---|---|---|---|---|---|---|---|---|---|---|
| 1970 | | | | 127 | 195 | 3090 | 1453 | 853 | 1519 | 453 | 1 | 0 |
| 1971 | 0 | 0 | 0 | 0 | 0 | 7 | 189 | 2165 | 2391 | 1700 | 791 | 1481 |
| 1972 | 1692 | 2364 | 527 | 77 | 9 | 0 | 141 | 10 | 15 | 23 | 27 | 28 |
| 1973 | 51 | 3 | 19 | 325 | 49 | 136 | 272 | 30 | 24 | 39 | 25 | 0 |
| 1974 | 13 | 19 | 5 | 11 | 42 | 31 | 3 | 0 | 0 | 359 | 31 | 0 |
| 1975 | 0 | 0 | 0 | 0 | 0 | 0 | 0 | 7 | 0 | 0 | 0 | 0 |

**Table 9.23** CS gas projectiles fired in Northern Ireland, January 1970–August 1975

| | Jan. | Feb. | Mar. | Apr. | May | June | July | Aug. | Sept. | Oct. | Nov. | Dec. |
|---|---|---|---|---|---|---|---|---|---|---|---|---|
| 1970 | 0 | 0 | 0 | 140 | 354 | 3496 | 1700 | 928 | 1705 | 497 | 1 | 0 |
| 1971 | 0 | 1 | 0 | 0 | 0 | 15 | 258 | 2404 | 2779 | 2169 | 962 | 2243 |
| 1972 | 2112 | 2771 | 694 | 95 | 19 | 0 | 235 | 16 | 30 | 30 | 37 | 76 |
| 1973 | 73 | 5 | 29 | 366 | 58 | 166 | 357 | 43 | 55 | 63 | 28 | 0 |
| 1974 | 18 | 21 | 6 | 13 | 68 | 32 | 6 | 1 | 1 | 957 | 41 | 0 |
| 1975 | 0 | 0 | 0 | 0 | 0 | 0 | 0 | 7 | 0 | 0 | 0 | 0 |

**Table 9.24** Death count in Northern Ireland, August 1969–December 1976

|  | Jan. | Feb. | Mar. | Apr. | May | June | July | Aug. | Sept. | Oct. | Nov. | Dec. |
|------|------|------|------|------|-----|------|------|------|-------|------|------|------|
| 1969 |  |  |  |  |  |  |  | 8 | 2 | 3 | 0 | 0 |
| 1970 | 0 | 0 | 0 | 0 | 0 | 11 | 6 | 2 | 2 | 0 | 3 | 1 |
| 1971 | 1 | 12 | 6 | 0 | 4 | 0 | 4 | 35 | 19 | 32 | 21 | 39 |
| 1972 | 26 | 22 | 39 | 22 | 40 | 35 | 95 | 55 | 40 | 39 | 20 | 34 |
| 1973 | 17 | 37 | 30 | 16 | 30 | 30 | 17 | 21 | 10 | 8 | 20 | 14 |
| 1974 | 19 | 15 | 26 | 14 | 25 | 14 | 12 | 14 | 12 | 19 | 35 | 11 |
| 1975 | 8 | 19 | 13 | 36 | 11 | 21 | 15 | 29 | 23 | 31 | 24 | 17 |
| 1976 | 47 | 27 | 17 | 20 | 26 | 37 | 28 | 20 | 12 | 28 | 23 | 11 |

**Table 9.25** Security forces personnel killed in Northern Ireland, October 1969–December 1976

|  | Jan. | Feb. | Mar. | Apr. | May | June | July | Aug. | Sept. | Oct. | Nov. | Dec. |
|------|------|------|------|------|-----|------|------|------|-------|------|------|------|
| 1969 |  |  |  |  |  |  |  |  |  | 1 | 0 | 0 |
| 1970 | 0 | 0 | 0 | 0 | 0 | 0 | 0 | 2 | 0 | 0 | 0 | 0 |
| 1971 | 0 | 4 | 4 | 0 | 2 | 0 | 2 | 7 | 8 | 15 | 11 | 6 |
| 1972 | 8 | 7 | 12 | 8 | 9 | 19 | 20 | 21 | 13 | 9 | 9 | 9 |
| 1973 | 5 | 10 | 16 | 7 | 13 | 4 | 6 | 3 | 2 | 4 | 9 | 5 |
| 1974 | 6 | 1 | 9 | 4 | 3 | 4 | 4 | 4 | 1 | 4 | 7 | 3 |
| 1975 | 1 | 1 | 1 | 0 | 2 | 1 | 6 | 2 | 0 | 4 | 11 | 2 |
| 1976 | 5 | 4 | 5 | 5 | 6 | 3 | 4 | 3 | 1 | 4 | 8 | 4 |

**Table 9.26** Baton rounds fired in Northern Ireland, August 1970–December 1976

| | Jan. | Feb. | Mar. | Apr. | May | June | July | Aug. | Sept. | Oct. | Nov. | Dec. |
|---|---|---|---|---|---|---|---|---|---|---|---|---|
| 1970 | | | | | | | | 12 | 27 | 199 | 0 | 0 |
| 1971 | 259 | 1033 | 255 | 243 | 50 | 27 | 1718 | 2975 | 3292 | 3419 | 1554 | 1927 |
| 1972 | 1563 | 3813 | 1588 | 2170 | 2588 | 1560 | 3480 | 2545 | 1429 | 1649 | 573 | 405 |
| 1973 | 1416 | 2289 | 1032 | 2013 | 1152 | 1507 | 1843 | 847 | 314 | 219 | 75 | 58 |
| 1974 | 92 | 210 | 170 | 437 | 265 | 105 | 32 | 152 | 20 | 1209 | 134 | 2 |
| 1975 | 0 | 17 | 4 | 303 | 97 | 145 | 50 | 2383 | 573 | 26 | 41 | 39 |
| 1976 | 7 | 541 | 49 | 108 | 66 | 192 | 171 | 2137 | 63 | 71 | 22 | 37 |

**Table 9.27** Kneecappings of Catholics in Northern Ireland, January 1973–December 1976

| | Jan. | Feb. | Mar. | Apr. | May | June | July | Aug. | Sept. | Oct. | Nov. | Dec. |
|---|---|---|---|---|---|---|---|---|---|---|---|---|
| 1973 | 7 | 6 | 7 | 4 | 1 | 0 | 3 | 9 | 5 | 5 | 4 | 2 |
| 1974 | 7 | 11 | 5 | 11 | 5 | 7 | 13 | 11 | 8 | 2 | 2 | 2 |
| 1975 | 7 | 11 | 9 | 16 | 7 | 8 | 8 | 19 | 7 | 35 | 10 | 1 |
| 1976 | 10 | 2 | 1 | 3 | 3 | 4 | 9 | 12 | 5 | 2 | 6 | 5 |

**Table 9.28** Kneecappings of Protestants in Northern Ireland, January 1973–December 1976

| | Jan. | Feb. | Mar. | Apr. | May | June | July | Aug. | Sept. | Oct. | Nov. | Dec. |
|---|---|---|---|---|---|---|---|---|---|---|---|---|
| 1973 | 1 | 4 | 3 | 2 | 4 | 0 | 0 | 1 | 1 | 0 | 3 | 2 |
| 1974 | 1 | 8 | 2 | 5 | 3 | 3 | 3 | 2 | 3 | 4 | 6 | 4 |
| 1975 | 4 | 7 | 3 | 3 | 6 | 2 | 2 | 6 | 5 | 8 | 2 | 2 |
| 1976 | 0 | 1 | 1 | 3 | 3 | 3 | 6 | 7 | 3 | 4 | 1 | 4 |

**Table 9.29** Suicides in Northern Ireland, 1966–75

|      | Jan. | Feb. | Mar. | Apr. | May | June | July | Aug. | Sept. | Oct. | Nov. | Dec. | Tot. |
|------|------|------|------|------|-----|------|------|------|-------|------|------|------|------|
| 1966 | 4 | 8 | 9 | 5 | 8 | 9 | 4 | 5 | 6 | 4 | 12 | 8 | 82 |
| 1967 | 4 | 5 | 7 | 14 | 7 | 8 | 12 | 6 | 8 | 7 | 15 | 5 | 98 |
| 1968 | 7 | 8 | 7 | 7 | 6 | 5 | 14 | 11 | 11 | 8 | 5 | 10 | 99 |
| 1969 | 7 | 7 | 8 | 6 | 7 | 7 | 6 | 9 | 16 | 8 | 5 | 9 | 95 |
| 1970 | 6 | 6 | 3 | 2 | 8 | 6 | 2 | 8 | 7 | 3 | 8 | 1 | 60 |
| 1971 | 2 | 7 | 5 | 3 | 0 | 7 | 7 | 4 | 7 | 2 | 3 | 6 | 53 |
| 1972 | 3 | 3 | 1 | 1 | 5 | 6 | 5 | 5 | 2 | 6 | 3 | 7 | 47 |
| 1973 | 10 | 3 | 5 | 5 | 6 | 7 | 4 | 7 | 2 | 8 | 6 | 7 | 70 |
| 1974 | 5 | 9 | 10 | 3 | 3 | 6 | 5 | 3 | 8 | 6 | 1 | 3 | 62 |
| 1975 | 3 | 2 | 8 | 7 | 5 | 1 | 6 | 5 | 4 | 6 | 4 | 5 | 56 |

**Table 9.30** Children born with defects and total live births, 1966–75

|      | Jan. | Feb. | Mar. | Apr. | May | June | July | Aug. | Sept. | Oct. | Nov. | Dec. | Total Children born with defects | Total live births |
|------|------|------|------|------|-----|------|------|------|-------|------|------|------|------|------|
| 1966 | 86 | 77 | 86 | 91 | 94 | 72 | 92 | 88 | 71 | 76 | 62 | 74 | 969 | 3322 |
| 1967 | 79 | 74 | 100 | 77 | 83 | 88 | 91 | 56 | 73 | 80 | 74 | 67 | 942 | 3341 |
| 1968 | 89 | 65 | 68 | 73 | 84 | 80 | 99 | 77 | 83 | 78 | 82 | 66 | 944 | 3317 |
| 1969 | 118 | 87 | 94 | 79 | 96 | 98 | 91 | 71 | 92 | 93 | 61 | 55 | 1035 | 3242 |
| 1970 | 89 | 76 | 92 | 106 | 104 | 97 | 74 | 84 | 89 | 85 | 84 | 63 | 1043 | 3208 |
| 1971 | 100 | 99 | 90 | 86 | 90 | 89 | 76 | 73 | 87 | 65 | 72 | 68 | 995 | 3176 |
| 1972 | 74 | 86 | 91 | 85 | 82 | 67 | 77 | 66 | 67 | 70 | 81 | 65 | 911 | 2999 |
| 1973 | 79 | 71 | 68 | 89 | 65 | 63 | 71 | 61 | 49 | 34 | 44 | 31 | 725 | 2920 |
| 1974 | 72 | 58 | 62 | 66 | 73 | 59 | 60 | 75 | 64 | 55 | 49 | 52 | 745 | 2716 |
| 1975 | 72 | 57 | 55 | 62 | 58 | 54 | 53 | 51 | 52 | 44 | 44 | 52 | 654 | 2613 |

*Source:* Registrar General's Reports 1966–1975

during the nearly twenty years of this study, we find that only a few have identified themselves as 'terrorists'. On the other hand governments, courts and scholars have identified all of them as 'terrorist'. In Northern Ireland, one of those who identified himself as a 'terrorist' was a former member of the Royal Marine Commandos. At the time of his psychological evaluation he was a member of an illegal loyalist group that belongs to the UDA umbrella organisation. He was interviewed and examined in 1978, after being released from arrest and interrogation in Belfast. He described his career as having been involved in 'terrorism'. He was trained in counter-insurgency warfare while in the British army and had served in Borneo and the Middle East. While serving in Northern Ireland, he married a woman from East Belfast and subsequently settled there when he retired from the army. He was training working-class Protestants, identified as 'loyalists', in terror and anti-terrorism tactics. He defined his current membership as 'terrorist organisation'.

Other than this British army alumnus of élite counter-insurgency units, no one in the various paramilitaries had identified their organisational affiliation even when to do so was not a threat to their liberty. If they characterised their activities under any sobriquet, it was as 'guerrillas' or 'freedom fighters'. Each member of a paramilitary organisation identified himself or herself as a 'patriot'. They had no difficulty identifying opposition militants as terrorists, but never themselves.

In 1979, when he was the subject of an extradition hearing in San Francisco, McMullen was 32 years old and a self-defined 'political terrorist'. He was also referred to by the Irish media as 'Pete the Para'.

## DEVELOPMENT OF THE TERROR MENTALITY

At the early developmental level of the formulation of the individual and group self is the need to identify some people as allies and others as enemies. Volkan writes that this need evolves from the individual's efforts to protect:

> his sense of self, which is intertwined with his experiences of ethnicity, nationality and other identifying circumstances. When

threatened by political or military conflict, man clings evermore stubbornly to these circumstances in an effort to maintain and regulate his sense of self. Members of any given group revert to childhood ways of reinforcing their bonding, developing shibboleths and investing objects with mystical value . . . the psychological cogency of man's need to have enemies as well as allies, and his stubborn adherence to identification with a group when undergoing hardship and danger. This need is the basis of political psychology, connecting the public arena of political action with individual psychological development. (p. 219)

John Mack (1979) described a phenomenon he called 'the egoism of victimisation' in which there is no empathy for suffering experienced by a group's enemies, although it may be as severe or more severe than the suffering of the group itself.

The effects of chronic humiliation, political stress and oppression on childhood development, both affective and cognitive, are uncanny echoes, as Peter Olsson (1987) points out, of pre-oedipal-based power of chronic political, military, economic oppression, humiliation and stress. As Olsson says, 'we see the externalised intrapsychic derivatives of ethnicity and nationality'. (p.11) Ethnic victimisation is described by Joseph Montville as the phenomenon that occurs:

when the traditional structures which provide an individual sense of security and self worth through membership in a group is shattered by aggressive, violent political outsiders. Victimhood can be characterized by either an extreme persistent low-level sense of moral vulnerability. (Montville, 1986)

Jeanne Knutson interviewed members of militant ethnic organisations engaged in acts of political violence and concluded:

One never erases the identity of a victim. The first blows make the victim permanently on guard for the next attack but the victimizer . . . A life preserving, primitive belief in personal safety has been breached. Once having been terrorized, a victim thus simultaneously grieves over the past and fears the future . . . this intense anxiety over future loss is driven by the semi-conscious inner knowledge that passivity ensures victimization. The genesis of political violence is [in believing] only continued activity in defense of one's self (one's group) adequately serves to reduce the threat of further aggression . . . when the act of affirmative violence takes place there simultaneously emerges . . . emotional awareness of intense rage . . . it is the point of no return for those who engage in continuing campaigns of political violence. (Knutson, 1981)

Jerold Post, a psychiatrist, reviewing the literature on the psychological characteristics of members of terrorist organisations in several different societies, argues that:

> Political terrorists are driven to commit acts of violence as a consequence of psychological forces, and that their special psycho-logic is constructed to rationalize acts they are psychologically compelled to commit . . . individuals are drawn to the path of terrorism in order to commit acts of violence and their special logic which is grounded in their psychology and reflected in their rhetoric, becomes the justification for their violent acts. (Post, 1987, pp. 2–3)

But terrorism, and terrorist acts, are multi-causal with different dimensions and involve, not only the psyche of the individual and the relationship between individual and group ideology, but also the history and nature of the politico-legal forces operating in arenas of oppression. Besides that, it is a dynamic rather than a static process definition, because of the natural shifts and changes in all of these elements in relation to each other.

At the same time it is true that not all children from all systems characterised by turmoil and violence grow up to become terrorists. We have only to look at the post-war young adults of continental Europe to see that the 1950s French, German, Dutch, Italian and Scandinavian young adults whose childhood was spent in the nightmares of occupied Europe with bombings, strafings and fixed battles were not a terrorist generation. On the other hand, there is every kind of evidence that youthful Irish and Palestinians are more likely to become involved in terrorist actions than were their parents. Therefore, the ordinary person in Northern Ireland and in the Middle East is more likely to become a victim of terrorism. Statistically, incidents of terrorism are more probable in these two places, and, therefore, increasingly people in North America and Europe are also more vulnerable, but more likely to become victims of highway accidents.

Post's psychiatric analysis of terrorists suggests that those individuals who are driven to take violent action are not emotionally healthy and well balanced 'despite their flawless logic once the basic premises are accepted'. He views the crucial connection between the individual so driven and the group with whom he can identify as the catalytic mechanism that must somehow be aborted in order to thwart terrorism. Post also wants mental health professionals and others deliberately to facilitate individuals leaving such groups by creating pathways out, thus implying that once the individual is separated from the group dynamic, he or she is more amenable to reason. Post implies that once caught up in such a group and terror tactics as a way of life, the individual is unable, alone, to find and choose a way out of terrorism.

Peter McMullen (and many of his peers in Northern Ireland and the rest of the world) opted out and has struggled against enormous obstacles and threats to stay out. This example in contradiction of Post's thesis serves only to underscore the diverse and dynamic nature of the social and psychological processes involved in membership of terror organisations and enactment of terrorist programmes. It is only lately that mental health scientists established the practice of describing symptoms as behaviours rather than pathologies. This is done because, over and over again, research has demonstrated that the same individual may appropriately be diagnosed under several different categories, depending on the particular phase and condition he or she is in when the diagnostician makes that examination.

## THE PSYCHOLOGICAL PROFILE OF A TERRORIST

Nobody can tell in advance who is likely to become a terrorist. The objective for psychological study is to recognise the variables that contribute to the violent act. In this way, it may be possible to alter some of the contributing conditions to thwart the probability of a violent outcome. McMullen's developmental history is typical in some ways of the process through which one moves from terrorised to terrorist.

His earliest experiences of prejudice made him aware of his vulnerability as a member of a negative identity group (Irish Catholic). Since his religious Catholicism was so important to him, he was continually reinforced for this identity and vulnerability. Peter's marriage to a woman whose family tradition incorporated republican activism provided for him a role model for action. The imports of his Thematic Apperception Test projective stories indicate that he is achievement oriented, but has few skills in interpersonal relationships and expects that conflict results in destruction and death. He sees himself trying to escape his own destruction but feels directionless, frightened and pessimistic. These themes are prevalent in the projective productions of children and adults in Northern Ireland who have been subjected to many years of political chaos and violence. Having identified with the victim group, Peter personally experienced as a threat the articulated intention of his commanding officers to attack the unarmed, mostly Catholic civil rights marchers two weeks hence. He likewise heard the screams of the victims of interrogation tortures in the context of his own vulnerability. This identification with the helpless, powerless victim, resulted in his belief, in 1972, that the only recourse for himself as victim and his identity group, was to use violence to fight violence.

Psychological test data derived from studies of a thousand children, aged six to sixteen in Northern Ireland in seventeen years of semi-annual and annual time sampling, provide insight into the dynamics of psychological development as children identify themselves as vulnerable prospective victims, threatened by hostile out-groups. These dynamics of truncation, of development, of political socialisation and moral judgment at the level of vigilante morality transcend the cultural diversity of the sample. Additional test data from members of paramilitary organisations, the IRA and the UDA, demonstrate continuity with these findings on the cognitive and affective development of children. The grown-up version of children truncated at the second level of cognitive development shows that such individuals are well within the normal limits on measures of personality and cognition, but are at the extreme in State and Trait Anger, low in Anxiety and higher than average on Curiosity. In other words, they are not anxious about their angry actions and tend towards innovation in group and individual behaviours. They are self-righteously indignant because they see their identity group as threatened and vulnerable (see Tables 9.31 and 9.32).

Significantly, the psychological test data reveal a range of normal characteristics in intelligence and personality. Some individuals come at either extreme of any continuum, but the

**Table 9.31** Corrections among STPI State and Trait Scales for members of a paramilitary organisation (N=28) in Northern Ireland

| Scale | State anxiety | State anger (N=27) | State curiosity | Trait anxiety | Trait anger | Angry temperament | Angry reaction |
|---|---|---|---|---|---|---|---|
| State anger (N=27) | .34 | | | | | | |
| State curiosity | .05 | −.10 | | | | | |
| Trait anxiety | .56** | .09 | −.45* | | | | |
| Trait anger | .00 | .56** | −.03 | .22 | | | |
| Angry temperament | −.21 | .26 | −.18 | .20 | .78*** | | |
| Angry reaction | .22 | .50** | .15 | .17 | .77*** | .23 | |
| Trait curiosity | −.08 | −.19 | .76** | −.43* | .03 | .01 | .08 |

\* p < .05
\*\* p < .01
\*\*\* p < .001

**Table 9.32** Mean and median scores on STPI scales for members of a paramilitary organisation in Northern Ireland

| Scale | N | Mean | Median | Standard deviation | Range | Percentile |
|---|---|---|---|---|---|---|
| State anxiety | 28 | 16.37 | 16 | 4.82 | 10–28 | 44 |
| State anger | 27 | 14.09 | 14 | 3.85 | 10–23 | 69 |
| State curiosity | 28 | 30.69 | 31.5 | ·5.19 | 21–39 | 71 |
| Trait anxiety | 28 | 15.87 | 15.5 | 3.63 | 10–23 | 38 |
| Trait anger | 28 | 20.84 | 20.5 | 5.61 | 10–30 | 76 |
| Angry temperament | 28 | 7.54 | 8 | 2.63 | 4–14 | 85 |
| Angry reaction | 28 | 9.11 | 8 | 3.03 | 4–16 | 58 |
| Trait curiosity | 28 | 29.73 | 30.5 | 5.27 | 20–39 | 64 |

majority fall within the mid-range of normal differences. This range is maintained graphically on the State-Trait Personality Inventory (STPI – a standardised, internationally-normed personality factor scale), with striking common features at the upper levels of State and Trait Anger and lower levels of State and Trait Anxiety (see Tables 9.31 and 9.32).

If we examine McMullen's psychological history and PIRA actions, it is not at all certain that his accessibility to group membership facilitated or catalysed his violent actions, or even rationalised them. Even more striking in contradiction to Post's formula for diminishing terrorism, is the fact that no one facilitated McMullen's exit from the PIRA and he made a difficult and nearly fatal choice to resign. Nothing has, in the years since he made that decision, facilitated or provided a pathway for McMullen out of terrorism, yet he has remained firmly committed to making a new life for himself.

This raises a major issue for investigation. What is his current psychodynamic status and how does that compare with his affective and cognitive condition at the time of his group actions?

Many theses about terrorism and terrorists are based on uni-dimensional and limited data. This leads to overgeneralisations and deals too simplistically with complex issues – psychologising – rather than psychologically analysing the diverse and complex phenomenon that is defined as 'terrorism'. In the long run, this kind of simplistic analysis gives the terrorist more power. The complexity and diversity of the real persons initiating and executing these actions are badly underestimated and thus unpredicatable. With all McMullen's uniqueness, there are, none the less, factors in his psycho-social development and environment that correspond with those of other members of paramilitary organisations. It is by compiling the hundreds of psychological case studies of such members, and the thousands of case studies of two generations of children, that these factors may be identified.

## AN ABBREVIATED LIFE

McMullen was the fourth of seven children of Catholic parents. His father, a non-com in the British military, took his family with him while he served at bases in England, the Isle of Man and Cyprus. Peter's earliest memories of school in England were good, and he says 'I felt English'. But when he was about six or seven, and was living in England he became aware of being Irish and being Catholic because of, as he says, 'stupid remarks about my accent . . . I had to fight'. As he became more anglicised, he told me, this didn't crop up again until he joined the army at the age of fifteen. He wanted to be a priest when he was eleven but his father did not agree, and although he was so committed to his religious vocation that he continued to take an aptitude test for admission to the White Fathers (Redemptorist Missionary Order) and assisted at Mass, Peter ultimately accepted his father's decision that he should join the army as he himself had done.

Peter says his father was very distant from him, and only close with his youngest sibling many years later. Peter describes his father as having been very intelligent and having had some bad breakdowns when he was very young. But he identified himself as English, became a drill sergeant and a gunnery instructor, and was well known for being 'tough' on everybody and known to be 'aloof''. Home life for Peter was 'rough'. His father wanted him to participate in the most physically tough, competitive sports.

Peter at a later stage wanted to be a chef or a draughtsman. He applied for admission to an academic programme in architecture but was refused, he said, 'because of my religion'. After joining the army at 15 (school-leaving age at that time), Peter completed six months of service and then got a medical discharge for his flat feet. He was in Belfast at the time, and went to live with a grandparent and took on odd jobs. He did not really know what he wanted to do when, in 1964, he got a job as a barman and met Eileen Loughran, a waitress. They became friends but dropped their relationship after a few weeks of dating. However, when Peter got drunk, failed to get to work and was fired, the relationship picked up again.

Peter went to live with a sister in Ripon, North Yorkshire (home of the Claro Barracks, which he has been charged with having bombed in 1974). Eileen quit her job and followed him to England. Her parents, who, Peter describes as more middle-class, were not at all happy about her going to England. Her brothers and sisters were all staunch republicans, but Eileen was pregnant and she and Peter decided to get married. They returned to Belfast where Peter worked as a cook in the Territorial Army from 1964-7. In 1967 he was transferred into the Parachute Regiment and returned to England for basic training.

In 1969 when Peter returned to Belfast with that regiment they were deployed during the riots along the Shankill and the Falls Roads in Belfast (Protestant and Catholic enclaves respectively). They were to play a role in maintaining the 'peace line' which at that time was not the ten foot corrugated metal with barbed wire on top wall that was erected later. The 'line' was a barricaded demarcation point on the footpath and road. During that period his commanding officers wanted to identify him according to his religion. The fact that he was Roman Catholic began to make a difference in deployment and associations. There was a question of whether he could be ordered to patrol on the Protestant side, and he was transferred to other responsibilities in the artillery corps and again returned to England for training. He was sent back yet again to Palace Barracks in Belfast in September 1970. At that time the SAS (the British equivalent of the US Green Berets) were incorporated into his regiment and also stationed at Palace Barracks in Belfast.

By that time, the McMullens had four children and a house opposite what had become the interrogation centre, not more than fifty yards away.

In mid-1970, the IRA was minuscule and fragmented about military policy. But the British army was already operating on the basis of Brigadier Frank Kitson's book, *Low Intensity Operations*, and was trying to subvert, intimidate, humiliate, compromise and penetrate the largely republican Catholic community that surrounded its headquarters. By that time Peter could no longer defend the army to his in-laws, as the necessary defender of the Catholic population. The army had not only failed to come to the rescue of the besieged minority during the riots and pogroms of 1969-70, but by 1970, Palace Barracks had become the site of detention and interrogation. At night Peter could hear the screams and smell the stench of that abomination not sixty yards away.

In 1971, when internment came in, his father-in-law and three brothers-in-law were among the 3,000 people lifted and interned for various periods of time that year. Peter says that he and his family kept to themselves then, and he worked in the officers' mess. In that capacity he overheard and knew about torture in the interrogation centre and finally, in early 1972, learned about the army's plans for confronting civil rights marchers at a demonstration planned for 30th January in Derry. This was the day that became known as Bloody Sunday, when the army killed fourteen unarmed civilian demonstrators (thirteen died on the spot and one died later from wounds inflicted that day). That was when Peter travelled down to Dublin, warned the IRA and joined them.

McMullen had been trained by the British army in counter-insurgency operations, mining and bombing as well as shooting.

He had been brought up to consider the IRA a terrorist organisation and he defined himself as a freedom fighter from the moment he joined the IRA. He deserted his regiment and participated in blowing up part of Palace Barracks, an act that caused considerable plant damage as well as embarrassment for the British army.

Between 1972 and 1974, the British government alleges that McMullen assumed a high-level position with the IRA and participated and planned operations in Northern Ireland and England (including the bombing of the Claro Barracks in Ripon, England). In December 1974, he was convicted by the government of the Irish Republic of being a member of the Provisional IRA and was sentenced to three years in Port Laoise Gaol for membership and a firearms violation.

Eventually, McMullen wanted to resign from the PIRA and told the leadership in Dublin that he would no longer participate in IRA activities. He was brought before a PIRA court of inquiry and found guilty of failing to obey an order. A few days later he was surreptitiously informed that he had been sentenced to death. He fled Dublin immediately and eventually entered the United States, using a false name and a fake passport.

McMullen had been in the States before. He was, he says, sent over earlier to organise, acquire and transport weapons back to the IRA. Now, he says, he came under surveillance by the British authorities and by the IRA members assigned to assassinate him. He tried to give himself up by first calling the FBI, who, much to his chagrin, seemed totally uninterested in meeting him. They suggested he call the Bureau of Alcohol, Tobacco and Firearms (BATF), who were very interested in his story, but could not grant him political asylum. For that they appealed to the FBI. At that point, either through their surveillance or by direct information from the FBI, British intelligence joined the FBI's interrogation of McMullen. They were able to join in the questioning by claiming that they wanted his 'help for intelligence purposes', and so extracted from him his admission of membership of the IRA and participation in bombing actions. The subsequent extradition request was adjudicated in northern California, where he had been apprehended, during the last quarter of 1979. The British government was denied their extradition application, and

McMullen was subsequently held over to be tried on illegal-entry charges.

Pete the Para won status as a political refugee but the Immigration and Naturalization Service (INS) kept appealing against each favourable decision. For the next six years, Peter McMullen lived free. He worked at various trades staying mostly in small towns and cities in the west, always wary of a PIRA assassination initiative or an INS deportation order. His Irish wife and children remained in Belfast and the couple were soon divorced. Peter then married an American woman he met while working and living in Hawaii. In mid-1986 the appeals court ruled in favour of the INS motion for deportation, and the papers were served on him in the small town in Utah where he was working in a jewellery shop.

He was summarily transported to New York to be flown to Dublin, Ireland, on 23rd December 1986. However, the new extradition treaty between the United States and Great Britain had come into effect the previous day, and as McMullen and his escorts were boarding a plane, a federal marshal served notice of extradition proceedings. McMullen was transported to Otisville, New York's federal detention centre, to await another trial for extradition under the new rules.

Some six years after the fact of the precedent-setting McMullen case, President Ronald Reagan, engaged in an effort to gain international co-operation for his declared 'war on terrorism' (apparently in exchange for British agreement for the use of bases in England to bomb Libya) signed into law a new extradition treaty that excludes fugitives from the United Kingdom from claiming status as political refugees. Although the British government had originally been denied their request for McMullen's extradition to the United Kingdom, the United States has now formally rejected the legitimacy of political opposition in Northern Ireland. But will it now recognise the findings of both the State Department and a congressional sub-committee, which have ruled that police and military actions in Northern Ireland have been a violation of human rights? Once again, McMullen's fate hinges on a series of precedent-setting legal arguments in his country of asylum. However, in the current situation, he would not be sent to Ireland – he would be extradited to England to face charges.

# THE SECOND GENERATION OF VIOLENT SOCIETIES

The psychological development of McMullen and several hundred thousand others like him in many parts of the world today, are candidates for membership of groups that enact terrorism. Many will not reach McMullen's level of activity, but, by virtue of their lifelong experience in places where intergenerational intercommunal violence is commonplace, they are susceptible. Most of these children are experiencing victimisation through ethnic prejudices as a daily routine.

Peter McMullen's own children, born in the late 1960s are now virtually adults. They are the second generation growing up in the current round of violence in Northern Ireland. This extensive longitudinal study supports the following conclusions:

1. The younger the child at the onset of violence/vulnerability, the less likely they are to develop a level of legal/political socialisation and moral judgment beyond the level of vendetta/vigilanteism (Fields, 1977). At this level, there is a pervasive 'righteous indignation' that is manifested as elevations in both State and Trait Anger with low anxiety about angry behaviour (Fields, 1986).

2. Children who identify with a lachrymose victim ethnicity experience vicariously the trauma of their identity peers especially when they have personal experience of vulnerability and violence (Fields, 1984).

3. Feelings of helplessness and parental inefficacy lead to children's selection as role-models/heroes members of paramilitary groups who enact terrorism against the dominant authority system. This results in intergenerational conflict and anachronistic behaviours among the younger generation (Fields, 1984).

4. Personal experiences of traumatic stress usually precipitate volunteers into organisations that enact violence (Fields, 1986).

5. Prolonged violence promotes factionation within groups and promotes proliferation and accelerations of radical xenophobia – polarisation between different groups (Khalaf, 1986).

According to this finding on the truncation of development of moral judgement in children between the ages of six and fifteen growing up in Northern Ireland since 1971, there is nothing surprising about the fact that the bombers and gunmen of Belfast are most frequently adolescent youths – boys and girls of working-class families.

The first six years of this study, in which 350 Northern Irish children and 300 members of paramilitary organisations were tested, provided dramatic indicators to the future of that tragedy.

In those early years of the data collection, the subjects were the children, between the ages of four and six, whose houses were burned down around them by angry mobs augmented by uniformed members of the 'security forces'; whose fathers and sometimes mothers, too, were dragged off to interrogation centres and returned to them a day or a year later, physically and morally broken; whose older siblings were interned or assassinated by terror squads and who, in telling their stories (on the TAT) see no one having control over their fate (see Table 9.33).

There have been changes in the stories, direction and dynamics evidenced through the psychological measurements applied to Belfast working-class children at semi-annual intervals for almost twenty years. One of the most dramatic has been the steady downward drift of the Motivation Index scores on the Story Sequence Analysis of the TAT. The mean scores were below the normed average at the beginning, and lower, too than those of age peers in Dublin (see Figures 9.1 and 9.2 and Tables 9.33 and 9.34).

Responses scored to the Tapp-Kohlberg questions have indicated that among these children there is not the expected progression from Level I through Level III. A few children manage to reach Level II at about age 12, but only ten children, 2 per cent of the entire sample, managed to reach Level III.

## CONCLUSION

Between 1971 and 1972 Pete the Para was undergoing the galvanising experience of his life as a Belfast Catholic while in the uniform of his people's historic oppressors. His children and all of their generational contemporaries will be even less likely to experience a range of choice behaviours than he did.

**Table 9.33** Response percentages on questions relating to political socialisation: comparison with US sample

| | Educational groups | | | | | | | |
| | Primary (6–10) | | | | Middle school (11–14) | | | |
| Levels: categories | DUB | TK | BEL 71–72 | BEL 73–74 | DUB | TK | BEL 71–72 | BEL 73–74 |
|---|---|---|---|---|---|---|---|---|
| **What would happen if there were no rules?** | | | | | | | | |
| I: violence/crime | 55 | 50 | 89 | 95 | 50 | 57 | 85 | 90 |
| II: personal desires not principles | 20 | 15 | — | — | 25 | 20 | — | — |
| II: anarchy/dis- order/chaos | 30 | 25 | 11 | 5 | 60 | 57 | 15 | 10 |
| II: impossible to imagine | — | — | — | — | 10 | 7 | 5 | 5 |
| III: man as self- regulatory (nothing would happen) | — | — | — | — | — | — | — | — |
| **What is a rule?** | | | | | | | | |
| I: prohibitive | 76 | 60 | 92 | 98 | 36 | 30 | 80 | 90 |
| II: prescriptive | 17 | 20 | 7 | — | 40 | 40 | 12 | 10 |
| II: enforcement | — | — | 1 | — | 24 | 10 | 12 | 5 |
| III: beneficial/rational | — | 15 | — | — | 15 | 27 | — | — |
| **What is a law?** | | | | | | | | |
| I: prohibitive | 78 | 60 | 92 | 92 | 90 | 43 | 90 | 96 |
| II: prescriptive | 20 | 20 | — | — | 10 | 43 | 12 | 5 |
| II: enforcement | — | 10 | — | — | 10 | 23 | 8 | — |
| III: beneficial/rational | — | — | — | — | 5 | 13 | — | — |
| **Why should people follow rules?** | | | | | | | | |
| I: avoid negative consequences | 53 | 50 | 60 | 82 | 25 | 13 | 50 | 90 |
| I: authority | 15 | 5 | 27 | 20 | 30 | — | 25 | 15 |
| II: personal conformity | 30 | 35 | 6 | — | 41 | 13 | 14 | 5 |
| II: social conformity | — | 10 | 13 | 5 | 10 | 53 | 12 | 3 |
| III: rational/bene- ficial/utilitarian | — | 5 | — | — | — | 27 | 4 | — |
| III: principled | — | — | — | — | — | — | — | — |
| **Why do you follow rules?** | | | | | | | | |
| I: avoid negative consequences | 65 | 60 | 94 | 96 | 26 | 47 | 89 | 90 |
| I: authority | 28 | 10 | 12 | 5 | 60 | 10 | 10 | 12 |
| II: personal conformity | 15 | 20 | — | — | 15 | 40 | 10 | — |
| II: social conformity | — | — | — | — | 10 | 40 | 10 | 5 |
| III: rational/bene- ficial/utilitarian | — | — | — | — | 5 | 7 | 2 | — |
| III: principled | — | — | — | — | — | — | — | — |

Table 9.33 continued

| Levels: categories | Educational groups | | | | | | | |
| --- | --- | --- | --- | --- | --- | --- | --- | --- |
| | Primary (6–10) | | | | Middle school (11–14) | | | |
| | DUB | TK | BEL 71–72 | BEL 73–74 | DUB | TK | BEL 71–72 | BEL 73–74 |
| **Can rules be changed?** | | | | | | | | |
| I: no | 40 | 20 | 98 | 98 | 46 | — | 64 | 70 |
| II & III: yes | 60 | 70 | 2 | — | 54 | 100 | 36 | 30 |
| **Are there times when it might be right to break a rule?** | | | | | | | | |
| I: no, unqualified | 80 | 55 | 95 | 95 | 20 | 7 | 70 | 80 |
| I: yes, unspecified | — | 25 | — | — | 10 | — | — | 10 |
| II: morality of circumstances | 20 | 20 | 5 | 5 | 60 | 73 | 25 | 10 |
| III: Morality of rule | — | — | — | — | 10 | 17 | 30 | — |

*Note:* all questions except 'Can rules be changed?' and 'Are there times when it might be right to break a rule?' are multiple coded; therefore, percentages may total over 100 per cent. Where answers were idiosyncratic or uncodable, the categories were omitted from the table. Level number indicates increasing cognitive maturity (adapted from Tapp and Kohlberg, 1971, p. 76).

TK = Tapp and Kohlberg    BEL = Belfast sample    DUB = Dublin

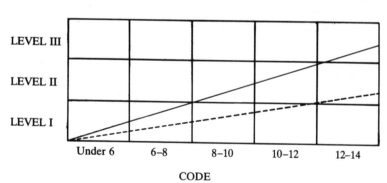

CODE

——————— = Expected development of moral judgement under normal conditions

– – – – – – = Development of moral judgement under conditions of violence

**Figure 9.1** Tapp-Kohlberg questions

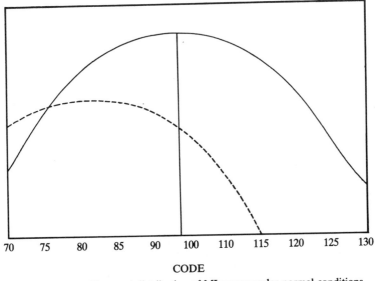

CODE

——————— = Expected distribution of MI scores under normal conditions

------ = Distribution of MI scores under conditions of violence

**Figure 9.2** Story sequence analysis motivation

**Table 9.34** Mean MI scores (Belfast), 1971–74

|  | Working class | | | | Middle class | | Repeat tested | |
|---|---|---|---|---|---|---|---|---|
|  | Prot. | N | Cath. | N | Cath. | N | Prot. | Cath. |
| 1971 | 85 | 12 | 80 | 12 | — | — | — | — |
| 1972 | 82 | 13 | 72 | 13 | — | — | — | 68 | 6 |
| 1973 | 74 | 26 | 70 | 26 | — | — | — | 64 | 12 |
| 1974 | 72 | 24 | 69 | 26 | — | 4 | — | 66 | 5 |
| Totals | | 75 | | 77 | | 4 | | 23 |

Parallel with the Northern Ireland research – psychological test data on members of paramilitary organisations and on children from six to sixteen – has been research in Israel, the West Bank, Lebanon and South Africa.

The data collection in these places has been less prolonged, but demonstrates that despite cultural differences among this wider sampling, terrorism, as a strategy and as a psychology, is a consequence of intercommunal prejudice and violence.

Palestinian children tested in 1982, scored significantly below the norms. They, like their age peers in Northern Ireland, saw the world as a hostile place in which people and even animals and insects related with each other mainly in mutual destruction.

Israeli children probably showed the greatest range and variety of responses. From 1974 to 1982 inclusive, kibbutz-raised children consistently scored at or above the norms on all of the tests. Not so their countrymen. Children in Kiryat Shmona, a new city close to the border with Lebanon were experiencing daily flight to underground shelters to avoid katusha rocket bombardments. They lived in a community that was, in the seventies, incohesive and disorganised. People in Kiryat Shmona had emigrated from Arab countries and carried enormous antipathy against those who, in some cases, were their tormenters.

Black South African youths, who describe themselves as 'comrades' were examined while they were in sanctuary, in most instances, far from their homes with little prospect of returning. Members of the group were aged between thirteen and twenty, but none had reached Level III and few were motivated for achievement. Hardly surprising, when we remember these young people came from the generation of adolescents that invented 'necklacing' – killing by hanging a tyre filled with petrol round the neck of the victim and setting it alight. In such a society every black person becomes brutalised by the escalating levels of violence.

They are growing up terrorised in Northern Ireland, Israel, the West Bank, Lebanon and South Africa, and probably in many other places as well. On the West Bank, young Israeli Jews and Palestinians have often carried out terrorist attacks on each other without even the order or sanction of an organisational membership.

Eighteen-year-old Israeli soldiers in an army of occupation are brutalised as they confront the objectified 'enemy other'. They have grown up in a culture that has consistently associated the identities of 'Palestinian' with 'terrorist'. They confront Palestinian youths whose anger and frustration are an immediate reinforcement that fuels the stereotype they were taught.

Israeli children report nightmares in which they and their parents are in concentration camps and the guards are Arab-Palestinian terrorists. Young Palestinians' nightmares are revivifications of the Sabra/Shatila massacre (which was carried out by Lebanese Christian paramilitaries against the Palestinian enclave in West Beirut in 1982) with themselves and their families victims of Jewish soldiers.

Israeli Arab children in Beit Safafa who had never seen or heard a gunshot or bomb in 1981 (they were too young to have any memory of the Six Day War in 1967) were traumatised in 1983 when TNT (the Jewish terrorist underground) set a bomb at the mosque.

Children who have been terrorised and truncated at an early level of legal socialisation are unable to function in an open democratic society. Samir Khalaf recognised the consequences of such developmental experience, when he described Lebanon as 'the pathology of democracy and pluralism'. Each new round of violence sends individuals and groups back to their community of origin and fearful of freedom (Khalaf, 1986).

These findings contradict Marxist theories which predicate progressive social change on the synthesis growing out of conflict between two contradictory systems. Instead, the insecurity, alienation and anomie that are the individual developmental psychology of childhood experiences of violence and prolonged traumatic stress devastate social organisation and xenophobically polarise the population.

Common sense and experience can tell us that people who are badly treated and/or unjustly punished will seek revenge. It should not be surprising then that adolescents who have themselves been terrorised become terrorists, and that in a situation in which they are provided consensual sanction by their community because of the actions of an unjust government their resort to terror becomes the way of life for the whole society. Traumatisation is not limited to the immediate participants in violence. It extends to everyone who identifies with the victimised group.

The experience of children becomes the political behaviour of adults, into yet another generation of intercommunal violence.


## REFERENCES

Fields, R. M., *Society Under Siege* (Philadelphia, Pa.: Temple University Press, 1976).

'Psychological Profile of a Terrorist', paper presented at the American Psychological Association Convention (1986).

'Terrorized into Terrorist', in Ochberg and Soskis, *Victims of Terrorism* (Westview Press, 1982).

'Children of Violence', paper presented at the Third International Conference on the Psychological Effects of War and Peace, Jerusalem, Israel (January 1983).

Khalaf, S., *Lebanon's Predicament* (New York: Columbia University Press, 1987).

Knutson, J. A. 'Political Violence', unpublished monograph (1982).

Mack, J. 'Forward' in *Cyprus: War and Adaptation* by Volkan, V. D. (University Press of Virginia, 1979).

Montville, J. V. 'Nationalism, Sectarianism and Political Violence . . .', paper presented at the Woodrow Wilson Center Interdisciplinary Research Conference on The Psychology of Terrorism (March, 1987).

Ollson, P. A. 'A Developmental Self Psychology Perspective on Terrorism', paper delivered at the Southwestern Psychiatric Association meetings (1987).

Post, J. 'Narcissism and the Charismatic Leader–Follower Relationship', *Political Psychology*, vol. 7, no. 5 (1986), pp. 675–88.

Tapp, J. and L. Kohlberg, 'Development of Legal Socialization', *Journal of Social Issues* (Dec. 1971).

Volkan, V. 'The Need to Have Enemies and Allies', *Political Psychology*, vol. 6, no. 2 (1985).

# 10 · WAR OF WORDS: THE *BELFAST TELEGRAPH* AND LOYALIST[1] POPULISM

The *Belfast Telegraph* occupied a unique place in Northern Ireland in the 1970s. At the height of its popularity[2] the paper probably penetrated virtually every household in the province; as commonly read by Protestants as by Catholics,[3] and was from 1960 the only paper generally circulating in Northern Ireland without an overt, direct connection with one of the major national, political or religious groupings.[4] Formal control of the paper had been lost by Unionists, who, through an intricate network of restrictions and relationships, had sustained a monopoly on ownership, management and editorship for half a century.[5] The new owner, the Canadian Roy Thomson, never again set foot in Northern Ireland; the local management, headed for the most part by a succession of English chief executives, and including a place on the board for a Dublin-based bank, was overseen by a parent company in London;[6] and the editorial ethos was largely driven by commercial concerns and methods imported from North America.[7] Thus the *Belfast Telegraph* was most normally seen as standing apart from 'the all-pervading tribal attitudes' many regarded as endemic in Northern Ireland and its press.[8]

The *Telegraph* had dropped its formal title as a Unionist organ in favour of a declaration of political independence,[9] and had replaced its Unionist, if liberal, editor-in-chief Jack Sayers, incumbent in the editor's chair at the time of Thomson's take-over, with an Englishman, Eugene Wason, hurriedly transferred from the *African Daily News,* where he had proved too liberal for the ruling white regime in Southern Rhodesia.[10] Yet alongside the suggestion that the protracted and litigious negotiations Thomson had to undertake to buy the *Telegraph* represented an effort by Unionists to retain control of Northern Ireland's most widely read paper in the face of an 'advance of liberalisation',[11] must be ranged Thomson's underlying commercial objectives in acquiring what he no doubt shrewdly considered a potentially lucrative property. The purchase of the *Belfast Telegraph* was *au fond* a business transaction.[12] By 1973 the *Telegraph* displayed the major characteristics of a Thomson paper; practically undistinguishable from 'any other to be found in the larger cities of the United Kingdom',[13] and heavily dependent on a large section of classified advertising, which tied the fortunes of the paper more directly to the local economy, through a reliance for a major part of its revenue on the flow of small ads, and especially employment advertising, rather than editorial attitude.[14] Thomson explained his philosophy of newspaper ownership in these terms:

> Newspapers create their own personalities and find their own individual levels and characteristics of audiences, which in turn determine the volume and nature of the advertising which finds its way into them. In this way, the common will can determine which newspapers it wants to continue and which it does not, and what particular role it wants each of them to fill. I do not see that any case can be made for riding roughshod over the common will . . .[15]

The effect, noted elsewhere in Thomson papers, was to increase the tendency towards more popular journalism.[16] If the *Telegraph* was to sustain, or even enhance its dominant role among the press in Northern Ireland, it clearly had to appeal not only to its traditional, mainly Presbyterian, Protestant working-class and lower middle-class audience;[17] but also to 'a new generation of relatively prosperous Catholics'.[18]

Something of an echo of Thomson's marketeering approach was found in the 'ideology of modernisation',[19] which underpinned liberal Unionist policies during the 1960s, with its day-to-day emphasis on practical rather than political issues.[20] One objective was to make Northern Ireland more attractive to outside investors, altering the image of the Unionist business community as 'political rather than commercial' as Thomson had found them,[21] an effort, not then regarded as being particularly handicapped by a commitment to 'a more systematic approach to economic planning', involving attempts partly to address the imbalance of

Northern Ireland's economic development, which highly favoured Protestants,[22] and partly to effecting more efficient arrangements with the Republic of Ireland. Some Catholics clearly appreciated that any benefits forthcoming might accrue somewhat to them, signalling a wane of more virulent nationalist sentiment[23] and the rise, in its place, of civil rights agitation for simple 'British rights for British people'.[24] In sum, '. . . sophisticated Catholics were becoming more interested in improving their lot within Northern Ireland than dismantling it as a political unit, and sophisticated Protestants seemed able to contemplate with equanimity closer ties with Eire *(sic)'.*[25] These tentative movements in Northern Ireland were played out against a backdrop of parallel alterations in the relationship between the Republic and Britain to one of reduced hostility and greater equality.[26] In a pattern familiar in more clear-cut colonial situations,[27] Britain in Ireland appeared to be tempering its favoured collaboration with Unionism with an increasing assuagement of the long-held concerns of bourgeois nationalism.

## CHALLENGE AND CONFRONTATION

After the failure of Unionist attempts 'to create a more united society',[28] the points of stress within unionism which they had exposed became a pivot around which unionists debated their future, and the editorials of the *Telegraph* in 1973, a year of heightened political sensitivity after the collapse of the Stormont government, were couched predominantly in terms of this disunity; a partisan examination of the disaffection of a sizeable section of its readership with the *Telegraph*'s commitment to the exploration of methods for Northern Ireland 'to break out of its political straightjacket . . .'.[29] Pervading the argument was a thematic discourse in which the paper editorialised that the complex political, social, religious and economic relationships of Northern Ireland, which opponents of the liberal experiment characterised as now inevitably leading to the reunification of Ireland, were, rather, most likely to do so because of the intransigence of Protestant loyalist populism.

At times almost daily the paper threw down challenges to 'those whose siege mentality is ingrained . . .' (12 Jan.). Central was the struggle for control of Unionism, principally articulated in the Assembly election in June, which could 'almost be reduced to two discrete components, a contest to decide who would represent Protestants and another to decide who would represent Catholics',[30] with part of the Unionist electorate clearly imbued with 'a community ethos distrustful of their own political leadership . . .'.[31] This friction contained obvious class undertones: many Protestants felt themselves inextricably excluded from the liberal schema.[32] Social control in the ghetto could be fragile: the Orange Order, the medium for advancement through the Unionist hierarchy,[33] was weakest in working-class areas,[34] and where the provision and regulation of services began to falter, paramilitaries provided substitutes.[35] Nevertheless, the Protestant proletariat was inclined only 'to displace Conservatism whilst remaining within a fundamentally Unionist, anti-nationalist and, at times, sectarian framework'.[36] When the Unionist Prime Minister Terence O'Neill aspired to 're-establish the Unionist Party's hegemony over the Protestant working-class',[37] it was the loyalist Revd Ian Paisley who rose to be its champion.[38] There was equally a fundamental ghetto assumption in 'the right symbolically to demonstrate . . . dominance';[39] Protestantism on the march with the UDA, in protest with Paisley and rallying with Vanguard, a Unionist pressure group.[40]

The 'tradition of militant Protestant populism'[41] was closely related to the existence of urban working-class communities in competition with, yet isolated from, Catholics.[42] These Protestants prized 'the maintenance of . . . [their] social and economic privilege',[43] which could be but threatened when Catholics attempted to 'shoot . . . [their] way into status positions equal with Protestants'.[44] In addition, politically and theologically subversive motives were ascribed to Catholics: civil rights was an IRA front, and every Catholic was a Fenian (a peculiarly loaded description in loyalist typology).[45] Thus Protestant militancy could be projected as, and often originated in, essentially defensive reaction, commonly evolving from vigilante activities.[46] The prime role of the so-called security question to such Protestants can hardly be overstated,[47] but ran the considerable risk of unbalancing the institutionalised reciprocation of responsibilities to the union as viewed by Unionists.[48] What motivated many loyalists was the belief that the future of the union was in doubt,[49] and that Britain had betrayed them.[50] However, there were few feelings of having themselves betrayed Britain.[51]

As the liberal Unionist experiment foundered in 1973, the *Telegraph* sought to exploit the potential contradistinctions of the situation. It associated Protestant militancy with physical force republicanism, and even with instigating it in reprisal or imitation: both the Provisionals and loyalists were 'wreckers': '. . . the men of violence on both sides are combining forces to tear the community apart . . .' (12 Nov.), and: '. . . there is no future for anyone in a country divided into armed camps, run by madmen' (29 June).[52] Vanguard,[53] was regarded similarly: 'The Craig faction is groping for a policy alternative to co-operation with Britain, but there is none, except Republicanism' (13 Feb.).[54]

Intransigent Orangemen could be 'rebels' (27 Apr.), a particularly potent word in an Irish context. The other side of the same coin was alienating a Britain which had demonstrated its commitment to the Union (22 Feb.) and produced 'reasonable' constitution proposals in the March White Paper (21 Mar.), but whose patience was not inexhaustible (28, 30 June). Continued rejection of the concept of power-sharing, enshrined in the British proposals was '. . . nothing short of a revolt against the will of the British parliament, and in such a confrontation there could be only one loser' (4 July). Power-sharing amounted simply to 'the price . . . to pay for . . . continued British citizenship' (8 Oct.). The paper ended the year 1973 with a 'stark' re-iteration of its basic message: if loyalists rejected British terms, '. . . Britain's backing for Northern Ireland, political and financial, must decline' (31 Dec.).

In 1973 the paper also felt it could attack loyalists for subverting the will of the (Protestant) majority they professed to be defending; a charge given more credibility since there was no election in Northern Ireland between 1970 and May 1973. Neither politicians nor paramilitaries had a 'valid mandate' (17 Jan.). At best loyalist extremists were backwoodsmen (27 Apr.) and undemocratic (22, 29 Nov.; 17 Dec.); at worst, 'fools and thugs . . . bully boys . . . a Fascist fringe . . .' (6 Dec.). They had 'no viable alternative plan . . . [except] second-class citizenship for Ulster people' (21 Nov.); they certainly did not have 'Ulster's best interests at heart' (10 Oct.), all of which, again, suggested a parallel with the Provisional IRA in attempting to prevent a constitutional settlement (12 Nov.). The *Telegraph* enthusiastically enjoined the Unionist leader Brian Faulkner, not just to repudiate and isolate the right (19 Feb.), but even to promote what it recognised to be the inevitable split in the party in order to 'give Unionist voters a clear choice' (28 Mar.). The value of ensuring that moderate opinion found a rallying-point was central to much of the paper's argument:

> A depressing aspect of the propaganda war is the way in which the militants take to themselves the role of protectors of the people . . . Protestants and Roman Catholics worthy of the name of their religion have nothing whatever in common with men who wish to put forward their point of view, or see others put it forward, with the gun, the bomb and the boot. (5 Feb.)

However, the paper's belief in the efficacy of its approach was rigidly founded on a particular estimation of the intent of Northern Ireland's electorate: '. . . sooner, rather than later, the ordinary people must get a chance at the ballot box to say "No" to violence and to rally round leaders with principles' (8 Feb.).

The paper looked to applaud the triumph of commonsense from below (10 Oct.; 10 Dec.), and was prepared to let Unionist 'voters . . . make up their minds whether they want to support candidates who are for or against the system' (23 Mar.). There was even a flirtation with community politics, the formation of the Greater West Belfast Residents' Association being greeted with 'There is a gaping void where there should be leadership. The people must step into the breach themselves' (28 Feb.). By comparison, the Loyalist Association of Workers (LAW), later a component of the Ulster Workers' Council, was simply self-appointed (17 Jan.); indulging in 'political blackmail' (22 Feb.), and responsible (in striking on 7 February, which the *Telegraph* called 'Black Wednesday' [9 Feb.]) for unleashing 'unparalleled thuggery' (8 Feb.). Vanguard was impractical, if not downright sinister (19 Feb.), and when talks with the SDLP over independence, which the *Telegraph* constantly denigrated as 'UDI', began, the paper was dismissive: 'If Protestants and Catholics could unite in a new Ulster, they should be able to give power-sharing a try in the old Ulster' (7 Mar.). That might not be within Unionism (2, 27 Apr.), or as a result of the traditional electoral arrangements; but proportional representation, employed for the first time in the district council elections at the end of May 1973, the *Telegraph* was confident would lead to a breakdown of the old sectarian politics and herald a new era of consensus (3 Mar.; 22 Nov.). Not that the paper had no reservations of any kind. 'Ulster is heading into the most critical period of her history, and all the odds are stacked against her' (5 Feb.) and ' . . . the people themselves should recognise the dangers they run, if they don't step back' (22 Feb.) were caveats entered early in the year. Moreover, there was repeated recognition that, while Protestants generally might be seeking an alternative to a return to the old style of Stormont (10 Apr.), loyalist dissidents had the power to stall any progress in that direction (19, 30 Nov.). Perhaps as a counterweight, the *Telegraph* was at times at pains to praise both the restraint and potential statesmanship of the SDLP (23 Mar.; 27 Nov.), and politicians in the Republic, too, could be both realistic and farsighted (27 Feb.; 15 Mar.). The paper supported British suggestions for the legalisation of Sinn Fein (30 Mar.), adding: 'Republicanism cannot be destroyed but if its supporters leave aside the gun, society can accommodate them' (9 Apr.). Ultimately, then, 'It should not be impossible to devise a brand new constitution at some future date, which would at least blur the divisive issue of sovereignty' (12 Mar.).

Given what the paper detected to be popular feelings of revulsion at the rejection of Faulkner's leadership by the Unionist party (25 Apr.), it was likely that moderates could coalesce in a new unionist centre alignment of some influence (2 Apr.). There was certainly, because of the perfectly acceptable British proposal for power-sharing, no going back to ascendency rule (17 Jan.; 13 Mar.): 'The people are willing their representatives on to some kind of honourable conclusion, and they must be made to feel this weight of public opinion' (16 Oct.).

Even the disappointment of an opinion poll, commissioned for the paper in February 1973, and confirming the reflection in political preference of sectarianism,[55] failed significantly to shake the *Telegraph's* underlying faith: ' . . . Protestants and Catholics are bidding for high stakes . . . but they are not prepared to risk all to achieve them' (19 Feb.). Looking, perhaps desperately, for a glimmer of hope, the paper identified only thirteen per cent support for moderates, and a vague priority for reconciliation (22 Feb.); and, despite all, later, the 'real bonus' of Britain's White Paper proposing power-sharing was that it meant an election (21 Mar.). If neither that Assembly ballot, nor the one a month earlier to elect the local authorities, confirmed the *Telegraph*'s optimism,[56] at least talks on power-sharing got under way, culminating in the Sunningdale agreement, to leave the paper eulogising at the close of 1973, ' . . . the year when reason began to take. over from emotion, and politicians learned the art of politics . . . The prospects have never been better . . .' (31 Dec.).

## CONFUSION AND COMPROMISE

Nevertheless, the *Telegraph*'s tone was significantly modified in 1974.

The stridency of its earlier condemnations gave way to less forthright rebukes: the analogy between loyalist and republican extremism, in particular, was much less keenly drawn. Loyalists were in some cases still referred to as 'wreckers' (6 May), implying a communality of intent, and on the eve of that year's Ulster Workers' Council strike a British ministerial announcement of an IRA plan to 'take over' Belfast[57] prompted the paper to warn against loyalists reacting in kind; but even with the strike under way, and the 'Troops Out Movement' launching in Britain, the *Telegraph* remained comparatively cautious: '. . . the majority still have confidence that a compromise can be reached between the two traditions, without recurring violence . . . ' (17 May). This clearly reflected the effect of the first of two general elections in 1974 in February, in which ' . . . a sweeping victory . . . [for anti-Sunningdale unionists had signalled] a powerful set back to the Assembly, the Executive and everything that has been achieved over the past eight months' (2 Mar.).[58] In January the *Telegraph* had continued to pursue its argument regarding the undemocratic and unrepresentative nature of loyalist populism (3 Jan.), and wholeheartedly supported Faulkner over his resignation from the Unionist leadership in the expectation that he would then head an alternative 'non-sectarian, democratic and progressive . . .' party (8 Jan.). The paper reckoned to identify 'a vast residue of public support . . .' (7 Jan.) for both Faulkner and the Assembly (21 Jan.), confident that the election would act as a referendum on 'the brave new world of Stormont politics' (2 Jan.);[59] 'This election will be judged in the number of votes for and against the Sunningdale proposals' (11 Feb.).

Indeed, returning to another familiar theme, the paper emphasised that votes in a particular direction would '. . . convince
Britain that men and money invested in Northern Ireland is *(sic)*
not wasted' (19 Feb.), while the anti-Faulkner Unionists were
'. . . headed straight for a confrontation with Britain' (27 Feb.).
However, the paper did enter caveats: the Republic had yet to
'provide evidence of its good faith', which seemed to indicate a
wavering of support for Dublin's efforts. Moreover, the Executive
itself had to 'give a lead' (25 Feb.). The paper was sure there was
enough material for 'a selling campaign', and itself emphasised a
Faulkner-Fitt delegation to London on the theme 'Ulster means
business' (7 Feb.). If there was '. . . little representation of the
Protestant working-class point of view' (28 Jan.), however
prescient a notion that may have been, the Executive had ' . . .
shown itself as an administration that cares more than most for
ordinary people' (28 Feb.). Even if, despite the liberal rhetoric,
there were not a majority vote for pro-Sunningdale candidates, the
*Telegraph* argued, it was by no means the end of the line (27 Feb.):
the practicalities of the proposals had yet to be worked out in
detail. Recognising that the creation of a Council of Ireland could
prove a major stumbling block (25 Feb.), and that first-past-the-
post elections were 'unsuited to Ulster conditions' (8 Feb.), the
paper reaffirmed that: 'Every vote for pro-Assembly candidates is
a vote for peace, progress and good relations with Britain' (27
Feb.).

In the light of the actual results there were further adjustments
to *Telegraph* editorials, which now urged reconciliation of loyalist
demands (4 Mar.); blamed the Republic for failing to produce
necessary improvements in security (5 Mar.), and called for
official talks between the new British secretary of state, Merlyn
Rees, and loyalist politicians (6 Mar.). The proposals for a Council
of Ireland were again highlighted as a problem area (20 Mar.): 'the
tide is turning against . . . the popular concept of Sunningdale as a
North-South deal' (5 Mar.). Appeasement had to be offered to
loyalists: the Executive's main shortcoming was its lack of
'representation of the loyalist masses' (13 Mar.). Naturally, this
admission blew a rather large hole in the *Telegraph*'s previous
insistence on a silent majority for political co-operation. It felt
compelled to confess 'Sunningdale is no longer seen as Holy Writ.
It represents a broad agreement on an institutional framework that

can be modified or brought into operation by easy stages, as public opinion allows' (13 Mar.). All the same, the paper stuck with the contention that 'a realistic re-assessment' (2 Mar.) was not tantamount to a renunciation of power-sharing; that loyalist intransigence was still to the detriment of the security effort, and that loyalists, who had no tangible alternative to offer (20 Mar.), were no less headed for confrontation with Britain (18 Mar.; 6 May). The greatest threat to Sunningdale remained violence, whatever its source (29 Mar.): 'The struggle is on for the hearts and minds of the Unionist electorate, and there is still everything to play for, despite the Westminster election results' (6 May). The Ulster Workers' Council strike later that month was to prove a turning-point.[60]

Unsurprisingly, the *Telegraph* vehemently opposed the strike as a 'dictatorship on the people' (15 May) and 'economic sabotage' (28 May), and, once it became obvious that the stoppage was not going to 'peter out' (16 May), the paper issued further dire warnings of the potential damage it was doing to the union (23, 27 May). At the end of the first week the *Telegraph* felt confident enough to question what it saw as the real motivation behind the strike:

> The suspicion is that they [the strike leadership] are playing for higher stakes, and want a return to the Stormont of old, without power-sharing. But they should be tested and made to show their hand . . . in the course of discussions, the picture will become clearer, and the people will be able to make up their own minds (22 May).

This assertiveness, however, was founded on additional concessions; the paper was urging that the British government accommodate loyalist sensibilities, if only to demonstrate that popular Protestant conceptions of Sunningdale were mistaken (20 May). In any event, full implementation of the constitutional proposals, the paper accepted, was highly unlikely, especially following the Stormont vote for ratification, which immediately preceeded the strike (15 May). More than that, both the Constitution Act, previously sacrosanct in the *Telegraph*'s eyes (cf. 2 Apr. 1973), and the agreement, the paper announced, were now negotiable (22 May). The intent was to save at least part of Sunningdale: 'If the lights go out . . . even power-sharing might be lost. The stakes are too high for the Government to defer an initiative to get talks going' (21 May); and '. . . a great many are also opposed to the very existence of the power-sharing Executive. Indeed, its destruction is a principal objective of the Ulster Workers' Council and of Mr West, Mr Craig and Mr Paisley' (27 May). If that meant sacrificing the Council of Ireland, so be it: that suggestion was 'effectively torn up. It lies in shreds' (loc. cit.). Recognising that there was no longer any justification for appealing to a silent majority – 'the objectives of the strike are supported by thousands of people who are neither thugs nor bullies, much less Fascists' (loc. cit.) – the *Telegraph* accepted that: 'The Sunningdale blueprint was based on the most optimistic assessment of the security situation and the public mood. It failed to stand the test of time' (23 May). Later, the paper spelled it out clearly: the Council of Ireland 'has even less support than ever . . . the time has come to save the Executive and most of the Sunningdale agreement' (8 Apr.).

The indissolvable union of continued membership of the United Kingdom and acceptance of power-sharing as a basis for devolved government had been a fundamental principal of liberal unionism (10 Apr.; 22 Oct. 1973): 'The victory of the Ulster Workers' Council strike was won at the cost of massive British disenchantment with Northern Ireland' (30 May). Failure to reach some kind of compromise would signal 'the end of membership of the UK' (5 July). The only 'viable policy' was both pro-union and pro-power-sharing (8 Aug.). Even a continuing direct British administration of Northern Ireland was the antithesis of unionism (20 Feb.; 7 Mar., 1973): 'a tunnel with no light at the end', as the paper quoted Harold Wilson, the prime minister (29 May). 'The Ulster solution will be found in Ulster by Ulstermen, or it will drag on indefinitely' (14 Oct.). This echoed the *Telegraph*'s assertion 18 months previously that the original White Paper on power-sharing was 'the first step on the road back to restoration of democratic processes' (16 Mar. 1973), and the paper continued to hope for a second power-sharing experiment (1 July), albeit one of modest scope (30 May), and which took account of loyalist feelings: 'as . . . people begin to pressure their politicians for some kind of settlement, to restore a degree of self-government to Northern Ireland, attitudes may change . . . There is nothing for democrats to fear, except that the voters may not fully understand the choice which is before them' (6 June). Independence and integration were 'madcap' and 'dangerous' (17 June; 29 Apr.). Moreover, attempts to circumvent the question of partition[62] were doomed to failure: 'sooner or later there has to be reconciliation' (7 Oct.). The greater danger lay in attempting thereby to stifle legitimate aspirations (30 Aug.); alienating all Catholics (19 Nov., 1973), and scuppering the SDLP (25 Oct. 1973). There was a need for Catholics to demonstrate that power-sharing could deliver 'peace and whole-hearted co-operation' (2 Oct.), while a major fault of the 1973 proposals had been what the British also accepted as the unattractiveness of imposition from Westminster (13 June; 30 Aug.). Yet, as devolved government on those British terms became less likely (8, 11 Nov.), even the idea of a Stormont administration was ditched by one of its previously most devoted adherents.

What the *Telegraph* had regarded as nothing more than an 'interim solution', a kind of punishment for an unruly populace (30 May) turned, after the second general election of 1974 in October,[63] into a much more acceptable alternative (23 Oct.). The paper began identifying redeeming features of the present direct rule (loc. cit.); suggested greater compatability of legislation over a range of subjects between Britain and Northern Ireland (28 Oct.; 28 Nov.); tentatively offered support for an increase in the number of Northern Ireland MPs (12 Nov.), and praised the contribution to stability in Northern Ireland made by British industry (29 Oct.). Direct rule was now seen as *the* alternative to power-sharing. The *Telegraph* underscored its even-handedness, and, therefore, its appeal to Catholics (loc. cit.). From repeating warnings of the dangers of British withdrawal, the paper moved to composing a catalogue of reasons why Britain ought *not* to disengage from Northern Ireland (25 Nov.). In a period of 'further polarisation', when the British Green Paper on a Constitutional Convention[64] appeared to have little hope of success (21 Nov.), it was now up to Britain to hold the ring indefinitely.

## COMMERCIAL CONSIDERATIONS

The *Telegraph*, in common with all liberal unionists, had been driven into a corner politically just as it was wrestling with commercial difficulties. There was little profit in finding itself at odds with a considerable portion of its traditional readership during a period of falling circulation.[65] However, since loyalists by and large accepted there was to be no return to ascendency rule, and saw direct rule was at least a partial guarantee of the union,[66] by adopting that stance, the paper could perhaps help solve its pressing problems. In the meantime the case for the favoured popular loyalist alternatives collapsed once Britain reaffirmed its commitment to the union,[67] and the Unionist stranglehold on the state apparatus was broken.[68] Nevertheless, the danger remained that the toleration for direct rule would rapidly disintegrate into demands for a return of majority government.[69] Thus the *Telegraph* was left rigorously defending an arrangement that had been anathema to it only months earlier. The paper had correctly identified the struggle to represent unionism as the major confrontation. That had been comprehensively lost, but not necessarily at the cost of a reconstituted loyalist Stormont. In backing down on the Council of Ireland, a position which the SDLP had adopted anyway,[70] the paper was only adjusting to reality. Yet underlying Catholic objectives remained anti-partitionist,[71] and support for indefinite direct rule, even in the *Telegraph*'s terms, was a denial of nationalism. Its advantage was that it was everyone's least worst option,[72] and held particular appeal to the Protestant bourgeoisie and working class.[73] The paper acknowledged this by underlining the British economic commitment to Northern Ireland. The benefits of that accrued, naturally, chiefly to Protestants in the most industrialised areas.[74] At the same time the fragmentation of urban working-class loyalism following the strike, and in particular the inability of Paisley to secure lasting proletarian support,[75] offered an opportunity to re-address a wavering audience.

The *Telegraph*'s dependence on an urban readership, especially in the Belfast travel-to-work area, arose from its nineteenth century origins in the burgeoning of the provincial daily press in the period following repeal of the Stamp Acts and of falling illiteracy.[76] A paper of 'moderate political opinions', it professed itself devoted 'with spirit to questions affecting the moral and social condition of the working-classes'.[77] Yet in a 'prolonged period of prosperity' for the provincial press during the early 1970s,[78] the *Telegraph* lost 44.8 per cent of the total circulation losses it sustained over the 20 years from 1967 (see Table 10.1).

**Table 10.1** *Belfast Telegraph* circulation, 1967–87

| Year | Jan.–June | (annual % +) | July–Dec. | (annual % +) | 6 mo % + |
|------|-----------|--------------|-----------|--------------|----------|
| 1967 | 219,874 |          | 212,454 |          | −3.37 |
| 1968 | 214,380 | (−2.5)   | 211,274 | (−0.56)  | −1.45 |
| 1969 | 215,866 | (+0.7)   | 213,287 | (+0.95)  | −1.19 |
| 1970 | 212,070 | (−1.76)  | 205,752 | (−3.53)  | −2.98 |
| 1971 | 205,781 | (−2.97)  | 201,351 | (−2.14)  | −2.15 |
| 1972 | 204,221 | (−0.76)  | 190,936 | (−5.17)  | −6.51 |
| 1973 | 190,687 | (−6.63)  | 182,942 | (−4.19). | −4.06 |
| 1974 | 186,001 | (−2.46)  | 177,148 | (−3.17)  | −4.76 |
| 1975 | 178,069 | (−4.26)  | 170,567 | (−3.71)  | −4.21 |
| 1976 | 171,640 | (−3.61)  | 163,571 | (−4.1)   | −4.7 |
| 1977 | 162,836 | (−5.13)  | 154,231 | (−5.71)  | −5.28 |
| 1978 | 156,247 | (−4.05)  | 151,353 | (−1.87)  | −3.13 |
| 1979 | 156,271 | (+0.02)  | 152,082 | (+0.48)  | −2.68 |
| 1980 | 156,306 | (+0.02)  | 149,273 | (−1.85)  | −4.5 |
| 1981 | 153,272 | (−1.94)  | 147,086 | (−1.47)  | −4.04 |
| 1982 | 150,995 | (−1.49)  | 144,705 | (−1.62)  | −4.17 |
| 1983 | 150,402 | (−0.39)  | 143,396 | (−0.9)   | −4.66 |
| 1984 | 151,564 | (+0.77)  | 142,682 | (−0.5)   | −5.86 |
| 1985 | 151,799 | (+0.16)  | 143,768 | (+0.76)  | −5.29 |
| 1986 | 149,377 | (−1.6)   | 144,237 | (+0.33)  | −3.44 |
| 1987 | 147,470 | (−1.28)  |         |          |       |

*Source:* ABC

The paper's circulation decline in the second half of 1972 was the largest officially recorded during those two decades, and, subsequently, 1973 showed the biggest annual fall in readership of the period. The deterioration continued through the next five years. (Between 1970 and 1978 the *Telegraph*'s circulation fell by just over 26 per cent.) This crisis coincided with a falling-off in revenue experienced by Thomson Regional Newspapers as a whole, although profitability was reasonably buoyant[79]. In 1970 59 per cent of Northern Ireland's population read the *Telegraph*.[80] The paper's circulation, however, was heavily concentrated in urban areas (see Table 10.2). In 1984 63.4 per cent of the readership was among around a third of households located in the five most urbanised district council areas.[81]

The loss over four years of one in six of its readers came at a time when the UK newspaper industry as a whole was experiencing structural problems in retaining an increasingly urbane audience,[82] and, under TRN's influence, by 1975 the *Telegraph* had adopted the sort of national media criteria, with their

**Table 10.2** *Belfast Telegraph* penetration (1984), urbanity and level of non-Catholic population (1981) by rank

| District council | Penetration of BT sales | Urbanity | Non-RC population |
|---|---|---|---|
| Belfast | 1 | 1 | 13 |
| Lisburn | 2 | 5 | 7 |
| Castlereagh | 3 | 3 | 1 |
| Newtownabbey | 4 | 2 | 4 |
| Carrickfergus | 5 | 4 | 2= |
| Londonderry | 6 | 7 | 25 |
| North Down | 7 | 6 | 2= |
| Ards | 8 | 10 | 5 |
| Antrim | 9 | 12 | 12 |
| Larne | 10 | 9 | 9 |
| Craigavon | 11 | 8 | 14 |
| Banbridge | 12 | 16 | 11 |
| Down | 13 | 15 | 22 |
| Newry | 14 | 14 | 26 |
| Armagh | 15 | 20 | 15 |
| Ballymena | 16 | 13 | 6 |
| Coleraine | 17 | 11 | 8 |
| Limavady | 18 | 17 | 16 |
| Cookstown | 19 | 21 | 17 |
| Dungannon | 20 | 22 | 18 |
| Strabane | 21 | 18 | 23 |
| Moyle | 22 | 23 | 19= |
| Ballymoney | 23 | 24 | 10 |
| Magherafelt | 24 | 25 | 19= |
| Omagh | 25 | 19 | 24 |
| Fermanagh | 26 | 26 | 21 |

*Sources:* Bruce (1986); Where? (1985).

emphasis on 'human interest' as well as 'professionalism', which was bound to affect the paper's long-standing political role. After all, as one observer noted, 'To a large extent commercial considerations have ironed out partisan bias among the national news organisations'.[83] Moreover, the importation of TRN techniques for newspaper sales, despite some hesitancy,[84] was also likely to be reflected in the *Telegraph*'s editorial columns: 'The contents [of newspapers] are heavily influenced by sophisticated surveys of what different types of reader require . . . Newspapers, through their advertising columns, have always clustered around the interests, customs and priorities of their readers . . .'[85]

It can be assumed that the attraction of newspapers as vehicles of entertainment rather than political ideas was as great in

Northern Ireland as elsewhere in the United Kingdom,[86] and during the 1970s the *Telegraph* pursued an increasingly non-political populism in its journalism, with the familiar emphasis on coverage of the more trivial, and eventually even abolishing the post of political editor.[87] The movement of middle-aged, higher-skilled urban Protestants from Unionism to loyalism[88] and the concomitant shift of Protestants generally out of manual occupations to more skilled work, and from Belfast and other town centres to suburban housing is likely to have been a key factor in determining this policy. At the same time middle-class Catholics, concentrated occupationally in the construction and service industries providing a growing proportion of employment (even in Belfast) as the decline in the old staples accelerated, were also in a position to benefit from direct rule. For working-class Catholics, however, the situation was quite different: 'in comparison with Protestants . . . [they] are no better off . . . than they were under the Unionist regime.'[89] Whatever the reality behind that kind of comment, the perception of their abandonment by liberal Unionists loomed large among the Catholic proletariat, and led to 'a deepening sense of alienation' from the status quo in Northern Ireland.[90]

## CONCLUSION

Undoubtedly the *Telegraph* miscalculated the strength of loyalist opposition to the arrangements proposed at Sunningdale and showed little appreciation of the underlying fears of British withdrawal which drew many loyalists into supporting alternative constitutional schemes and, subsequently, into abandoning them when the continuation of the union had been secured. Moreover, like many liberal unionists, the paper failed to foresee Britain's willingness to accommodate loyalist intransigence after May 1974. It may be argued that the *Telegraph* in consequently adopting a more conciliatory attitude to direct rule was simply adjusting to the realities of the situation, perhaps not least significantly in line with the twists and turns of British policy.[91] Direct rule also had its attractions in being relatively popular, and at the same time an option not favoured by any of the leading loyalist parties. Even the jettisoning of the Council of Ireland had been foreshadowed by the SDLP itself. Precisely what role commercial considerations played in the process is difficult to determine with any real accuracy, although, whatever its circulation performance, the *Telegraph* would surely have found it impossible to sustain its position as a major component of the Northern Ireland media while remaining so clearly at odds with so many of its readers, unless, of course, its owners were prepared to retrench at a time of general expansion (though not without uncertainty) in the provincial press. Furthermore, the downgrading of politics within Northern Ireland which accompanied direct rule suited a more popular type of journalistic approach, concentrating on more ephemeral interests. At the same time many, perhaps a majority, of the *Telegraph*'s readers might be seen as making positive gains from the constitutional arrangement. What was sacrificed, however, was the central core of liberal unionism: the commitment to devolved community government, and the acceptance therein of the fundamental legitimacy of nationalist aspirations in Northern Ireland.

Until more is known about this significant voice within the unionist community, it will be difficult to determine with any precision the real motives behind this shift. Similarly, the work now promised on the Catholic proletariat in Northern Ireland should throw light on the subject from the opposite direction, as it were. Nevertheless, it may be unsurprisingly suggested that middle-class Protestants were more inclined to align with their Catholic counterparts than their proletarian co-religionists, and that to sustain their primary position as collaborators with the British, they were willing to accommodate the vacillations of successive governments in London. Meanwhile, British perceptions of the *Telegraph* as somehow laudably aloof from the cruder sectarianism of Northern Ireland may indicate a recognition of the role of liberal unionists in defusing Protestant working-class opposition to a policy of assuaging nationalism. Ultimately, when the first part of this formula fell apart, the second went by default. Then liberal unionism was useful in making palatable an arrangement which offered economic stability for ambitious middle-class Catholics in Northern Ireland, while holding out promises from London directly to Irish nationalists in Dublin, but which further alienated the Catholic working-class in the North.

## NOTES

1. Nomenclature is problematical when dealing with Ireland. In this article Protestant and Catholic are used to denote the main groups perceived to exist in Ireland. Unionist = a supporter of the Ulster Unionist Party and its successors, while unionist = a supporter of unionism. Similarly Nationalist and nationalist. Loyalist = a unionist or other supporter of partition. These forms are employed purely for the sake of clarity and imply no judgement.
2. Six-monthly records of the *Belfast Telegraph*'s (BT) circulation are held by the Audit Bureau of Circulation (ABC). In 1967, the daily circulation for January–June (ABC, Jan–Jun 67) reached 219,874.
3. Elliott, Philip, 'Reporting Northern Ireland: a study of news in Great Britain, Northern Ireland and the Republic of Ireland', *Ethnicity and the Media* (Paris: UNESCO, 1977) p. 274.
4. Elliott, op. cit. (1977), p. 273.
5. Thomson of Fleet, Lord, *After I was 60* (London: Hamish Hamilton, 1965), pp. 89–90.
6. Author's own experience, *Belfast Telegraph*, 1976–87.
7. Thomson, op. cit. (1965), p. 89. Goldenberg, Susan, *The Thomson Empire* (London: Sidgwick and Jackson, 1985), p. 169.
8. Rees, Merlyn, *Northern Ireland: A Personal Perspective* (London: Methuen, 1985), p. 338.
9. *Newspaper Press Directory* (London: Benn, 1971).
10. Ibid (1970); Thomson, op. cit. (1985), p. 94.
11. Thomson, op. cit. (1985).
12. Ibid. With characteristic colourfulness Thomson wrote, 'With a paper, if it turned out to be a stumer, you could at least find a customer and get some of your money back', p. 202.
13. Elliott, op. cit. (1977), p. 279; Goldenberg, op. cit. (1985), p. 162.
14. Goldenberg, op. cit. (1985), p. 169.
15. Thomson, op. cit. (1965), pp. 219–20.
16. Jenkins, Simon, *Newspapers: The Power and the Money* (London: Faber and Faber, 1979), pp. 89–90.
17. *Where? Regional Press Marketing Handbook* (London: Regional Newspaper Advertising Bureau, 1985).
18. Boyle, Kevin & Tom Hadden, *Ireland – A Positive Proposal* (Harmondsworth: Penguin, 1985), p. 64.
19. Bew, Paul & Henry Patterson, *The British State and the Ulster Crisis: From Wilson to Thatcher* (London: Verso, 1985), p. 16.
20. Buckland, Patrick, *A History of Northern Ireland* (Dublin: Gill and Macmillan, 1981), p. 113. Bew and Patterson, op. cit. (1985), p. 25.
21. Thomson, op. cit. (1965), p. 89.
22. Buckland, op. cit. (1981), pp. 110–13.
23. Bew and Patterson, op. cit. (1985), p. 4.
24. Whyte, John, 'Interpretations of the Northern Ireland conflict' paper read at the Irish Association, 4 Mar. 1976.

25. Harris, Rosemary, *Prejudice and Tolerance in Ulster: A Study of Neighbours and 'Strangers' in a Border Community* (Manchester: Manchester University Press, 1986), p. 224.
26. Arthur, Paul, *Government and Politics of Northern Ireland* (Harlow: Longman, 1984), p. 106.
27. Low, D. A., 'The contraction of England', inaugural lecture, University of Cambridge, 22 Oct. 1984 (Cambridge: CUP, 1984), pp. 1–7.
28. Harbinson, John F., *The Ulster Unionist Party, 1882–1973: Its Development and Organisation* (Belfast: Blackstaff, 1973), p. 165. Bew and Patterson (1985) contains a detailed account of this failure.
29. *Belfast Telegraph* editorial (18 Apr. 1973); further references in parentheses in text.
30. Laver, Michael, *The Theory and Practice of Party Competition: Ulster, 1973–1975* (London: Sage Publications, 1976), p. 23.
31. Arthur, op. cit. (1984), p. 122.
32. Nelson, Sarah, *Ulster's Uncertain Defenders: Loyalists and the Northern Ireland Conflict* (Belfast: Appletree, 1984), p. 53.
33. Harbinson, op. cit. (1973), p. 86ff.
34. Whyte, op. cit. (1976).
35. Nelson, op. cit. (1984), p. 77ff.
36. Patterson, Henry, *Class Conflict and Sectarianism: The Protestant Working-Class and the Belfast Labour Movement, 1882–1920* (Belfast: Blackstaff, 1980), p. xii.
37. Bew and Patterson, op. cit. (1985), p. 11.
38. Taylor, D., 'The Lord's Battle: An Ethnographic and Social Study of Paisleyism in Northern Ireland (Ph.D thesis, Queen's University, Belfast, 1983, unpub.), pp. 93–4.
39. Ibid, p. 44.
40. Ibid, p. 65; Nelson, op. cit. (1984), p. 101.
41. Bew and Patterson, op. cit (1985), p. 32.
42. Taylor, op. cit. (1983), pp. 12, 102.
43. Ibid, p. 44; Arthur, op. cit. (1984), p. 122.
44. Harris, op. cit. (1986), p. 203.
45. Nelson, op. cit. (1984), pp. 73, 102. Bruce, Steve, *God save Ulster!: The Religion and Politics of Paisleyism* (Oxford: OUP, 1986), p. 100.
46. Bruce, op. cit. (1986), p. 105; Bew and Patterson, op. cit. (1985), p. 32ff.
47. For the SDLP's appreciation of this, see White, Barry, *John Hume, Statesman of The Troubles* (Belfast: Blackstaff, 1984), pp. 150–1.
48. Harbinson, op. cit. (1973), p. 165.
49. Nelson, op. cit. (1984), p. 114.
50. Ibid, p. 108ff.
51. Ibid, p. 115.
52. See also, 2, 3 Jan.; 6 Feb.; 31 May; 17 Oct.; 2 Nov. 1973.
53. Nelson, op. cit. (1984), p. 104.
54. See also 25 Oct. 1973.
55. *Belfast Telegraph;* 'What Ulster thinks: Faulkner and Hume take poll honours' (20 Feb. 1973).

56. Bruce, op. cit. (1986), p. 104; The *Belfast Telegraph* immediately recognised the 'polarised vote' in the Assembly elections (BT ed., 2 July 1973).

57. *Belfast Telegraph*, 'PM exposes IRA takeover', (13 May 1974). See also Wilson, Harold, *Final Term: The Labour Government, 1974–76* (London: Weidenfeld and Nicholson, 1979), p. 73.

58. Anti-Sunningdale unionists took 51 per cent of the popular vote, compared to 32 per cent in the Assembly election, to Faulkner Unionists' 12.5 per cent. The vote for the centre parties collapsed, too, from 16 per cent in May, 1973 to 6.2 per cent, while support for all power-sharing parties was down from 63 per cent to 41 per cent. See *Belfast Telegraph*, 'Loyalists weigh up bargaining power' (2 Mar. 1974); Laver (1976), pp. 14, 35.

59. The paper appears to have had a change of mind soon after. 'It would be a mistake to regard the contest as a straight Sunningdale referendum . . . ' (19 Feb. 1974); and the election was 'merely an interim opinion poll' (27 Feb.).

60. In fact, the strike was a turning-point in many ways. The most comprehensive description is in Fisk, Robert, *The Point of No Return: The Strike That Broke the British in Ulster* (London: Andre Deutsch, 1975). See also McAllister, Ian, 'Political parties; traditional and modern' in Darby, John (ed.), *Northern Ireland: The Background to the Conflict* (Belfast: Appletree, 1983), p. 69.

61. John Hume's view was that the British destroyed the liberal unionist concept of power-sharing as the sole basis for a continuation of the union (White, op. cit. (1984), p. 175).

62. Bew and Patterson, op. cit. (1985), p. 78.

63. Faulkner's Unionist Party of Northern Ireland polled a 'derisory' 1.9 per cent in October (White (1984), pp. 176–7).

64. Arthur, op. cit. (1984), p. 118.

65. Audit Bureau of Circulation.

66. Bew and Patterson, op. cit. (1985), p. 105.

67. Ibid, p. 100; Bruce, op. cit. (1986), pp. 111–12.

68. Bew and Patterson, op. cit. (1985), pp. 101–2.

69. Bruce, op. cit. (1986), p. 113.

70. White, op. cit. (1984), pp. 165–6.

71. Arthur, op. cit. (1984), pp. 105–6.

72. A *Belfast Telegraph* opinion poll identified 32 per cent of Protestants and 21 per cent of Catholics in favour of continued direct rule, or full integration (21 Feb. 1973). Boyle and Hadden, op. cit. (1985), p. 75.

73. Bew and Patterson, op. cit. (1985), p. 104.

74. Boyle and Hadden, op. cit. (1985), p. 66ff.

75. Nelson, op. cit. (1984), p. 161ff; Bruce, op. cit. (1986), pp. 276–82.

76. Williams, Francis, *Dangerous Estate: The Anatomy of Newspapers* (Cambridge: Patrick Stephens, 1984), p. 95; Beckett, J. C. *The Making of Modern Ireland, 1603–1923* (London: Faber and Faber, 1981), p. 313.

77. *Newspaper Press Directory* (London: Benn 1873).

78. Rogers, Frank, 'The provincial press and its future', *UK Press Gazette Souvenir Issue* (3 June 1985), p. 70.
79. Thomson Regional Newspapers revenue from job advertisements is estimated to have fallen by £20m. between 1973 and 1981/2, although overall profits rose sevenfold between 1972 and 1979 (Goldenberg (1985), pp. 163, 169).
80. Elliott, op. cit. (1977), p. 273.
81. *Where? Regional Press Marketing Handbook.*
82. *The Times,* 'Quest for the magic middle' (1 July 1987).
83. Elliott, op. cit. (1977), pp. 279, 303–4, 310, 312.
84. Goldenberg, op. cit. (1985), p. 169; Rogers op. cit. (1985), p. 70.
85. Smith, Anthony (ed.), *The British Press Since the War* (Newton Abbott: David and Charles, 1974), pp. 14, 16–17.
86. Elliott, op. cit. (1977), p. 274.
87. Author's own experience, 1976–87.
88. McAllister, Ian, *The 1975 Northern Ireland Convention Election* (Glasgow: University of Strathclyde, 1975), p. 23.
89. Boyle, Kevin, Tom Hadden & Paddy Hillyard, *Ten Years on in Northern Ireland* (London: Cobden Trust, 1980), pp. 8, 10, 12, 108.
90. Boyle and Hadden, op. cit. (1985), pp. 76–7. There has been disagreement over the British government's possible motives, especially in dealing with the Provisionals. See Holland, Jack, *Too Long a Sacrifice: Life or Death in Northern Ireland since 1969* (New York: Dodd Mead, 1981), 131–6, and McCann, Eamon, *War and an Irish Town* (London: Pluto, 1980), pp. 142–5.
91. The *Telegraph* concurred with most government initiatives and observations during this period, while relations between the government and BBC Northern Ireland deteriorated to a state in which government ministers felt they could no longer rely on the broadcasters; see Cathcart, Rex, *The Most Contrary Region: The BBC in Northern Ireland, 1924–1984* (Belfast: Blackstaff, 1984), p. 233, and Curtis, Liz, *Ireland, the Propaganda War: The British Media and the 'Battle for Hearts and Minds'* (London: Pluto, 1985), p. 106.

# 11 · CATHOLIC WOMEN AND THE NORTHERN IRISH TROUBLES

The origins and nature of the conflict that scars the people and landscape of contemporary Northern Ireland have been analysed extensively over the past decade, making writing about 'the Troubles' one of the few growth industries in the economically devastated province. However, until very recently, scholars have neglected to examine the role of women in the conflict as well as the impact of the conflict on the lives of ordinary Northern Irish women. With the exception of Bernadette Devlin McAliskey, whose meteoric rise in the civil rights movement lead to a Westminster seat in 1969, and the founders of the Peace People, Mairead Corrigan Maguire and Betty Williams, Northern Irish women have remained virtually hidden from the history of the Troubles.[1] Such scholarly reticence reflects a very low rate of formal female participation on both sides of the Northern Irish political and sectarian divide. In this article the analysis will focus primarily upon women in the Catholic/nationalist community, and their response to the revival of militant republicanism and British government efforts to defeat it over the past two decades.

## I

The lack of formal political status for Northern Irish women is the product of the confluence of island-wide historical, cultural and religious forces that have generally constricted the role of women, producing a society that is extremely male dominated. Indeed, in her *The Unmanageable Revolutionaries,* Margaret Ward documents a consistent tendency within Irish nationalism to exclude women from positions of leadership despite the crucial service they have rendered to the nationalist cause. For instance, although women were active in organising community opinion against the landlords and their agents during the land wars of the 1870s and 1880s, sustained the widespread agitation against Irish conscription during World War I, and provided important courier services during the Irish War of Independence from 1919–21, they were never rewarded for these contributions. With the establishment of the Irish Free State in 1922, Irish women were expected to, and generally did, return to their traditional roles.[2]

Within Northern Ireland and especially in the large working-class areas of Belfast and Derry, the patriarchial influences pervade the very air that all Ulster women breathe. The influences of the churches, the schools and an economic structure that keeps those few women who do work in sex-segregated, low-paying and primarily part-time jobs reinforces the male domination, and collectively ascribes the primary role of women to be that of sacrificing mother, obedient wife and servicer of male needs.[3]

The Catholic and Protestant church structures and ideologies form mirror images in their insistence upon women's nurturing roles and privatised status. The limited educational opportunities and curriculum offered to young Northern girls compounds the situation, since until very recently, most left school at the age of fifteen. Bernadette Devlin's university education was unusual, while Mairead Corrigan's departure from school at fifteen for full-time employment was more reflective of the experience of most Northern girls in the 1960s. In the Catholic community the cult of the Virgin Mary presents a very passive role-model for Catholic womanhood. Polly Devlin, describing her youth in rural Derry in the late 1940s and 1950s, recalled this Catholic tradition when she wrote: 'Mary, the Holy Mother and Blessed Virgin, standing in utter resignation at the foot of the Cross waiting to receive the battered body of her son, was presented as the perfect role-model; her passivity, her lack of protest, was the only way to greet adversity and evil.'[4] Visual evidence of this influence is apparent in one West Belfast gable painting that depicts a fallen Provisional IRA soldier, draped with the green, white and gold tricolour, being held by his mother in the fashion of Michael-angelo's Pieta. Yet on the other hand, devotion to Mary has been an important source of strength and endurance to many Catholic women whose families have been affected by the on-going violence or whose sons or husbands have been imprisoned or killed. In so far as the cult of Mary gives mothers a special status in Catholic tradition and family life, and places an especially strong emphasis upon the Virgin Mary's role as intercessor to secure salvation, the strong devotion to Mary in Irish Catholicism has been an important catalyst in motivating many women whose relatives have been affected by the Troubles to engage in political activities that previously they would have thought inappropriate or beyond their capabilities. For instance, Mary Nelis, a Sinn Fein supporter from Derry City, who had two sons in Long Kesh in the mid-1970s, including one on the 'dirty protest', travelled all over the country bare-footed and clad in only a blanket to protest against the withdrawal of political status from republican prisoners in March 1976. She recalls feeling '. . . like Mary, the Mother of Jesus, doing the Stations of the Cross in her bare feet, and wrapped in a blanket on the hill of Calvary.'[5]

Clearly Northern Irish women have not been indifferent, and many have responded energetically, courageously and with acute political intelligences to the economic, political and judicial issues that have affected their immediate families and communities. Given that a long history of Catholic unemployment, deplorable housing conditions and humiliating poverty had been sowing seeds of discontent in the broad Catholic community since the foundation of the Northern state in 1921, and that in communities like Derry the women historically often provided the sole family income, Catholic women tended to be politically more aware than their Protestant neighbours. It is perhaps not surprising then that many Catholic women became politically active when the Northern Irish Civil Rights movement foundered on the rocks of flagrant abuse of police powers by the Royal Ulster Constabulary and of the refusal of the Stormont regime to concede any of the demands of the civil rights movement. Much of this response, particularly in the early stages of the Troubles was through informal activity at the community level. For instance, when Derry's Bogside was under frequent tear-gas attack in 1969, some of the women devised home-made gas-masks from nappies soaked in lemon-juice, vinegar and water to distribute to the menfolk who were protecting their community. Eileen Doherty, wife of Paddy

'Bogside' Doherty, converted her kitchen into a virtual cafeteria from which Bogside defenders were provided with tea, soup and bread.[6] It was women who defied the first curfew imposed on West Belfast in July 1970 because it prevented them from obtaining the bread and milk needed by their families. (On this occasion, it was notable that some Protestant women from the Shankill Road were observed bringing the necessary supplies over to their Catholic neighbours on the Falls Road.) Women were the principal organisers of the rate and rent strike in 1971 in protest over the introduction of internment by the Stormont administration in August 1971.[7]

By late 1970 and early 1971 Catholic urban neighbourhoods found themselves virtually under siege, and the women became more politically active in direct response to loyalist attacks on their homes, widespread internment, and the repressive methods subsequently employed by the security forces in the search for the men and weapons of a newly revived IRA. The invasive house-searches conducted by the security forces during the 1972–3 period, which featured the smashing down of doors at 5 a.m., the ripping up of floorboards, the ransacking of closets and cupboards, and the beating of men in front of their wives, mothers and children only served to sharpen and quicken a growing political consciousness among the Catholic women who witnesed them. (In 1973 alone, there were 72,000 house-searches.)[8]

Between 1971 and 1976, the impact of wide-scale arrests and more and more men going on the run emptied the Catholic neighbourhoods of men, leaving the women of these communities increased responsibility as the standard bearers for nationalist identity and as the principal protesters against the policing and surveillance methods employed by the Stormont regime and eventually the British government. Many women began organising community protests, which nurtured in them a growing sense of self-confidence, and as a result they began to participate more actively in politics.

## II

The political response of Catholic women to these developments in the early 1970s reflects the broad historical divisions within Irish nationalism, that is, the tension between those who espouse a constitutional, gradualist approach and those who are convinced that violence is the only appropriate weapon in the long historic campaign to achieve independence for the entire island of Ireland. Women advocating the constitutional approach would generally support the Social Democratic and Labour Party, which has the support of most Northern Catholics. Generally having the advantage of more financial security and education, women in the SDLP are often more politically active than their sisters in the working-class districts. Indeed, the SDLP is distinguished by the large number of women who hold seats on the local government councils. Brid Rodgers, who began her political involvement in 1967 with the protests by the Committee for Social Justice over the poor housing allotted to Catholics in predominantly Protestant Portadown, eventually rose to the position of SDLP party general secretary in the early 1980s, and was a party representative at the New Ireland Forum. In the Westminster election of June 1987 she ran as the SDLP candidate against Harold McCusker, MP, the sitting Official Unionist Party representative for the Armagh constituency. Although she did not win, her candidature drew more votes to the SDLP within the district than the party had won in the three previous elections.

Female support for republican Sinn Fein and its military wing, the Provisional IRA, has been and is primarily based in the working-class ghettos of West Belfast and Derry. It was in these areas especially that the political effects of internment and the invasive surveillance methods created a strong sense of community solidarity, a 'prison culture', which drove wives, sisters and mothers into sympathy with republican Sinn Fein and the Provisional IRA. The majority of women engaged in local community protests, such as in October 1976, when the women of Turf Lodge estate, using the traditional tactics of rattling dustbin lids and blowing whistles, kept the army out of their district for a month in the wake of the shooting by a British soldier of thirteen-year-old Brian Stewart. Indeed, bin rattling was a frequently employed means of warning men in the nationalist areas that the army or police were arriving to conduct search operations.[9] Although it was quickly absorbed into Sinn Fein, the Relatives Action Committee, which spearheaded protests against the end of political status for paramilitary prisoners on 1 March

1976, was initially formed by a few women from West Belfast's Ballymurphy districts. Women remained the chief organisers and participants in the protests over conditions in the H-Block (the republican name for the Maze Prison in Belfast) protests that took many women all over the island. Maire Drumm, vice-president of Sinn Fein, and Miriam Daly were prominent figures in the anti-H-Block movement before they were assassinated by loyalist paramilitaries respectively in 1976 and 1979. In the subsequent public demonstrations from March to August 1981 in support of the hunger-strikers in Long Kesh, women were especially prominent. As David Beresford has shown in his recent book on the 1981 hunger strikes, *Ten Men Dead,* it was largely the women visiting their menfolk who smuggled the 'comms' in and out of Long Kesh (the IRA name for the Maze), so setting up a courier system by which the Army Council of the Provisional IRA and Sinn Fein could communicate regularly with the prisoners and their principal leaders.[10] In recent years women have been the principal agents in organising protests and demonstrations against the use of super-grasses, or paid informers, to obtain convictions, and against strip-searching of female prisoners.[11]

Under the stimulus of this prison culture and the sense of empowerment gained from involvement in community protests, some women were drawn deeply into Sinn Fein politics, and a few younger women became politicised to the extent that they joined the IRA. Lily Fitzsimmons, a mother with five children, who lived in the Turf Lodge estate of West Belfast, protested in the initial demonstrations against internment, but she became more deeply involved when her sixteen-year-old eldest son Sean was interned in 1974, and she subsequently joined the anti-H-Block campaign when her son went on the dirty protest. After the 1981 hunger strike, Lily formally joined Sinn Fein and has been an active party member. Her experience took her into electoral politics and onto the Belfast City Council. Sisters often were drawn into involvement with Sinn Fein or with republican paramilitaries after their brothers had been arrested and imprisoned. Bernadette Sands, sister of Bobby Sands, and Marie Fitzsimmons, daughter of Lily Fitzsimmons and sister of Sean, became actively involved in the Provisional IRA after the arrests of their brothers.[12] Likewise, Marie Gibson, who witnessed her brother's arrest when she was only thirteen, said she felt such anger and bitterness afterwards that, 'Any soldier I saw in the street after that, I automatically just wanted to go for his throat. I identified them with my brother being inside, and if it wasn't for them he wouldn't have been there.' Sentenced by a Diplock court to three years in Armagh gaol on charges of rifle possession, Marie went on protest immediately since she did not consider herself a criminal or guilty of any offence. Marie recalled that survival amidst the dirty conditions during the Armagh 'no wash' protest was possible only because the women developed a strong, disciplined and almost family-like support structure among themselves. They fought off the boredom of twenty-three hours in the cells by giving each other lessons in Gaelic, lectures on Irish history and folklore and feminism.[13]

Mairead Farrell, who was killed by the SAS in Gibraltar in March 1988, is another example of a Catholic woman who was sucked into political activity and eventually paramilitary work as a result of the pervasive grip of the 'prison culture' in the early 1970s. Her mother, in attributing her daughter's initial involvement in the IRA, said: 'She was strongly affected by different girls' fathers and brothers being arrested, being interned, for no reason at all. That had a big influence on her, I think. She went up to visit numerous people in Long Kesh, such as boys she knew from Andersonstown, of whom there were plenty interned. There would hardly have been a family she knew that didn't have at least a couple inside, and she went to Long Kesh regularly to visit them.'[14]

As a result of her paramilitary activities, in 1976 Mairead was sentenced to fourteen years in Armagh gaol, where the women republican prisoners had established a command structure similar to that of the IRA men in Long Kesh. She moved into a leadership position as OC in the gaol, eventually becoming the driving force behind the six-year 'no work protest' over the ending of political status. Along with her Andersonstown neighbour, Mary Doyle, and Margaret Nugent from Greencastle, she joined in the first hunger strike, which lasted from 27th October to 18th December 1980. Mairead undoubtedly would have joined in the second strike initiated by Bobby Sands had the Army Council given its approval. The Army Council apparently wanted full media attention to be concentrated on the men in Long Kesh, and therefore insisted that the Armagh women return to the support role traditional within

Irish republicanism. Despite the Army Council's decision Mairead considered herself '. . . a volunteer in the Irish Republican Army' and '. . . a political prisoner in Armagh jail . . . prepared to fight to death if necessary to win the recognition that I am a political prisoner and not a criminal'.[15]

Mairead Farrell's actions and attitudes suggest that many republican women seem to have felt it incumbent upon them to prove to the male-dominated leadership not only the sincerity and steadfastness of their republican convictions, but also their willingness to endure the most extra-ordinary sacrifices in the long tradition of Irish republicanism. Maire Drumm Og, daughter of the Sinn Fein vice-president assassinated in 1976, declared as much in 1979 when she said, 'I will conclude by assuring the leadership of the Republican movement that in the days to come when the war to eject the British reaches a successful conclusion, women will not be found wanting. Indeed, if you show any signs of weakening we will take over.'[16] The militaristic and macho features of the parade dress of the units of the Cumann na Ban (Irish Women's Council, founded in 1914) in republican parades also reflect a tendency to emulate the male-dominated values associated with republicanism. Many women who experienced gaol sentences found that their psychic health and survival depended upon suppressing their emotions and femininity and adopting very hard attitudes.[17] Thus the Armagh women found inspiration to sustain their 'no wash' protest and hunger strike from the example of Terence MacSwiney, the Lord Mayor of Cork, who died on hunger strike in Brixton prison in 1920 during the Irish War of Independence. The MacSwiney legend, combined with the Catholic tradition that suffering ultimately brings sanctification and resurrection, provided a powerful leitmotiv to the women in Armagh as well as to the men on the blanket and on hunger strike in Long Kesh. It is perhaps significant that one of the most treasured objects of the relatives of the imprisoned were handkerchiefs that had the images of Christ and a hunger-striker painted on them by the incarcerated men. Given an almost relic-like status, these handkerchiefs would be especially valued by a Catholic population familiar with the story of St Veronica, said to have wiped the face of Christ when he was on the way to his Crucifixion, leaving the image of his face on the veil she used.

Obviously the violent tactics of the republican paramilitaries create a very complicated and ambivalent relationship between the

Catholic church and those of its flock who support or are directly involved in Provisional IRA operations. While the Catholic hierarchy have on many occasions implored the British government to address the causes rather than just the symptoms of nationalist alienation, they have been unequivocal in their condemnation of Provisional IRA violence. The moral dilemma posed by paramilitary violence and the Christian commandment 'love thy neighbour' is solved by many PIRA men and women by identifying with the liberation theology that has become so prominent in Central and South America. (It is not unusual to see Che Guevera portrayed with Irish republican soldiers in republican areas of Belfast.) For example, Lily Fitzsimmons, who retains her identity as a Catholic and found recitation of the rosary with her neighbours on the street corners a source of comfort during the H-Block and hunger-strike protests, is able to dismiss the hierarchy's condemnation of Sinn Fein support of the armed struggle by saying: 'The church has always sided with the establishment.'[18] While selective Catholicism enables many women to resolve the contradictions between their Catholic loyalties and their maternal and political instincts, some have left the church. For instance, Mary Nelis of Derry, who in her younger days often attended daily Mass, was very bitter that the church did not take a more forceful stand against the British government over prison conditions, and after having read the writers of the feminist canon, has ceased to be a practising Catholic. Like many younger women whose exposure to higher education introduced them to Marxist feminist theory, Mary sees the church as a bulwark of capitalist imperialism, and believes that there is an integral link between national liberation and women's liberation.[19]

The influence of the Marxist feminist theory has been reflected in recent years in the internal campaigns that younger Sinn Fein women have waged to gain wider influence and power in the party. As early as 1979 some militant republican women were beginning to eye positions of leadership within the movement. The experiences of the Armagh women and the crucial role that women took in organising H-Block protests and – most especially – demonstrations in support of the hunger-strikers raised the aspirations of many young women to be included in the party's governance structure and to have women's issues specifically addressed in the party platform. A Sinn Fein Women's Committee was formed in

1978, and by the 1980 Ard Fheis (annual conference), the availability of contraception, family planning and divorce was advocated in the party platform. The views of young women in Sinn Fein on the relationship between republicanism and feminism were succinctly stated by Rita O'Hare in 1980 when she declared:

> It is only when the Republican Movement recognises the oppression of women, and sees clearly where it comes from – imperialism, social and economic – that the selflessness, the dedication, and the ultimate sacrifice paid by women volunteers . . . will be truly recognised . . . This year's Sinn Fein Ard Fheis, for the first time ever is going to be asked to approve a policy document specifically on *Women in the New Ireland* and on Sinn Fein's involvement in the women's struggle until a new Ireland is established. This is a development of major significance, however late we may be in reaching it . . . We cannot wait for the end of British rule, nor can we merely make promises about the things we will do in the new Ireland. We must work, as we must on other social and economic issues, in hammering at the oppression of women now.[20]

In the past few years, Sinn Fein has made a deliberate effort to augment its political programme by addressing the economic and social issues of most immediate concern to its membership, specifically the issues of housing, unemployment and health services and benefits. Rita O'Hare's call for action on these issues did not leave women in the background, for women in West Belfast, and particularly some within Sinn Fein, have been active in conducting investigations and surveys which have established irrefutable evidence of the deplorable housing conditions that have pertained in the Divis Flats and Turf Lodge estate in West Belfast. Between 1985 and 1987, Sinn Fein women co-operated with a team of university social scientists to assess the impact of these conditions on the health of the families living in badly built and poorly maintained estates.[21] In June of 1986 the British government announced its decision to demolish the Divis Flats, and while this decision may have been made under the pressure of new circumstances arising out of the Anglo-Irish Agreement of November 1985 and concerted efforts by the SDLP leadership to draw attention to the plight of the Divis residents, the women of the area provided crucial service in marshalling the facts and figures to present to the government authorities.

By 1983 some of the goals articulated by O'Hare in 1980 were accomplished. A separate Women's Department was established, and women were guaranteed eight out of thirty-two seats on the Ard chomhairle, the Sinn Fein executive committee. A women's centre on the Falls Road was established and provides information to neighbourhood women on health and welfare benefits. Since 1983 'Eira Nua' has advocated educational programmes to eliminate the evils of domestic violence and rape. The party supported the idea of shared parental child care, and an end to the concept of illegitimacy. The endorsement of some of these items from the feminist agenda has not been accomplished without stress and strain, as was reflected in the party's handling of the abortion issue. The personal beliefs of male members of the executive as well as fear of alienating grass-roots Catholic support kept the party from endorsing abortion until 1985. The Ard Fheis of November 1985 featured a hot debate on the issue, and a resolution that 'We are opposed to abortion as a means of birth control. We recognise that women have a right to choose,' was passed narrowly by 77 to 73 votes on a second ballot. (It is noteworthy that the eight women members of the executive were also opposed to this resolution.) With the support of the party leadership, that policy was amended at the 1986 Ard Fheis, when the wording recognising women's right to choose was deleted, thereby restoring a basically Catholic orientation to Sinn Fein policy on this issue. While it is clear that the Sinn Fein leadership has recognised the need to address women's issues, knowledgeable observers believe that tactical considerations were the primary motivators in persuading the leadership to address women's issues, and that there is a huge gap between stated party policy on women's equality and the views and actions of the party rank and file.[22]

It is clear that women within Sinn Fein have had to wage a tough struggle for the gains they have made in the last five years. Some of their gains have been significant, such as the seats guaranteed on the national executive, and the fact that Rita O'Hare and Sile Darragh, both former republican prisoners, respectively hold positions as editor of *Republican News* and head of Sinn Fein Foreign Affairs Department. Notwithstanding these gains, continued paramilitary violence and British use of extraordinary police and judicial powers give the political/constitutional question an overriding priority that eclipses issues on the feminist agenda.

The very nature of the political situation tends to heighten Catholic consciousness in republican areas, and the Irish Catholic clergy, as was evident by its position on the Irish Republic's abortion and divorce referendums of 1983 and 1987, appears determined to uphold the traditional roles of women in the Irish social and family structure.

Sectarianism and the isolation of working-class women in their communities makes contact between Sinn Fein and middle-class feminists difficult if not impossible, so that it is likely that feminism within republicanism will continue to have a difficult road ahead. Yet the experiences of some republican women have steeled their nerve, and their determination not to retreat into traditional roles was evidenced by this 1984 comment of Mary Nelis of Derry: 'Women have fought their way to the front, and now that we are there we won't be taking a back seat again.'[23]

It is important to note that not all Catholic women living in nationalist areas support Sinn Fein republicanism. Indeed, if electoral evidence, especially in the Westminster elections of 1986 and 1987 is any guide, the moderate nationalist party which supports a constitutional resolution of the Northern conflict, the SDLP, continues to hold the support of most Catholic women. Some Catholic women have eschewed formal party politics and involve themselves in programmes at community centres designed to keep children off the streets in order to protect the youth from harassment by the security forces and the possibility of para-military recruitment. Many Catholic women involve themselves in community reconciliation work at the local level or at the more widely known Corrymeela centre. The Peace People, although significantly diminished in numbers since 1978, continues to have a few Catholic women who are active in its various projects, ranging from providing transport to the prisons to providing counselling services and minimal financial help to many ex-prisoners and their families. Moreover, there is still a large percentage of women in the nationalist neighbourhoods, who, given the heavy pressures of family responsibilities, have no time or energy left from their daily struggle to give to political activity.

Finally, as in the Protestant community, there are a few women in the Catholic community whose feminism has lead them to put the traditional political issues of nationalism and unionism in abeyance while they campaign for legal and social reforms that would influence directly the everyday lives of their Northern sisters.

Eileen Evason of the University of Ulster at Coleraine, Inez McCormack, head of the Northern Irish branch of the National Union of Public Employees and Mary Clarke Glass of the Equal Opportunities Commission have been successful in drawing support from many Catholic women in their campaigns to highlight the disabilities that all Northern women suffer in the areas of wage, job and educational discrimination. Co-operative efforts by feminists have lead to the establishment of refugee centres for victims of domestic violence, strengthened laws against rape, as well as some improvement in the state medical benefits available to women.[24] Admittedly the number of Northern women, either Catholic or Protestant, whose feminism takes priority over the political/constitutional issues is still very small. The depth of the political-sectarian division, especially in Belfast and Derry, makes it extremely difficult to build a broad-based feminist consensus, and thus any ecumenical feelings that may have developed at the work-place or at women's meetings are especially fragile once the women return to the politically and religiously divided ghettos.

## III

So long as Ulster politics retains its sterile, confrontational, triumphalist style, the goals and aspirations of women will be ignored and marginalised. Northern Irish women will have a limited impact in helping to build a peaceful and just society until Northern Irish men show a willingness to engage in constructive dialogue across both the political and the sexual divides.[25] Obviously, this will not happen until the British government effectively addresses the legitimate economic, judicial, and political grievances of the minority community. Judging from the political developments between 1985 and 1988 – the Protestant reaction to the Anglo-Irish Agreement, the Provisional IRA's refusal to abandon the bomb and the bullet, the Tories' firm stand against any major alteration of the Diplock court system, and the united opposition of the male political leaders within the North to a serious consideration of women's issues – it appears that

Northern Irish women, be they Catholic or Protestant, nationalist or unionist, will continue to face tough and difficult times for the foreseeable future.


## NOTES

1. The few works published to date include Ward, M., and M. T. McGivern, 'Images of Women in Northern Ireland', *Cranebag,* vol. 4, no. 1, pp. 66–72; Fairweather, E., M. McFadyean and R. McDonough, *Only the Rivers Run Free* (London: Pluto Press, 1984).
2. Ward., M., *The Unmanageable Revolutionaries* (Dingle Brandon Books, 1983). See also Beale, J., *Women in Ireland: Voices of Change* (Dublin: Gill and Macmillan, 1986).
3. Kramer, J. D., and C. A. Curry, *Attitudes Towards Women in Northern Ireland* (Belfast: Equal Opportunities for Northern Ireland, 1985). Indeed, the rapid demise of the Peace People movement in 1977 was partially caused by the total lack of experience and training in leadership skills of its two founding members, and their acquiescence at an early stage in accepting some male leadership in any effort to confer legitimacy on their movement in the eyes of the community. Ironically, some observers at that time commented that it was the hidden agendas introduced by the intruding male leadership that caused the collapse of the peace movement (Ann McCann, interview, June 1987).
4. Devlin, Polly, 'All of Us There', Frank Ormsby (ed.), *Northern Windows* (Belfast: Blackstaff Press, 1987), p. 214.
5. Interview with Mary Nelis, July 1985.
6. Interview with Eileen Doherty, July 1985.
7. Ward and McGivern, op. cit., p. 70.
8. O'Malley, P., *The Uncivil Wars: Ireland Today* (Boston: Houghton Mifflin, 1983), p. 259.
9. Ward and McGivern, op. cit., p. 70.
10. Beresford, D., *Ten Men Dead* (London: Grafton Books, 1987), p. 30.
11. *Republican News,* 14 Mar. 1985; *Irish News,* 16 Nov. 1984; D'Arcy, M., *Tell Them Everything* (London: Pluto Press, 1981).
12. Interview with L. Fitzsimmons, July 1987. Bishop and Mallie assert that 80 per cent of those now involved in the PIRA have entered through family connections, Bishop, P. and E. Mallie, *The Provisional IRA* (London: Heinemann, 1987), p. 3.
13. Fairweather, *et al.,* op. cit., pp. 215–18, 223; D'Arcy, op cit., p. 121. (D'Arcy recalls that when the ancient myth of the Irish warrior Cuchulain was recounted in these sessions a good deal of emphasis was placed upon the goddess Scuthach, who had tutored Cuchulain in his martial skills.)
14. D'Arcy, op. cit., p. 18.

15. Fairweather, *et al.*, op. cit., p. 229.
16. *Republican News*, 18 Aug. 1979.
17. Beresford, op. cit., p. 19.
18. Interview with Lily Fitzsimmons, July 1987.
19. Interviews with Mary Nelis, June 1985, July 1986.
20. D'Arcy, op. cit., p. 12.
21. Interview with M. Osborne, July 1987; *Fortnight*, (June 1987), p. 5.
22. Interviews with I. McCormack, M. Clark Glass and M. McMahon, June 1986, Jan. 1987.
23. Mary Nelis, Nov. 1984, statement in Armagh prison box file, Linenhall Library, Belfast.
24. Interviews with E. Evason, I. McCormack and M. Clark Glass, July 1986; Jan. 1987.
25. An example of such male opposition would be the anti-abortion meeting in Belfast (Sept. 1987) that brought together on the same platform representatives of the SDLP and the DUP.

# GLOSSARY AND WHO'S WHO

**Alliance Party:** Non-sectarian democratic party in Northern Ireland.

**Anglo-Irish Agreement:** Accord between United Kingdom and Irish Republic, signed in November 1985.

**Anglo-Irish Treaty:** Settlement reached in December 1921 establishing a self-governing regime in the 26 counties.

**An Phoblacht:** Sinn Fein journal.

**Ardoyne:** Protestant section of East Belfast.

**Armalite rifle:** Popular weapon employed by IRA and Loyalists.

**Army Council:** Council of the IRA Military Command.

**Assembly, Northern Ireland:** Short-lived representative body which was abandoned in 1974.

**Blanket protest:** Refusal to wear prison clothing.

**Bloody Friday:** Date in 1972 when 11 people were killed in Belfast bombings.

**Bloody Sunday:** Date on which deaths were caused by British army in Derry, 1972.

**Bogside:** Catholic area of Derry.

**B Specials:** Mainly Protestant part-time police, regarded as sectarian force and much disliked by Catholics. Disbanded early in the conflict.

**Church of Ireland:** Anglican Church in Ireland.

**Civil Rights Association:** Movement for civil equality in housing, jobs, etc. in Northern Ireland.

**The civil war:** Between Republican groups in early 1920s.

**Michael Collins:** Irish leader assassinated in 1922.

**Council of Ireland:** Body of representatives for North and South of Ireland.

**Creggan Road:** Catholic area in Derry.

**Dail Eireann:** Parliament of the Republic of Ireland.

**Derry/Londonderry:** Alternative names for province's second city – Derry is the name used by Catholics and Londonderry by Protestants.

**Bernadette Devlin (McAliskey):** Civil rights leader and MP 1968–74.

**Diplock Courts:** Legal procedure functioning without jurors and using special rules concerning evidence and conviction.

**Direct rule:** Government from Westminster.

**DUP:** Democratic Unionist Party, the Revd Ian Paisley's group.

**Easter Week Rising:** Republican revolt which declared an Irish Republic.

**Eire:** Republic of Ireland.

**Emergency Powers Act:** Law allowing detention without trial.

**European Commission on Human Rights:** Body to which Irish Republic issued a formal complaint in 1976 about the treatment of suspects and prisoners in Northern Ireland.

**Falls Road:** In Catholic West Belfast.

**Brian Faulkner:** Sometime Unionist Prime Minister of Northern Ireland, died in 1977.

**Fenians:** Alternative name for Irish Republican Brotherhood – an oath-bound secret society to secure an Irish Republic in the nineteenth and early twentieth centuries.

**Fianna Fail:** Democrat Party in present-day Irish Republic.

**Fine Gael:** Democrat Party in present-day Irish Republic.

**Gerry Fitt:** Sometime leader of SDLP, member of House of Lords.

**Garret Fitzgerald:** Sometime Prime Minister of Irish Republic.

**Flags and Emblems Act:** Law to prohibit public display of Republican symbols.

**Free Presbyterian Church:** Splinter group from main body of Presbyterians. Revd Ian Paisley's group.

**Garda Siochanna:** Main police force of the Irish Republic.

**Charles Haughey:** Current Prime Minister of the Irish Republic.

**H-block:** Northern Ireland prisons holding convicted Republicans and Loyalists.

**Sir John Herman:** Chief Constable of Northern Ireland.

**John Hume:** Leader of SDLP.
**INLA:** Irish National Liberation Army – splinter group from the Official IRA.
**Internment:** Confinement of suspects without legal conviction.
**IRA:** Irish Republican Army.
**IRB:** Irish Republican Brotherhood, also known as the Fenians.
**IRSP:** Irish Revolutionary Socialist Party.
**Brig. F. Kitson:** Authority on counter-insurgence and terrorism.
**Lisburn:** District Council area south of Belfast.
**Long Kesh:** Internment camp for IRA suspects.
**Loyalists:** Mainly Protestant upholders of Northern Ireland as part of United Kingdom. Anti-Republican.
**Maze Prison:** An H-block prison.
**James Molyneaux:** Leader of Official Unionist Party and MP.
**Nationalists:** Supporters of an independent, usually united, Ireland.
**NICRA:** Northern Ireland Civil Rights Association.
**Noraid:** American-based propaganda and fund-raising vehicle for the IRA.
**Northern Ireland Act:** Lead to the formation of the state of Northern Ireland in 1920.
**Northern Ireland Office:** Administrative apparatus for the province.
**Offences Against the State Act:** Legislation pertaining to political anti-state activities.
**Official IRA:** Marxist wing of the IRA.
**Cardinal O'Fiaich:** Roman Catholic Primate of All Ireland and Archbishop of Armagh.
**Orange Order:** Militant Protestant lodge which is an oath-bound secret society.
**OUP:** Official Unionist Party.
**Ian Paisley:** Leader of Democratic Unionist Party and MP.
**Paramilitaries:** Units of Republican and Loyalist groups acting and sometimes dressing as formal military bodies.
**Peace People:** Supporters of 1970s non-sectarian peace campaign.
**Prevention of Terrorism Act:** Enacted 1974 and modified form made permanent in 1986.
**Provisional IRA:** Essentially non-Marxist wing of Irish Republican Army.
**The Province:** Northern Ireland. Historical province of Ulster is larger than the present state.

**Public Order Act:** Law allowing bans on parades, demonstrations, etc.

**Red Hand Commandos:** Protestant group in the early 1970s.

**Republicans:** Adherents of a united Irish Republic.

**Republic of Ireland:** 26 counties making up present-day Eire, declared a republic in 1949.

**RUC:** Royal Ulster Constabulary, the main police force in Northern Ireland.

**Bobby Sands:** First hunger striker to die (in 1981).

**SAS:** Special Air Service of British army, trained in commando tactics.

**SDLP:** Mainly Catholic Social Democrat and Labour Party. A rival of Sinn Fein.

**Shankill Road:** In Protestant West Belfast.

**Sinn Fein:** Political force for a united Irish Republic, linked to Irish Republican Army.

**Six Counties:** Northern Ireland.

**Special category status:** Prisoners in Northern Ireland prisons who, having been convicted of politically related offences, were given different status from ordinary criminals.

**Special Powers Act:** Legislation placing wide authority in the hands of the Minister for Home Affairs.

**John Stalker:** Former Deputy Chief Constable of Manchester, a Catholic, who was conducting an internal investigation of the RUC.

**Stormont:** Site in Belfast of the former Northern Ireland Parliament.

**Sunningdale:** Meeting place where agreement on a power-sharing executive was transacted in 1972.

**Supergrass trials:** Trials at which witnesses are used against their own group, and whose testimony is uncorroborated.

**Troops Out Movement:** British pressure group with Irish Republican sympathies.

**The Troubles:** Generally refers to the Anglo-Irish war of 1919–21.

**UDA:** Ulster Defence Association – a Loyalist paramilitary group.

**UDR:** Ulster Defence Regiment – provides mainly part-time support for the police.

**UFF:** Ulster Freedom Fighters – a Protestant paramilitary group.

**Ulster:** Old province, now usually used to refer to Northern Ireland.

**Ulster Workers' Council:** Protestant group which called a general strike against power-sharing in 1974.

**Unionist Party:** The Official Unionist Party, a legal constitutional party.

**UVF:** Ulster Volunteer Force, a Protestant paramilitary group.

**Vanguard:** Militant Protestant Loyalist movement.

**Visor:** British army magazine.

**West Belfast:** Mainly Catholic district.

**Widgery Commission:** Met in 1972 to report on the causes of violence in Ireland.

# INDEX